MW00669425

CABINET OF
CURIOSITIES

CABINET OF CURIOSITIES

A HISTORICAL TOUR of the UNBELIEVABLE, the UNSETTLING, and the BIZARRE

AARON MAHNKE

with HARRY MARKS

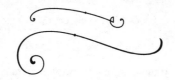

ST. MARTIN'S PRESS ♒ NEW YORK

First published in the United States by St. Martin's Press,
an imprint of St. Martin's Publishing Group

CABINET OF CURIOSITIES. Copyright © 2024 by Grim & Mild Entertainment, Inc.
All rights reserved. Printed in the United States of America. For information,
address St. Martin's Publishing Group, 120 Broadway, New York, NY 10271.

www.stmartins.com

Design by Jonathan Bennett

The Library of Congress Cataloging-in-Publication Data is available upon request.

ISBN 978-1-250-29120-2 (hardcover)

ISBN 978-1-250-29121-9 (ebook)

Our books may be purchased in bulk for promotional, educational, or business use.
Please contact your local bookseller or the Macmillan Corporate and Premium Sales Department
at 1-800-221-7945, extension 5442, or by email at MacmillanSpecialMarkets@macmillan.com.

First Edition: 2024

10 9 8 7 6 5 4 3 2 1

To the entire Grim & Mild team,
who share my deep passion for history
and the curious stories it contains

CONTENTS

PART FOURTEEN: WARTIME WONDERS

AN INTRODUCTION

We all have a favorite spot. Yours might be a bench that overlooks the ocean, shaded by twisted ancient trees. Perhaps it's a special restaurant you visit once a year. Or maybe it's just a humble room in your family home.

One of *my* favorite rooms in the world, if you're curious, is more than three thousand miles from my office. That certainly makes it difficult to visit, I know. Despite that, not a week goes by that I don't close my eyes—if only for a moment—and revisit it in my imagination.

The Enlightenment Room at the British Museum in London.

There's a texture to the place that's difficult to describe. It's actually a number of connected rooms, grounded by beautiful wood flooring and lined on both sides by tall antique bookcases. Many of the shelves are used in the traditional sense, holding hundreds of old leather-bound volumes, but others serve as a display for a wide assortment of objects.

It might be a national collection in one of the most prominent museums in the world, but it's impossible to *not* feel like you're also walking through someone's personal library. It is also, in a very real sense, a cabinet of curiosities.

Want to feast your eyes on the magical equipment of one of England's most legendary wizards? The Elizabethan alchemist Dr. John Dee used a number of tools in his pursuit of forbidden knowledge, and some of them are on display in this magnificent room.

His actual crystal ball still shines under the lights, right beside a mirror crafted from polished black obsidian brought to England all the way from Mexico. There's even a magical disc about the size of a dinner plate, made of wax and covered in mysterious drawings, that looks like a prop from a Doctor Strange movie.

How about a real mermaid from the 1700s? Of course, by "real," I simply mean one of the many handmade taxidermy projects that combined the upper body of a monkey and the tail of a fish. They were typically made in Japan and passed off to gullible European visitors—in exchange for money, of course.

Most of us know about the "Fiji Mermaid" that was part of P. T. Barnum's American Museum in New York City. But that specific example was only on display in 1842, and vanished shortly after in a fire. Thankfully, others still exist, and the Enlightenment Room is one place to get your fix.

Now, when I call this space a "cabinet of curiosities," I really do mean that literally. The practice of building a personal collection of curious objects goes back centuries, although it wasn't until the 1600s that they really started to take off in Europe. By the 1700s, the trend had spread even to England.

These "wonder rooms," as they were sometimes called, usually served two purposes. They offered a fun hobby for bored aristocrats to show off their wealth and well-traveled light fingers. Think of them as the private souvenir drawers of various European colonizers, with all the complex baggage that comes with that language.

But they were also bold attempts by these people to understand the world around them. Every time they stumbled upon some weird part of nature, they would bring it home, study it, and then put it on display. They were "curiosities" because they raised questions, rather than providing answers. And humans aren't very good at letting go of a mystery, are they?

At this point, you might be thinking that these old "wonder rooms" and "cabinets of curiosities" sort of sound like museums, and you would be correct. In fact, a lot of European museums began as gathering points of many personal collections. Over the years, these private cabinets were bought up, bequeathed, and donated until they became the large public collections that we call museums.

In fact, the Enlightenment Room is the oldest in the British Museum. It originally held the King's Library, a collection of sixty-five thousand books and documents gathered by King George III. And then, in 2003, the space re-opened as the cabinet of curiosities it is today.

A good chunk of the items you can see in there, as well as other objects across the museum, came from the personal collection of Sir Hans Sloane, who spent the better part of seven decades gathering a staggering collection of over seventy-one thousand pieces. In a very real way, the curiosity of one person led to the collection and preservation of an incredible amount of history.

One last thing. If you had the chance to slowly walk the length of this gallery, you would notice how all of the objects are grouped into themed collections. Geological samples are in one spot, relics from specific scientific expeditions can be found elsewhere, and there are even collections of fossils and bones.

The reason for this organization is pretty obvious: it helps visitors get a full experience. They can explore one particular category and really soak it in. Plus, seeing related items together on the shelf adds an extra layer of context to their individual stories. All of a sudden, they are more than just unique items—they become part of a bigger world.

Which is why this book exists. My team and I have spent the past five years gathering the most amazing, entertaining, and enlightening stories from history and placing them into a modern, digital cabinet of curiosities. Yes, every story is a little object sitting on a shelf by itself, and that's all well and good. But it's time for a bit of organization.

Like the Enlightenment Room, my goal here is to present these tales in the context of specific categories. This topical arrangement allows fans of curious history to more easily find what they are looking for, and to see just how interconnected the individual stories of the past really are.

So please, enjoy your tour through a new kind of cabinet of curiosities. Walk the width and length of our gallery, and take in the wonders that are on display. I've worked hard to curate this ever-evolving exhibit of the most fascinating tales from history, and I'm certain that you'll enjoy visiting these incredible places, unusual characters, and amazing events.

That is, of course, if you're more than a little . . . *curious.*

Aaron Mahnke
November 2023

CURIOUS

AMERICANA

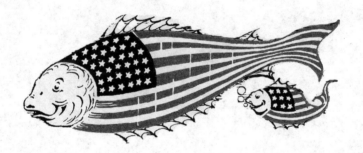

SECOND LIFE

It's one of many tales of the founding of America. Settlers from England were exploring more and more of the *New* World, and as they did, they set up new communities far from the comfort of home. We know these stories as well as the backs of our hands, if not in detail then at least in theme.

Most of the original states have a story that echoes these themes, but there's one tale in particular that I want to tell you. Some think it begins as far back as the late 1670s, when English settlers began to cross over the Appalachian Mountains. First there were dozens, then hundreds, and then thousands. They made their homes in an area that was part of the far western edge of the colonies of North Carolina and Virginia, settling along the Watauga River valley.

They farmed and hunted for years, making a new life for themselves, but in 1763 England declared it illegal to cross the mountains into the west, so they had a choice: They could either return to North Carolina's legal territory, or become united and support themselves. They had fought to be there, after all, defending themselves against the Cherokee tribe of Native Americans. They didn't want to give all of that up.

In 1772, they drafted a document that foreshadowed the coming Declaration of Independence. With it they formed the Watauga Association, set up courts and a militia, and continued to defend their territory. A few years later, the British sent troops over the mountains to attack them, but these frontiersmen were stronger than they seemed. They met the British at the foot of King's Mountain and sent them retreating back into the eastern colonies.

After the war was over, they tried their hand at being a satellite colony of North Carolina, but after being taxed almost as severely as they had under the Crown, they seceded to go it alone. In 1784 they set up their own state—America's fourteenth, in fact—and elected a governor named John Sevier. Thomas Jefferson even backed their move and helped them make a formal request to the government to be recognized as a new American state.

Sadly, the new state failed to get the approval necessary, and their entire enterprise fell apart. About four years after attempting to become an independent state, the land was repossessed by North Carolina and Sevier was arrested as a traitor. Which is why you've never heard of the first fourteenth state in American history, a state named after one of the heroes of the Revolution, Benjamin Franklin.

Yes, the state of Franklin was shut down before it could even begin its new, official life, but the spirit that gave birth to it—the strength of the frontier settlers and their fierce independence—helped keep the dream alive. In 1796—twelve years after their first failure—the people of the territory were successfully admitted to the Union as a state. They changed the name from Franklin to Tennessee, and it's stuck ever since.

Oh, and their first governor? None other than John Sevier. Naturally.

It's a powerful lesson, wrapped up in a bit of lost, bizarre history. Our failures often hurt, but over time most people will forget about them. What's truly important, it seems, is to never give up.

You never know how things will turn out in the end.

SHOTS FIRED

Theodore Roosevelt is remembered today as an icon of strength—and for good reason. He was a cowboy, a hunter, and a soldier before he ever stepped foot in the White House. But not everyone knows the truth behind the Bull Moose's tough demeanor.

Growing up, Teddy was sick. A lot. He battled asthma for most of his childhood and woke up many nights suffering from severe breathing problems, a feeling he compared to being smothered to death. As he got older, joining his father on hikes and camping trips, the attacks lessened. Teddy realized the secret to beating his asthma was in physically strengthening his body.

He took up boxing and studied biology. Hunting became a beloved pastime, especially on his ranches in North Dakota. His resilience carried him through college, where he studied naval history and strategy, even as he worked his way up through the New York State Assembly, governor's office, vice presidency, and then finally, the White House.

Teddy had grand plans for his presidency, and one of those plans included an unprecedented third term in office. It was the fall of 1912 in Milwaukee, Wisconsin, when he left his hotel to deliver one of the last speeches of his grueling campaign. He'd been on the road for weeks shaking hands and talking before crowds of hundreds, even thousands of voters. His voice had all but disappeared, but Teddy pressed on. There were bigger issues at stake and by this time, Teddy was known for speaking softly.

Clad in his thick Army overcoat, he stepped into a waiting car ready to whisk him off to the auditorium. Inside his breast pocket, Teddy had placed his folded-up speech—about fifty pages total—and his metal eyeglass case. The crowd cheered when they saw him, and Theodore Roosevelt—not one to disappoint his adoring constituents—stood to wave back at them.

He never saw John Schrank, the out-of-work barkeep, raise the Colt .45 to his chest. The shot rang out and Schrank was quickly tackled and arrested by Roosevelt's bodyguards. The would-be assassin claimed the ghost of William McKinley had visited him in a dream one night and told him to avenge McKinley's assassination by killing President Roosevelt.

Teddy—pale, but calm—touched his fingers to his lips. If the bullet had pierced his lung, he'd have blood coming out of his mouth. When his fingers came back clean, he instructed the driver to get him to the auditorium right away.

Once there, three doctors examined the severity of the president's wound. The bullet had, in fact, pierced his skin, and lodged itself in the right side of his chest. It had been slowed by the thick wad of paper and the metal case in his pocket, so much of the damage was superficial. Teddy pressed on, determined to deliver this important speech.

He sent one of his bodyguards out onstage to explain to the audience what had happened. Some didn't buy it. One man shouted an all too familiar refrain: "Fake!"

Teddy took to the stage, the bloodstained shirt on display for all to see. He held up the speech with the hole going straight through all fifty pages and just like that, the crowd fell silent. He spoke for an hour and a half before finally heading to the hospital. Doctors were unable to remove the bullet and Teddy lived with it inside his chest for the rest of his life.

His valiant efforts didn't win him any points with voters, though. One month later, Woodrow Wilson won the election, and became the twenty-eighth president of the United States.

But Teddy wasn't fazed by the attempt on his life. He'd been expecting something like that to happen for a while. When asked how he was able to remain so calm and deliver his entire speech, even after being shot, he said:

"In the very unlikely event of the wound being mortal, I wished to die with my *boots* on."

PONY UP

Its legacy is as American as baseball and apple pie. Its riders were fast, famous, and fearless. It has been the subject of over a dozen films and television shows, and it became the foundation of one of the largest banks in the world. When it came to speed and reliability in the 1860s, you couldn't beat the Pony Express.

As California began to boom from the gold rush, business owners and settlers needed a faster way to communicate with folks farther east. At the time, letters and packages took roughly twenty-five days to travel by stagecoach. Even longer if going by ship. The Pony Express more than halved that time with an average delivery window of about ten days.

Not everyone used the Pony Express, though. It was really expensive for the average person to send a letter. At five dollars per half-ounce of mail, the service was primarily used as a delivery method for newspapers, business correspondence, and government bulletins. Gold rush hopefuls just couldn't afford the speedy service.

And speedy it was. Ten days may have been the average time it took to deliver a letter, but it certainly wasn't the fastest. That record belonged to Robert Haslam. He'd earned the nickname "Pony Bob" and for a very good reason: he was responsible for the fastest delivery in Pony Express history.

Bob had come to the United States from England as a teenager just as the Pony Express was getting up and running. He'd gotten his start by building depot stations, but was soon given a route of his own from Lake Tahoe to Buckland's Station, a seventy-five-mile stretch of Nevada Territory all his own.

In May of 1860, with his deliveries in tow, Bob traveled on horseback from San Francisco to Buckland's Station where he got a taste of a growing war. Not the Civil War, mind you, but one that must have seemed equally as terrifying. The Pyramid Lake Indian War had found its way to Buckland's Station in a bad way. The relief rider who was supposed to carry Bob's mail east to Smith's Creek was too scared to ride due to the growing Native American threat.

Bob couldn't let the letters he'd been carrying go undelivered. He had to make a decision and quick, or his trip would have been for nothing. He mounted up and kept going. One hundred and ninety miles on horseback in just under nine hours without rest. He'd made it.

Bob slept all night before traveling back to Buckland's Station the next day. Once he reached the depot at Cold Springs, he noticed the war had finally arrived. The station keeper had been killed and everything inside had been taken. There was no time to stop. The longer he lingered, the more danger he was putting himself in, so he just kept going.

Three hundred and eighty miles later, Pony Bob had done it: he'd completed the longest round trip on record for the Pony Express in less than two days.

Bob Haslam rode for the Pony Express for months following his record-breaking journey, but the most important ride of his life was yet to come. In April of 1861, a very special delivery had to get from Fort Kearny in the Nebraska Territory all the way to Placerville, California. If it didn't make it, the fate of the entire country might be at risk, and only one rider was fit to carry such precious cargo: Pony Bob himself.

He picked up the bundle, tucked it into his saddlebag, and rode for 120 miles. His route took him through Paiute Indian territory, and as he traveled, he encountered a handful of braves who didn't take kindly to his trespassing on their land. One of their arrows found its way into his arm, while another flew straight into his jaw, knocking out several of his teeth. The attack didn't deter him, though, and his horse galloped faster until they were out of danger.

He made it to California in just eight hours and twenty minutes, and then delivered his package. You see, that precious cargo he'd been carrying had been Abraham Lincoln's inaugural address, which was to be telegraphed to Sacramento for publication up and down the West Coast. And if Bob hadn't made it in time, California might have chosen to side with the Confederacy at the start of the Civil War.

What's most interesting about the Pony Express isn't the roster of riders like Pony Bob Haslam or Buffalo Bill Cody, nor the blistering speed with which mail was delivered across the country. It wasn't even the dangerous conditions its riders faced, like mounting threats from Native Americans or harsh weather.

No, it's that this company, which has had such an enduring legacy as an icon of American industry, existed for only eighteen months.

BY A HAIR

Memento mori. It's Latin for "remember, you will die" and it has become a mantra for thrill-seekers and entrepreneurs to remind them to live life to its fullest. We have a limited number of years on this planet, so we must make the most of them. Some people repeat the phrase in their daily life, almost like a kind of mantra. Others carry a token with them, a tangible reminder that hardens the concept into something real.

Such tokens were common throughout history and were often fashioned into jewelry to be worn by the mindful . . . and the grieving. A ring with an ornate skull design might have been worn by a mournful widow to honor her late husband. A daughter might have gone about her life with a photo of her deceased mother in a locket around her neck.

One of the most famous mementos ever created, however, bears the last remaining vestige of an American icon. Born in Virginia in 1732, George Washington is best known as a Revolutionary War general and, of course, the first president of the United States. But he was also a devoted husband and friend.

He began courting Martha Custis in 1758, traveling more than thirty miles on horseback to spend time with her. Both parties were independently wealthy, attractive, and ranked high on the social ladder. They fell in love almost immediately and married one year later. Contrary to popular practices at the time, Martha didn't have her husband sign a prenuptial agreement to protect her assets from a previous marriage. They had found in each other someone to love and trust without question.

Though he had no children of his own, Washington happily helped raise Martha's son and daughter from her first marriage. They lived a happy life, with George turning their modest farmhouse at Mount Vernon into an eleven-thousand-square-foot estate. When he traveled, George left the home in Martha's care, and even though she was glad for the independence, she also missed him terribly.

She would occasionally visit him during the Revolution at his winter encampments, greeting soldiers along the way and acting as a beacon of light amid a dark and depressing time. Her effect on the troops was no doubt felt throughout the war, and her presence may have helped motivate her husband to succeed. Being apart for so long weighed heavily upon both their hearts.

After the war, George was elected the first president of the United States and moved the family to New York and then Philadelphia, the temporary capitals of the newly formed nation. They embraced their new roles, and it was during George's second term when he met another important person in his life: his friend and confidant Tobias Lear.

Lear had tutored the Washingtons' children and worked his way up within the family, from becoming the president's clerk to his eventual business partner. They shared meals and stories, and grew to be more like brothers than colleagues. And Lear remained in touch with his dear friend long after Washington retired back to Mount Vernon.

And it was at Mount Vernon where George and Martha spent their final years entertaining their grandchildren and hosting parties for American elites. Through distance and war and politics, the Washingtons had emerged more in love than ever before. Sadly, their love would not be enough to endure George's stubbornness.

In December of 1799, he set out on horseback to inspect his land in the middle of a snowstorm. He returned to the house for dinner later that night where Martha and several guests had been waiting. Not wanting to keep them from their meals any longer, he remained in his cold, wet clothes while he ate.

The next day, George complained of a sore throat, but continued his survey of the farm in the freezing weather. The sore throat turned into a chest cold, and twenty-four hours later, George Washington died in his bed at Mount Vernon. By his side were Martha and longtime friend Tobias Lear.

Washington was buried four days later. He'd secretly given Lear an order to wait so he would not be accidentally entombed alive, a common fear of that era. Lear obliged out of a deep love and respect for the man who had taken him under his wing. However, Washington had also given his friend something else. A memento of their friendship and a tribute to his meaning to the family.

It was a brooch. Composed of beveled glass and adorned with rubies along the top, it bore the words "token of my friendship" in French. And entwined behind that beveled glass were two locks of hair—one belonging to George, and one to Martha.

Their life together was one of passion and undying affection. Even in death, the two refused to remain apart. Not only were they entombed together within the Mount Vernon mausoleum, but their hair, the last evidence of their corporeal existence, was preserved as a reminder to Tobias Lear that life was to be lived as though every day might be your last, and if possible, to do it with your loved ones by your side.

Oh, and if you go out in the cold, wear a hat.

ACTING OUT

Ed was an actor. A pretty famous one at that. He was born in 1833 in Maryland to a family of actors. His father and two brothers had all performed Shakespeare onstage for adoring crowds, and Ed had made a bit of a name for himself.

He'd gotten his start in a performance of *Richard III* alongside his father, who favored a more outspoken acting style to Ed's quiet contemplation. Regardless of how they performed, one thing was certain: the family knew how to entertain. People came from all over to watch the men recite some of the most famous lines ever written for the stage.

Then, three years after their first performance together, Ed's father passed away. Ed chose to remain with the show for an international tour. And it was on this tour that he gained wide acclaim for his talents. People in the United States and Europe knew his name, and it became synonymous with "star."

But his homeland was changing. A conflict that had begun in the South had migrated north and embroiled the country in a war unlike any other. Fathers were pitted against sons. Mothers stopped speaking to their daughters. Blood was shed in fields and streams from Georgia to New York as the Union fought to end the scourge of slavery infecting the southern states.

It was time for Ed to come home. He boarded a ship bound for the US and rejoined his family, who had changed considerably in his absence. He and his brothers had found themselves on opposing sides, with Ed supporting the Union and his brothers in favor of the South. In fact, none of them appeared onstage together until 1864, when they participated in a charity to raise funds for a statue of William Shakespeare for Central Park in New York City.

Coincidentally, 1864 was also the year Ed would become a hero. He'd been standing on a train platform in Jersey City, New Jersey, when he caught sight of a boy just shy of adulthood beside him. A crowd had gathered to board the car and pushed him forward. Before he had a chance to get out of the way, the train began to move, spinning him off his feet at the edge of the platform. He nearly fell onto the tracks, but there was Ed, ready with lightning quick reflexes. He grabbed the boy's collar and pulled him back up next to him. The young man recognized his savior, and thanked him profusely for what he'd done.

Ed was only too happy to help, but had no idea who he'd actually saved. He wouldn't find out until months later, just before the country would enter a period of mourning for President Abraham Lincoln. Lincoln, as we all know, was shot during a performance at Ford's Theater by John Wilkes Booth. An actor.

Booth had had a brother. Two, in fact, both of them also actors. He'd fallen out with one, however. A Unionist named Ed. Edwin Thomas Booth.

Edwin hadn't known his brother was going to assassinate the president. To perform such an act was unthinkable, even to many of the very people who hated the man and what he stood for. But Edwin tried not to dwell on the dishonor his brother had brought to his family's name. Instead, he sought solace in one simple fact: he'd done some good.

You see, the young man Edwin had saved on the train platform that day wasn't some random boy. In a letter he'd received just before the president's death, the truth had become clear: the boy had told his story to a Colonel Adam Badeau, serving under General Ulysses S. Grant. The colonel then penned a letter of gratitude for rescuing his newest recruit, a young soldier named Robert Todd Lincoln. Abraham Lincoln's son.

Edwin Thomas Booth and Robert Todd Lincoln had managed to change the nation, one for the worse, one for the better. We'll never know what might've happened if Edwin hadn't been there to prevent Robert Todd Lincoln from falling, but we do know one thing: despite a lifetime on the stage, it was certainly the greatest performance of his life.

TIME TRAVELER

Our time on this earth is often short. Disease and unforeseen circumstances can make it even shorter. Compared with the red sea urchin, which is known to live as long as two hundred years, our lives can be seen as a blip, a gust of wind coming in and blowing out in an instant.

It's rare for a person to live past ninety years of age, even rarer for ninety-five. And one hundred is reserved for only the most special cases. Less than 1 percent of the American population lives to be a hundred and the percentage only goes down from there as their ages go up.

But one man beat the odds. If someone had written a novel about him, readers would have called it science fiction. He was a man out of time, with firsthand knowledge of experiences only read about in history books.

His name was Sylvester, and his story is one of a kind.

Born on a North Carolina plantation in 1841, Sylvester had a tough childhood. He was enslaved, as were his parents, and he worked alongside them until he turned nineteen. That's when his enslaver sold him to another plantation in Mississippi. When the Civil War started, he assisted his owner in securing guns for the Confederate army, which automatically made the young slave a Confederate soldier.

Yeah, Sylvester had unknowingly been enlisted to the side trying to keep him a slave. It's not like he had a choice, but he eventually got the upper hand a few years later when he escaped north and joined the Union army. Once away from his old life, Sylvester soon found himself alongside scores of other soldiers as part of General Grant's Vicksburg campaign and the Battle of Champion Hill. He had no fighting experience, and he'd never been in a war before, but he held on to his faith, which helped him calm some of the more frightened soldiers.

Freed by the war, Sylvester went back to Mississippi, where he found work on a farm, eventually settling down to work at a local sawmill. And that's where his story ended. Well, ended is the wrong word. Paused is more like it. You see, many years later, the people of Collins, Mississippi, held a birthday party for him. A five-layer cake was brought in adorned with a *lot* of candles. That's because this party was held in 1965.

Yes, the Civil War veteran had lived to the unheard-of age of 124. And naturally, his story reached a historian named Alfred Andrews, who helped get Sylvester classified officially as a veteran of the Civil War despite there being no record of his ever having served.

But Sylvester Magee didn't need a piece of paper saying he'd been a soldier. He told Andrews stories about the war, about specific battles no one else would have known. He spoke in exceptional detail about his experiences, establishing himself as the oldest and last surviving former American slave.

When you think about a life as long as Sylvester Magee's, you realize he didn't just survive one war. He also lived through two World Wars, the Korean War, and Vietnam, until finally passing away in 1971. And what makes his story even more powerful is what else he witnessed.

He began his life in servitude, only to see the end of the Civil War and the end of slavery in the United States. One hundred years later, he saw the signing of the Civil Rights Act of 1964, a law that prohibited discrimination based on race, color, religion, sex, or national origin. He watched the first Black woman win an Academy Award. He saw schools desegregate. And sadly, he lived to see the assassination of Dr. Martin Luther King.

Despite the bad he witnessed, though, there was a lot of *good,* too. And one thing is certain: Sylvester Magee lived a full life. Perhaps more than any other American citizen.

Time is a funny thing, after all. But if we manage to stick around long enough, there's no telling the kinds of stories we'll be able to tell.

Sylvester Magee knew that better than anyone.

AMERICAN ICON

Since the country's founding, the United States' flag design has followed a fairly standard formula each time a new state is added. The thirteen original colonies are represented by the seven red and six white stripes, while the current states themselves are represented by white stars against a field of blue in the upper left corner.

Some things change from flag to flag. For example, when Oregon became a state in 1859, several different versions of the flag existed, including one where the thirty-three separate stars were arranged in the shape of one big star, while another flag chose a diamond shape for them instead. But the blue background and thirteen stripes remained the same no matter what.

Despite calls for change to the status quo, it seems people still love and admire the flag's simple, yet iconic design. However, things were a bit different almost sixty years ago.

After Alaska and Hawaii were admitted as states in 1959 and 1960 respectively, it had been decided that such a drastic change to the country required an equally drastic change to its flag. A government employee named Stanley Pratt solicited ideas for new flag designs from a group of Ohio residents.

Within a week, he had flags of all shapes and sizes on his desk, and had one of the toughest jobs of his career ahead of him: judging every single submission. He wrote back to each entrant, explaining his decision. Almost everyone took it well, except for one.

Robert Heft felt he had put a lot of work into his flag. He didn't just draw it on a piece of paper. He spent twelve and a half hours sewing a full-size version for Mr. Pratt. He kept the thirteen stripes of red and white, as well as the blue rectangle in the top left corner. The stars he arranged in a kind of grid pattern with lines of five and six stars alternating until they numbered fifty.

Mr. Pratt's comments weren't entirely wrong. He said Heft's flag lacked originality, which it did, but Heft felt he had something special, something fit for a country, so he did what any self-respecting flag designer would do: he wrote his congressperson.

Ohio congressman Walter Moeller hoisted Robert's flag all the way up to the United States Congress for a vote. It didn't take much for him to convince his fellow congressmen of the flag's importance. They voted in favor of its design and it was formally accepted as the new symbol of the United States on July 4, 1960. Yeah, Independence Day. Poetic, right?

However, the story doesn't end there. In fact, it isn't even the whole story. You see, I haven't been completely honest about the flag's provenance. You might be asking why a government official went to Ohio to source a new design rather than open up the opportunity nationwide?

Well, it is true that Robert Heft designed the flag, but he didn't do it as part of a contest. And Stanley Pratt technically did work for the government, but not for any federal agency. The flag had been part of a class project. Pratt had been a high school teacher, and Robert Heft, his student.

Robert ended up getting a B minus on his project. Disappointed in his grade, he asked his teacher if there was anything he could do. After all, he'd spent an entire day stitching it together—it had to be worth more than a B minus. So, Mr. Pratt gave him a seemingly impossible task: he told him if he could get the United States Congress to accept his design as the official national flag, then he'd change his grade to an A.

Robert passed away in 2009, but his design lives on, flying over the White House and every government building across the country. Heft's family still possesses the original flag he made by hand, though museums and wealthy collectors have tried to purchase it. To the family, it isn't just a piece of history. It's a family heirloom.

And as for Mr. Pratt's promise? He made good on it. Robert got his A.

BONE TO PICK

Benjamin Franklin is best known as one of America's Founding Fathers, partly responsible for our independence from Great Britain. A politician, inventor, author, and polymath, Franklin was a man with an insatiable curiosity. However, behind his striking wit and boundless intellect beat the heart of someone with more than a few secrets.

Remember, Franklin's work took him all over the world. In 1764, he traveled to London to advocate on behalf of the American colonists against new taxes being imposed on them. For ten years he tried to make the case for lower taxes on his people back home, but found himself blocked at every turn.

However, while living in England during this period of time, Franklin needed to occupy his days with other pursuits. He was used to expanding his mind with scientific and artistic endeavors back in Philadelphia, so he continued to invent and write. But it was inside his London home that evidence of some of his more questionable "work" would be discovered over two hundred years later.

In 1998, a group calling themselves the

Friends of Benjamin Franklin House had started turning Franklin's former London abode into a museum all about him. A worthy pursuit and a noble cause, for sure.

A few weeks into the process, though, one of the construction workers who had been renovating the basement came across a pit in the floor big enough to hold a person. It was in the middle of a room devoid of windows and positioned far from the street. A room that was, for all intents and purposes, hidden and soundproof. And down in the pit, sticking straight out like a weed, was a human bone.

The worker called the police, who allowed the team to continue their work. Bit by bit, a team of workers carefully uncovered more than one thousand bone fragments in Franklin's basement, some of which had been carved into while others had been sawed straight through. And there was evidence someone had drilled into several of the skulls they found.

The shards belonged to ten victims, six of whom were children, all of which had died more than two hundred years earlier. Perhaps the charming diplomat who'd invented bifocals and the glass armonica had also pursued a career as a serial killer.

The police, upon learning of the age of the bones, chose not to pursue an investigation. After all, how do you prosecute a Founding Father? But historians were curious. They documented all the fragments and began running tests. It was clear something heinous had gone down in Franklin's home.

Well, heinous by today's standards. No,

Benjamin Franklin was not a serial killer. He didn't cut up people in his basement. He let his friend William Hewson do that. Hewson was a medical student with a passion for studying the internal workings of the human body. However, once he and his former teacher parted ways, Hewson was left without a laboratory in which to continue his work.

Luckily, his friend Ben Franklin lived nearby with a basement large enough for him to dissect his bodies in peace. Specimens were hard to come by, so Hewson resorted to grave robbing. He'd sneak the bodies in under cover of night, perform his work, then bury what remained so he wouldn't get caught trying to get rid of the evidence. He never killed anyone, but that didn't mean his methods were ethical.

It's not clear whether Franklin participated in, or even knew about, the experiments going on in his basement. When he returned to America, he continued to let Hewson use the house for his work. If only his friend had been more careful.

In the spring of 1774 while dissecting a cadaver, Dr. Hewson cut himself and contracted an infection, which eventually turned into sepsis. He died a short while later, but don't worry—his bones were not among the others found in Franklin's house.

Dr. William Hewson was given a proper burial in St. Martin-in-the-Fields Churchyard in London. And Franklin . . . well, he didn't really have any skeletons in his closet after all.

But he did keep quite a few in his basement.

CLOWNING AROUND

A good president needs to have a lot to win. They need to be likable. They must have sound policies that benefit the American people. And . . . well, none of that actually is true. Politicians are a rare breed. Mix a pinch of charm, a dash of authority, and a whole heaping bowl of hubris, and you'll eventually have yourself a red-blooded American individual with grand dreams of running the country.

One man had such a dream over 170 years ago when he tried running for president. His name was Dan Rice, and he made his living as an entertainer. He trained animals, satirized national politics, performed in stage shows, and parodied Shakespearean plays with his own humorous versions.

Early in his career, when he had no money to his name and only one horse, larger circuses and troupes made fun of his "one horse show." Although they had intended to insult him, the aspiring star flipped it around and used the phrase to advertise his surprisingly enjoyable performance.

As he gained in popularity, his show was able to generate more income, and was eventually dubbed "The Greatest Show on Earth" years before P. T. Barnum's own traveling circus would fly that flag. Legendary American author Mark Twain admired Rice so much that his description of a circus in *Adventures of Huckleberry Finn* was based on the performer's famous spectacle.

But Rice was best known for his enduring role as a circus clown. He didn't just run around and perform slapstick for cheering children, though. His was more like a stand-up comedy routine than your typical clowning around. He'd perform observational humor, and sing songs about the news, which let audiences in on another passion of his: politics.

Rice once invited then-candidate Zachary Taylor to campaign aboard his circus wagon, encouraging the future twelfth president to "jump on the bandwagon"—which, by the way, is how that phrase came to be. Later on, Rice decided to stop sharing the stage with other politicians, and enter the fray himself.

In 1864, he ran for the Pennsylvania senate, using his immense popularity to help power his campaign. But when it later appeared that he wouldn't secure enough votes to gain traction in the polls, he dropped out.

He didn't let the experience discourage him, though. Rice wanted to serve the people as best he could and—as they say—"the show must go on." When Rice tried again four years later to get elected to public office, he aimed higher. Much higher. You see, he wanted to be the *president*.

At first it seemed the papers were supportive of his plans. He was a national treasure, after all, beloved by audiences everywhere. Of course, Rice had his detractors, and not everyone thought the former circus clown had the ability to lead the people. A newspaper called the *Somerset Democrat* mocked his bid for the presidency, claiming he "had amassed wealth by catering to the tastes of the very lowest order of society in the disreputable capacity of a . . . clown and showman."

More papers followed with rebukes of their own, and although he tried to respond through open letters and opinion pieces, his efforts had little effect. It didn't help that a popular military general was moving up in the polls, no doubt bolstered by his impressive performance during the Civil War. When it became clear he wouldn't get the nomination, Rice withdrew from the race, allowing Ulysses S. Grant to go on and become the eighteenth president of the United States.

Dan Rice was an entertainer, a showman, and a patriot. He loved his country, and thought there was no better way to show that love than to become an elected public servant.

But don't think of him as a failure. He was incredibly patriotic, and those images of him with his long white beard went on to inspire a character we all know from the recruitment posters that were printed and distributed during World Wars I and II.

He might not have become president, but without Dan Rice, America wouldn't have its most famous mascot of all . . .

. . . Uncle Sam.

BATTLE PLANS

The 1980s were a wild time. Advances in technology had brought the personal computer to the masses, as well as fear about the future. We didn't have any idea of what the internet would bring. There was no warning about social media, and nobody was branding themselves as an "influencer."

But a war was brewing, one that would bring two world powers together in a display of unity not seen at any other time in history.

It began as the Cold War was ending. President Ronald Reagan and Soviet leader Mikhail Gorbachev had gone back and forth in an effort to end the global arms race. The Soviet Union had promised to eliminate ballistic missiles and Intermediate-range Nuclear Forces, or INFs, from Europe. In turn, the United States would promise not to continue their research into strategic defense initiatives for ten years.

But President Reagan wasn't interested in stopping research. While he hated the concept of Mutually Assured Destruction, his goal was to implement his Strategic Defense Initiative—a missile defense system that would prevent a ballistic missile attack—from space.

Neither side trusted the other, but that

didn't stop either of them from working on a possible solution. The talks came to a head in September of 1986 when Gorbachev suggested a meeting somewhere neutral where they could discuss matters in peace and perhaps come to some kind of agreement.

Reagan agreed and thirty days later, on October 11, the president of the United States and the leader of the Soviet Union gathered at a house in Reykjavik, Iceland, that had once been used as the British consulate. It was there where they would begin negotiations.

Things didn't go well at first. Gorbachev was described as "belligerent," wanting only to discuss ending the arms race. Reagan, on the other hand, had several problems he wanted remedied, including the Soviet invasion of Afghanistan and various human rights violations.

Unable to find common ground, the two men decided to leave the house and take a walk around the property with their interpreters. The discussion they had was heard only by the people present. History tells us nothing of value was mentioned, as the summit fell apart not long after. The Cold War wouldn't end for another five years.

However, Gorbachev certainly remembered what he and the former president discussed. You see, Reagan was an avid reader, specifically of science fiction. Edgar Rice Burroughs was a favorite, but so were some contemporary authors, two of whom ended up writing policy for the president's bold new initiative. Because Reagan saw space the way Gene Roddenberry had—as the final frontier.

Jerry Pournelle and Larry Niven, the co-authors of the 1974 bestseller *The Mote in God's Eye,* had been asked to join a new committee dedicated to advancing America's future technology efforts. It was called the Citizens' Advisory Council on National Space Policy, and was comprised of former astronauts, military personnel, scientists, and other science fiction authors.

Over three days, the Citizens' Advisory Council met at Niven's house, where they drafted a policy designed to combat Reagan's fears. Later, during his walk with Mr. Gorbachev, he brought those fears up in conversation.

President Reagan no longer saw Gorbachev or the Soviet Union as the US's ultimate enemy anymore. And although their talks fizzled in Reykjavik, the two men understood that at some point they'd need to put their differences aside and join forces. There was another threat on the horizon. One that would require as much firepower as our planet could muster.

President Reagan asked Mr. Gorbachev if he would help when the time came. Mr. Gorbachev, with the help of his translator, didn't laugh or scoff or insult the president in any way. He simply turned to him and said, "No doubt about it."

And just what battle were they preparing for, and where was that war going to take place? Nowhere, it turns out. Well, nowhere on *Earth,* that is.

They had agreed to help each other for the greater good, should a new enemy ever arrive to threaten their safety.

An enemy . . . from outer space.

WILD
COINCIDENCES

UPSIDE DOWN

We've all mailed a letter or two in our lifetime. Most of us understand that sending a letter has certain costs attached to it—like paying the mail carriers and the people who sort and organize it all—so there's a fee attached to each letter. Literally, in fact; since the 1840s, people have paid for the privilege of mailing a letter by purchasing stamps.

One beautiful spring morning, a man named Bill Robey left the post office with a sheet of stamps. There were one hundred of them all together, and he'd paid a whopping $24 for the lot of them. They were pretty, too, with a bright red border on a background of sky blue. And right there in the middle of the frame, flanked by the value of the stamp and a large "U.S. Postage" banner across the top, was an airplane.

They were hot off the presses, and were sort of a commemorative stamp, so to speak. You see, the airplane featured in the artwork was meant to represent a historic flight that was about to take place the very next day. The Postal Service was about to enter the era of airmail, transporting mail over hundreds of miles with the help of airplanes. It was a very big deal.

In fact, when the flight took place the next day, President Woodrow Wilson showed up to watch it. The plan was to fly from Washington, DC, all the way to New York City, and despite some early engine troubles, the flight finally took off under the guidance of Lt. George Boyle.

The plane, by the way, was a Curtiss model JN-4. "JN," of course, sounds a lot like "Jen," which is why most people called them "Jennys." And that Jenny took off and vanished over the horizon.

Anyway, the day before, when Bill Robey took those stamps home, he noticed something odd about them. The entire sheet appeared to have been printed incorrectly. The plane in the middle of each tiny frame was flying upside down, the product of a simple printing error involving a reversed plate. Most important, though, they were rare.

In fact, only nine of those upside down sheets were printed before the mistake was fixed, making them extremely rare. I think most people have seen them before, too. These stamps are a textbook example of how manufacturing errors can turn a common object into something that's incredibly desirable to collectors. And let me tell you, these things were desirable.

Bill ended up selling his $24 sheet a week later for $15,000. The man who bought it sold it a week later for $20,000. From there, the prices just skyrocketed. Over the years, the sheet was separated into blocks to sell off one or two stamps at a time, and by the 1960s, a single-stamp price was in the tens of thousands of dollars. By the 1980s, one stamp would run you nearly $200,000.

In May of 2016, the old "inverted Jenny"

set a new record, with a single stamp selling at auction for nearly $1.2 million. And honestly, I can't help but wonder at the power of rarity and time to make something as small as a postage stamp become worth more than a million bucks. It's crazy, for sure, but it's not the craziest part of this story.

These stamps were released on May 10 of 1918, just a few days ahead of the flight they were meant to commemorate. On May 15, the crowd gathered to watch the plane take off, and then watched it slowly disappear in the distance. Except, it headed the wrong way.

It was supposed to fly north, but instead headed south. The pilot, George Boyle, blamed it on a broken compass when he called his boss for help. You see, it turns out he had landed somewhere in Maryland and needed someone to come get him and the plane. And not just "landed"—Boyle actually crash-landed that Jenny, which was a bit more embarrassing.

The plane had crashed in a cornfield, and to be honest, it was a miracle that Boyle survived to talk about it later. That's because of the position the plane ended up in.

It was upside down.

THE RUNDOWN

Peter Karpin was a spy, there was no question about it.

He'd been captured by the French as he was trying to slip into their country in 1914, just as the First World War was beginning. Maybe his papers were clearly forged, or perhaps there was something about his accent, or the way he shifted his eyes when they asked him questions. We don't know why he was captured, only that he *was*.

Which meant that the French had a problem on their hands. They could toss him in jail—which they did right away—but then what? Alert the Germans that their spy had been captured? That was only going to force them to send another spy, or perhaps more than one. The French would have to be even more diligent with their border patrols after that, and no one wanted that. There were too many other things that needed their time and resources.

There was another option, though, but it was risky. Someone proposed actually keeping Peter Karpin's capture a secret from the Germans. They could send fake intelligence reports back to the man's superiors in Berlin and try to fool them into believing that Karpin was doing his job. So that's what they did.

For three years they sent back reports, and for three years the Germans replied with more instructions and requests. Of course, the French were feeding the Germans one false report after another, but the Germans hadn't noticed. They were even making military decisions based on those false reports. It was brilliant.

It gets better, though. You see, Peter Karpin needed an income to survive in France, so the Germans were sending him money on a regular basis. Sometimes it was for his own personal expenses, while other times it was funding for the projects they were tasking him with. And every time Germany sent that money, the French were intercepting it and putting it into a bank account.

In 1917, though, Peter Karpin escaped. I don't know how, but he managed to slip out of wherever they were holding him and vanish into the depths of France. More than likely he was going to head back to Germany, but without his money and papers, that was going to take some time. Oh, and speaking of money, that was when the French decided to spend the cash they'd been covertly stealing from the Germans.

They bought a brand-new car with it. Fancy, right?

A few years later, in 1923, France sent forces to an area of Germany that the Treaty of Versailles had declared to be a demilitarized zone. The Germans had failed to make all of the World War I reparation payments they'd agreed to and had instead formed a "passive resistance" that was creating tension. The French arrived as a sort of peacekeeping measure.

They brought the car with them, which was a bit poetic, I think. A car purchased by the French, with German funds, and now it was in Germany. Now, I don't know the exact circumstances, but at some point in the French occupation there in 1923, that car was involved in an incident. Maybe it was used in crowd control, or perhaps it was just being driven through the streets like anyone today would enjoy.

Whatever reason the car had for moving, it tragically struck a German citizen down, throwing him to the ground like a rag doll. The French driver of the car quickly climbed out, panic and grief painted across his face, and approached the body of the man he'd hit. It was too late, though; the man was dead.

Checking his papers for anything that would help them contact the man's relatives and inform them of the tragic accident, the French soldiers discovered something amazing. This man they had hit—the one who now lay dead in the street after being struck by the German-funded automobile— wasn't the random stranger they expected him to be. In fact, they knew him.

It was the spy himself, Peter Karpin.

THE GIFT

King Edward VII—like many of the wealthy elite of England—loved to hunt. In the 1860s, when his mother, Queen Victoria, was still on the throne and Edward was nothing more special than being the Prince of Wales, he would often gather his friends and take them fox hunting.

Among this group of friends was *another* man named Edward, this one being an actor by profession. The pair of Edwards were apparently very close, and at some point in their relationship the prince gifted the actor with a small golden matchbox, the sort that a gentleman would keep attached to his pocket watch chain for easy access and safekeeping. It even had Edward's name on it—the actor, not the prince.

Years went by, as they have a way of doing, and both men continued to enjoy their hunts. Sometimes it was together, but oftentimes Edward the actor, Edward Sothern, would hunt without his friends. And it was on one of those solo rides that he was thrown from his horse, and along with picking up a few bruises, something else happened. He lost the matchbox.

He was heartbroken. It'd been in his pocket for years, and he'd grown accustomed to its usefulness, so he had a replacement made and then moved on. Later in life he passed that second matchbox on to one of his three sons, a young man named Lytton.

Actually, Lytton was also an actor, just like his father, and eventually his own career took him overseas to Australia. While he was there, he made new friends in the world of theater, and one of his closest was a man by the name of Labertouche. When Lytton's time was up in Australia, he gifted his golden matchbox to Labertouche and went home to England.

Many years later, another of Edward's sons, named George, was on a foxhunt of his own. It had been a long time since he had hunted in his father's favorite area, so as he did, he took in the scenery with a bit of nostalgia. There's no record of how successful his hunt was that day, but he *did* happen to bump into the old farmer who worked the land, and introduced himself as George Sothern, Edward Sothern's son.

The farmer was astonished. Not only did he know the young man's father, but he had just been thinking about him that very morning. One of his farmhands had been out plowing in the field when a glimmer of something metal caught his eye. It turned out to be something Edward had dropped years before: his gold matchbox.

George went home that day with the matchbox in his pocket—the original one, mind you, gifted to his father by the Prince of Wales—as well as a fantastic story. He wanted to tell someone. So later that day George sat down and wrote a letter to his youngest brother Edward, who was traveling with a theater production in America.

This is the point where I stop for a moment and tell you, yes, there were three Edwards, and that's pretty confusing, I know. Edward the prince, Edward the friend, and Edward the son. Plus two other sons, right? It's complicated, but it's also worth it, trust me.

Edward the son received the letter from his brother George on the morning of a train ride, and waited until he was seated and the train was moving before he opened it. Across the seat from him was another actor, Lawrence by name, who had just joined up with the company that day, and they planned to get to know each other and prepare for their next stop.

Edward the son read the letter, and as he did, his eyes opened wide. Lawrence noticed this, and asked about it.

"My brother," he said, "has found our father's long-lost matchbox, gifted by the Prince of Wales himself."

And then he proceeded to tell Lawrence about how the matchbox was lost, how his father had a second one made, and how his brother Lytton had given that one away in Australia.

"I wonder," Edward muttered half to himself and half to Lawrence, "whatever became of that second matchbox. Does Labertouche still possess it, or has he, in turn, given it to someone else?"

Lawrence smiled at him from across the seat, and then reached into his pocket. When he pulled his hand back out, there in the middle of his palm sat a small golden matchbox. Turning it over, both men could clearly see the engraving on the back.

"Oh, he gave it to someone else," Lawrence answered. "And that someone else was *me*."

THE COIN FLIP

No one could agree on what to do. The three travelers had just finished up an appointment in Indianapolis on January 15, 1941. They planned to board a train the next morning and begin the long journey back to California.

It was really Jane Peters's trip, but she was traveling with her mother, Bess, along with a mutual friend. Jane was the one calling the shots, but had been happy to ride the train home until she received a message from her husband, who was eager to see her.

To be honest, she was just as eager to get home and be with him, too, so when he suggested they skip out on their train tickets and catch a commercial airliner home, Jane lit up with joy. The conflict arose when Jane's friends shook their heads and refused. They both hated the thought of flying, and would rather take the slower—but safer—route home by train.

In the end, they did what any group of indecisive travelers might do: they would flip a coin. Heads, they would follow Jane onto the airplane and get home faster. Tails, they would take the train as planned. Everyone agreed to let the coin decide for them, and

so they pulled out a coin and gave it a toss. The winner was the airplane.

They boarded TWA Flight 3 at 4:00 a.m. on January 16, and began the westward flight. Today, that airplane would have made it all the way to California without a problem, but in 1941, more frequent refueling stops were necessary, so they picked up a few more people along the way. St. Louis was their first stop, and then on to Albuquerque. After that, they headed to Las Vegas to refuel before heading west to California.

The plane took off from Las Vegas around 6:55 a.m. with twenty-two people on board. Thirteen minutes later, however, the captain made a navigational error, and somehow flew the plane into the side of Potosi Mountain. Everyone on board the plane died instantly, including Jane.

Jane Peters's husband, Clark, was heartbroken. He flew to Las Vegas to claim his wife's body, along with those of his mother-in-law and the family friend. Actually, the family friend was Clark's press agent. Clark, you see, was a fairly well-known film star named Clark Gable.

And Jane? Well, she was buried in Forest Lawn Memorial Park outside of Burbank near Hollywood, where she had spent most of her life. Jane, you see, was one of the most important Hollywood stars of the 1930s, and had just finished raising the modern equivalent of $33 million for the war efforts. She was adored, and would be sorely missed.

Most people don't know her as Jane Peters, though, because that was her *birth* name. Instead, her star on the Hollywood

Walk of Fame, along with the credits of all her films, bears her stage name: Carole Lombard.

She accomplished *so* much in her short life. But if it wasn't for a flip of the coin, who knows what else she might have done. Sadly, we'll never know.

NOT EVEN A KING

Most people today know at least the basics of the story of France's King Louis XVI. He was the last king of France, and when he died, the monarchy died with him. And of course, he was the grandson of Louis the Great, also known as the Sun King. Even his wife, Marie Antoinette, was well-known, with one of the more recognizable names from popular history.

But what most people tend to skip over is his childhood. Unlike his grandfather the Sun King, who ascended to the throne at the age of just four, Louis XVI didn't become king until he was nearly twenty. Which means he had a lot of time before that to experience life from a less lofty position.

One moment in particular stands out. As a child, Louis was approached by an astrologer, who asked if he could make a prediction. When Louis agreed, this astrologer warned the future king to be cautious on the twenty-first day of each month. This warning came with no further explanation, but despite that, it planted itself firmly in the boy's mind.

Later, after taking the throne in 1774, Louis organized his responsibilities as king around that childhood fear. He avoided doing any important business on the twenty-first of each month, assuming that if he never set wheels in motion on those days, there would be nothing to return and harm him. Then again, what was coming down the pipeline was something no one could have predicted.

When the American Revolution broke out in 1776, Benjamin Franklin approached Louis for help with defeating the British rule of the American colonies. King Louis agreed, and sent much support to their cause. And in the end, it worked. The British were defeated, and the French gained a new, powerful ally. But it also showed the French citizens that a country could exist without a monarchy.

In 1789, revolution broke out again—this time in *France*. Inspired in part by the Americans, the French overthrew their own king and set up a republic in its place. Which meant that King Louis XVI had to go. But here's where it gets weird.

King Louis did his best to fight off the revolution, but on June 20 of 1791, he and his family put on the clothing of servants and escaped into the night, while their servants remained behind, dressed as nobles. The following day, they were captured and arrested. That would be June *21,* for anyone keeping track.

A little over a year later, the new French government issued the official pronouncement that abolished the French monarchy forever. The date? September 21, 1792.

It would take another few months before Louis met his fate. It's the part most of us know the best. Louis was led out into the Place de la Concorde, where an enormous crowd had gathered to watch the execution. There, in front of the people he once ruled over, Louis gave a brief speech, and was then executed by guillotine.

The date? 1793. January 21, of course.

That old astrologer told Louis to avoid the twenty-first of the month, and looking back it seems like that was solid advice. The trouble was, he couldn't control everything.

No one—not even a *king*—can stop the march of time.

SOMETHING BORROWED

Tony had arrived in London to take part in the production of a new Hollywood film. It was an adaptation of a popular novel, and because of that, Tony really wanted to get a copy of the book for himself, to read and study and use as a resource for his own performance.

Shortly after arriving in the city, he headed out to a local bookstore to see if they had a copy, but left empty-handed. He checked a few more stores, but each visit resulted in the same outcome. Frustrated, Tony decided to call it quits and head back to his apartment, so he walked to the nearest subway station—Leicester Square—and headed inside.

While he waited for the train to arrive, he took a seat on one of the nearby benches. No one was sitting there, but as he sat down he noticed that someone had left a small pile of papers at one end. His curiosity drove him to pick up the pile and look through it, which is when he made a fantastic discovery. There, inside the papers, was a copy of the very same book he had been trying—and failing—all day to buy.

Tony took that book home and devoured it. It was clearly a well-loved copy, with handwriting scrawled in pencil throughout the pages. But it allowed him to fully understand the author's vision for his character, and that gave him the tools he needed to deliver his best as an actor. After the filming was complete, he left London and took the book with him.

Roughly two years later, Tony was in Vienna working on the film's production when he had a chance to meet the author of that elusive book. The writer, George Feifer, thanked Tony for his performance and help in bringing his novel to life, but also lamented that he no longer owned a copy of his own novel. Tony listened in surprise as George described loaning his last remaining copy to a good friend.

"But that friend," George added, "never returned my copy. In fact, she told me she lost it in the subway."

Tony smiled, and then reached into his bag and pulled out the copy of the book he still carried with him. The cover was still sharp, and the title of the book was printed across it: *The Girl from Petrovka*.

George Feifer took the copy in his hands with wide eyes, and then opened it up to look at the pages. There, scribbled in the margins, were his own personal notes.

"This is it!" he exclaimed, smiling wide at Tony. Tony, understanding his place in this wild coincidence, gladly passed ownership of the book back to George.

So that's how an author rediscovered his own missing novel. Lost by random circumstances, it had returned to him through the most unusual of events, and handed to him by one of Hollywood's most legendary lead-ing men.

Our hero the actor wasn't listed in the credits as Tony, but by the name all of us know him today: Anthony Hopkins.

LUCK OF THE IRISH

The saying "luck of the Irish" doesn't have one definitive origin. Some say it comes from successful Irish miners who had found their "pots of gold" while digging underground. Others claim its meaning was ironic, that the Irish had been treated so poorly abroad during the potato famine that emigrants were cursed with "the luck of the Irish."

Regardless of where it came from, the Irish are considered a lucky people, and none luckier than Violet Jessop. Born in Argentina in 1887 to Irish immigrants, Violet was the eldest of nine children. She took care of her younger siblings to help her parents until she was diagnosed with tuberculosis. Doctors gave her months to live, but Violet had a strength unlike some of her siblings, three of whom had already died young.

She fought the disease and won, only to lose her father not long after that. At sixteen years old, Violet moved to England with her mother, who took a job as a flight attendant aboard ships while Violet stayed home to raise her younger sister. Unfortunately, not long after they'd settled into their new home, their mother grew very ill and it fell to Violet to take over as the sole breadwinner for the family. With few other opportunities available, she applied to be a flight attendant like her mother and was hired in 1908 by the Royal Mail Line to work on a ship called the *Orinoco*.

Throughout her career as a flight attendant, Violet worked aboard numerous ocean liners, helping guests and even saving lives. She had come from nothing, only to find herself working on some of the fanciest, most luxurious ships ever created.

But there was something odd about Violet. It seemed wherever she went, disaster followed. Sure, some of her siblings died of disease and her father passed away when she was a girl, but the tragedies didn't end there.

After working for the Royal Mail Line, she took a job with the White Star Line. If that name sounds familiar, that's because the White Star Line built three of the most famous ships in history: the *Olympic,* the *Britannic,* and the *Titanic.*

All three would go on to be involved in devastating accidents and two now reside at the bottom of the ocean. But each one counted Violet Jessop as an employee . . . and a *survivor.*

During her time as a flight attendant on the *Olympic,* that ship collided with the British warship the HMS *Hawke.* Although it didn't sink, the ship was sliced below the waterline, and eventually had to have extensive repairs done to become seaworthy again.

Not long after, as the *Titanic* sank, Violet was handed a baby to look after. She escaped with the child in a lifeboat along with other passengers. Amazingly, that baby was eventually returned to its mother aboard the rescue ship, the *Carpathia.*

Oh, and just a side note: many years later—after Violet had retired, in fact—she claimed she received a telephone call from a stranger who asked if Violet had saved a baby the night the *Titanic* sank. When Violet answered "yes," the woman on the other end told her, "I was that baby," and then hung up before Violet could reply.

A friend of hers suggested that the call had been a hoax, but Violet knew better. She hadn't told anyone about the story before, so there was no way a random person would have known to call her with such a joke.

Finally, as a nurse on the *Britannic,* she'd jumped out of a lifeboat moments before it was sucked into the sinking ship's propellers and shredded into splinters.

Violet Jessop has been depicted in various movies, television shows, and stage productions over the years, though not always by name. Often blended into other characters, hers is a story that has slipped past the history books, though she did earn the nickname "Miss Unsinkable."

With all the fanfare surrounding the *Titanic*'s "Unsinkable" Molly Brown, it's easy to lose sight of an unsung hero of the White Star Line such as Violet. Well, you *might* call her an unsung hero. Others might call her cursed.

But I like to imagine that the woman who beat tuberculosis, outlived her siblings, and survived multiple shipwrecks . . . was a miracle of sorts. A one-of-a-kind person who became the very definition of that household phrase: the luck of the Irish.

PUT A RING
ON IT

When you think of movie stars, there are way too many to pick from these days. And each year, it seems, those names and faces get swapped out for a brand-new crowd. But a century ago, the list was a lot smaller. And sitting right at the top of it all was Rudolph Valentino.

He was the original pop culture icon. Born in Italy in 1895, he came to New York in 1912, where he worked odd jobs busing tables and gardening. It wasn't until he was hired as a dancer when his luck started to change.

He found work in a traveling musical that took him from New York all the way to California, where he went on to pursue a stage career. Although he'd only ever performed in front of live audiences up to that point, another actor took one look at Valentino and suggested he try his hand at films. With his striking good looks and his knack for wooing the ladies, Rudolph Valentino became known around Hollywood as the "Latin Lover," and eventually only by his last name: Valentino.

He came up in the era of silent movies, of which he performed in almost forty. Unfortunately, like other notable film legends, such as James Dean and Bruce Lee, Valentino's career was cut short. He died at the young age of just thirty-one.

More than a hundred thousand people lined New York City streets to pay their respects to him. There were reports of suicides by mourning fans, as well as a public riot. However, as strange and unexpected as his passing was, the circumstances surrounding it were even stranger. In fact, Valentino's death may have been the first of several linked to one common culprit: a ring.

That's right, a tiny piece of jewelry he wore on his pinkie. He'd bought it in San Francisco from a shopkeeper with a dire warning. The ring, a silver band with a stone in the middle, was cursed. Valentino didn't want to hear it. He was a success now, and he wanted something to show how far he'd come.

He purchased the ring despite the owner's cautionary tale, and it quickly became his signature. He wore it in publicity photos, and even in his motion pictures—most notably 1922's *The Young Rajah*. It was a commercial and critical flop, the first of several for the young actor.

His next three films were all box office disappointments despite Valentino's immense talents and dashing good looks. It seemed like the shopkeeper had been right: the actor's signature ring had been holding him back. Unfortunately for Valentino, it was too late.

While on tour to promote his last film, *The Son of the Sheik*, Valentino came down with a case of bleeding ulcers and required surgery. At first, all seemed to be okay, but doctors discovered he'd developed an infection known as peritonitis, an inflammation of lung tissue leading to fluid buildup inside the lungs. Nothing could be done. His condition got worse, and by the end of August 1926, he was gone.

The ring, however, did not go with him. Instead, it was passed down to his lover, another actor, Pola Negri. But she immediately fell ill after taking possession of it, and her career suffered. She managed to survive, though, and decided to pass the ring on to singer and actor Russ Colombo. Colombo had been described as a doppelgänger of sorts to Valentino and it turned out to be true in more ways than one. Days after he accepted Negri's gift, Colombo died after a bizarre shooting incident involving a friend.

The ring then bounced to another of Colombo's acquaintances, a man named Joe Casino, who was so afraid of the curse, he locked the ring away and refused to take it out for anyone. But the allure proved to be too great, and even Joe succumbed to its call. He'd been wearing the ring only a week when he was struck and killed by a truck.

Casino's brother, Del, was the next to claim the ring, and decided to lend it to a Rudolph Valentino memorabilia collector. Perhaps he hoped that the curse hadn't been a curse at all. Maybe the ring had just been an innocent part of a bunch of odd coincidences. Well, you might think that if the ring's journey ended there.

But it didn't. One night, Del came home to find his house had been robbed. Guess what had been taken. That's right, Valentino's ring. The thief was quickly caught by the police, but didn't go quietly. The officer fired a warning shot that ended up killing him instead.

Several years later, figure skater Jack Dunn slipped the ring on his finger for a screen test. The film? A biopic about the late Valentino. Ten days later, Dunn passed away from a rare blood disease.

After that, the ring was locked away never to be seen—or worn—again. Today, no one knows where it is, and Valentino's spirit is said to haunt many locations around Los Angeles in search of it.

That busboy from Italy certainly made a name for himself in his short time on Earth. While his career had not been as prolific as that of some of his peers, he's still remembered—and watched—to this day. And the name Valentino has become synonymous with the notion of the "Hollywood heartthrob."

After all, it does have a nice ring to it.

DAM IT ALL

It rises over the Colorado River, a concrete protector for the areas below. It irrigates more than 1.5 million acres of land in the United States and Mexico, where much of our fruit and cotton are grown. And it supplies water and hydroelectric power to Nevada, Arizona, and California without fail. The Hoover Dam is truly a wonder of the modern world.

Built in 1933, it took twenty-one thousand men five years and 4.4 million cubic yards of concrete to finish it. And like all great structures, it started out as little more than an idea.

As families began moving out west in the late 1800s, they found themselves at the mercy of all sorts of things, including the local wildlife, harsh weather conditions, and the most dangerous natural phenomenon of all, the Colorado River.

People living in the lower river valley often lost their homes, and sometimes even their lives, during the times when the Colorado flooded. So in 1922, a group of surveyors decided to do something about it. They saw what could be possible if a dam was built in just the right spot on the river, what it could do for the neighboring territories. No more devastating floods; instead, they could provide electric power for thousands—and a feather in America's cap as an agricultural innovator.

They considered blasting the walls of nearby Boulder Canyon, collapsing it into a sort of natural dam, but the method was untested and there were no guarantees it would save money in the long run. Instead, on December 20 of 1922—five days before Christmas—the surveyors set out to find the perfect spot to build their dam from scratch.

It was during this hunt when the Colorado River experienced a flash flood. No one saw it coming, especially not John Gregory Tierney, who was caught in the rush and washed away in the river. Though his remains were never found, John was presumed to be dead. He became the first of almost one hundred casualties of the Hoover Dam both before and during its construction.

John left behind a son, Patrick William Tierney, who learned to get by without his father there to guide him. Before the dam's completion, however, Patrick experienced the second worst thing to happen to his family since his father's untimely death: the Great Depression. Everyone was out of work and, without his father there to help make ends meet, it was up to Patrick to support the rest of the family.

He sought work wherever he could. Unfortunately, Patrick had no notable skills, and jobs were hard to come by. Then, one day, he came across an open position as an electrician's helper on a major construction project out west. You can probably guess what that project was, too. That's right; the

Hoover Dam. The wild endeavor his father never got to see get off the ground.

Patrick worked on the enormous intake towers responsible for moving water throughout the dam for irrigation and hydroelectric power. It was a good job, and he earned a lot of money doing it, but then the unthinkable happened.

In 1935, three months after President Franklin Roosevelt dedicated the dam in front of the American public, a freak accident sent Patrick falling off one of the intake towers on the Arizona side of the dam. He plummeted 320 feet to his death below.

Patrick was officially listed as the final casualty of the Hoover Dam's construction. The date of his death? December 20, 1935. Exactly fourteen years to the day his father, the very first casualty, was swept away by the Colorado River.

A tragedy, for sure, but you know what they say: like father, like son.

WIZARD'S COAT

We know it by heart. The iconic lines and songs live inside us and connect us back to a time when our wildest dreams lived just over the rainbow. We scowl at the Wicked Witch as she threatens Dorothy and her little dog, too. We chuckle as the Munchkins push each other out of the way to introduce themselves to their young savior. And we smile as the Scarecrow dances his way off his perch and onto the Yellow Brick Road.

While it has become a beloved part of cinematic history today, the film carries behind it a legacy of conflict, injuries, and ballooning budgets. It pulled in only $3 million during its box office run in 1939, well behind a little film you might have heard of called *Gone with the Wind*, which was reported to have grossed almost $200 million by the time it left theaters.

But after the success of Walt Disney's *Snow White and the Seven Dwarfs*, Hollywood saw fantasy as the next big thing. MGM pulled out all the stops for its adaptation of L. Frank Baum's novel, and put Judy Garland—one of its brightest stars—front and center, surrounded by a who's who of talent: Margaret Hamilton as the Wicked

Witch of the West, Ray Bolger as the Scarecrow, and character actor Frank Morgan as the wizard himself.

Actually, he was more than that. Yes, he played the wizard, but Morgan also portrayed the carriage driver, one of the Emerald City guards, and the Gatekeeper. You know, the guy who talks to Dorothy and her companions about horses of a different color?

But there was one role in the film of special import to Frank Morgan. Professor Marvel, the fortune teller at the beginning of the story. The role is small, only on screen for a few minutes, but there's something special about it that makes it one of the most magical moments ever captured on film.

You may remember Professor Marvel's costume from the movie, but in case you can't, allow me to jog your memory. He wore checkered pants, a white ruffled shirt with a high collar, and a wide, dark tie. Over his shirt he wore a patterned vest, and to top it all off, a long coat.

The vest looked like repurposed upholstery from an old couch. The pants and shirt? A mismatch of eclectic styles that appeared old even when they were new. And the coat—well, the coat was a serendipitous find, according to Mary Mayer, the publicist for the movie at the time.

The coat really brought the whole ensemble together and gave Professor Marvel a look of lost grandeur. He was a man with little to his name and, unlike the Scarecrow or the Tin Man—who required custom costumes due to their technical natures—Professor Marvel's was a hodgepodge of secondhand scraps. But the coat. The coat

needed to be something just a *little* bit different from the rest of the costume.

The director wanted the character to wear something that had once been nice, but was now tattered. Rather than make something new and weather it, the wardrobe department searched thrift shops all over Hollywood for the perfect coat. And soon enough, they found it.

It was a green Prince Albert jacket with wide lapels and long tails. It was the jacket of a man of stature. At least, it would have been at the turn of the century. Now, it was a hand-me-down for a fraudster in a Hollywood fantasy. And it was perfect.

Frank Morgan arrived at the studio for test shots a few months before his scheduled filming date. The costume and makeup people needed reference photos to use when it came time for him to shoot his scenes. They styled his hair and dressed him up in the various pieces they'd acquired to round out Professor Marvel's unique look, finishing it all off with that coat.

It was on one hot afternoon when Morgan decided to empty his pockets to lighten his load, and he came across something. It was a name sewn into the inside of the jacket pocket. No one could believe it. The costumer contacted the coat's tailor back in Chicago to verify the discovery and as it turned out, the piece of clothing they owned did, in fact, belong to someone intimately tied to the film they were working on.

The ratty coat hanging on Frank Morgan's shoulders had belonged to a man from New York who had passed away some years earlier. He had once advocated for the women's suffrage movement, and he had given the world fourteen fantastic tales of people and places living somewhere over the rainbow.

Frank Morgan's coat had been made for the man who had, in a way, given him the most important role of his career. A man . . . named L. Frank Baum.

BROTHERS GRIM

Coincidences happen all the time. If you've taken a tour through the Cabinet of Curiosities before, I'm sure you've noticed a few. Tales of unexpected meetings, or people in the wrong place at the wrong time. Sometimes those coincidences are just that: the unintended consequence of a random choice lining up with a specific moment. No premeditation, no effort. These things, as some might say, just happen.

And sometimes, the coincidence we find ourselves in is a little too perfect, almost as if fate had been planning it all along. That's how seventeen-year-old Erskine Ebbin might've described what happened to him. Erskine was a typical teenager in 1975. He went to school, he hung out with friends, and he swam in Bermuda's shimmering blue water every day. You know—the usual teenager stuff.

Okay, maybe not exactly typical. Erskine lived in Bermuda, a group of islands often thought of as paradise. White sandy beaches, water so clear you can see straight to the bottom, and more than three hundred shipwrecks lying beneath the waves. Yes, Bermuda is also home to one of the most mysterious and dangerous parts of the eastern seaboard—the Bermuda Triangle—but to the locals and thousands of yearly tourists, Bermuda is merely a beautiful collection of beaches and British history.

But it's definitely not like other places. Sure, people drive cars to get from point A to point B, but almost everyone travels by bus, bicycle, taxi, or—in Erskine's case—moped, a zippy little two-wheeler that allows citizens and tourists alike to navigate the island's narrow streets with ease.

On July 21, Erskine had been riding through the city of Hamilton, situated along one of Bermuda's main ports lined with colorful homes and shops along its wide roads. Summer was a busy time to be out and about on the island, and that meant that the roads were crowded. For a tourist, that could be a frustrating thing. But Erskine was no tourist.

No, he was a local. He'd lived there his whole life, and knew what to expect from the vehicles that whizzed by him each day. However, on this day, Erskine ran into some unfortunate luck. To be more specific, a bit of bad luck ran into him—in the form of a taxicab. On an island known for its high rate of traffic fatalities, Erskine became one of the twenty-six automotive deaths reported in 1975.

We don't really know what caused the accident. We don't know whose fault it was, or what sort of mistake the drivers made. Maybe Erskine was in the wrong place at the wrong time, or maybe it was the cabdriver who slipped up. We don't have answers to a lot of the questions we might want answered.

All we know is that Erskine collided with a taxicab as they both reached the intersection. He was thrown from his scooter, and died a short while later from his injuries.

Like I said, there are a few details we don't know about his accident. But there are other details we *do* know, and they are eye-openers, to say the least. Because this wasn't the first time this taxi driver had been involved in an accident.

One year earlier—almost to the day, in fact—the exact same taxi driver passed through the exact same intersection, colliding with another vehicle. Even more bizarre, the cab's passenger in both accidents was the same person, which should take the award for the most amazing coincidence. And it would, in any other story. But not this one.

Because the victim in the earlier accident had also been a young man riding the very same moped. Not the same model, or color—the *exact* same moped. It was all just too much of a coincidence to fathom, yet it happened nonetheless, which is why it's so memorable and so fascinating.

The same cab, the same passenger, the same driver hitting two men riding the same moped one year apart. Some might call it a coincidence, but others see it as something bigger. Some might even call it a curse.

Why? Because Erskine Ebbin actually knew the first man to die. Very well, in fact. You see, his name was *Neville* Ebbin.

Erskine's Ebbin's older brother.

THE
HAND-ME-DOWN

Hollywood has its fair share of iconic automobiles. The winged race car from *Chitty Chitty Bang Bang,* the Duke cousins' General Lee, and perhaps the most famous car ever to grace the silver screen, Doc Brown's DeLorean time machine from *Back to the Future.*

But there is another car. Its story is one of tragedy and horror, more like something out of a Stephen King novel than reality, but oddly enough, we've never seen it in a single film.

The 1955 Porsche Spyder was built as a racing car, meant for the tracks rather than the open road. Its design was iconic. Its sleek, aluminum body sat low on a steel frame, hugging the ground as 110 horses pulled it along. Two large, round headlights stared straight ahead almost in surprise at how fast such a tiny car could go.

In 1955, only one star had the audacity to drive such a machine outside the confines of a closed track. A cultural icon. A legend. A rebel himself: James Dean.

His story is one of misfortune. A young man taken far too soon, his legacy lives on in his films, which are still regarded as some of the most influential in all of cinema. And his car? Well, that has a legacy all its own.

It was in late September of 1955 when Dean's Porsche collided with a 1950 Ford Tudor, a hulking two-door sedan with chrome bumpers. He'd been on his way to Salinas, California, for a race, pushing the car to its limit. The Tudor had attempted to make a left, but didn't see Dean careening down the road in time.

The Porsche was a wreck, a crushed heap of metal and rubber that, following Dean's death, was bought by George Barris. If that name sounds familiar, it's because George Barris created some of film and television's most beloved cars, including Adam West's 1966 Batmobile.

Barris had been the one to customize the Porsche for Dean before his crash. He put stripes on the rear wheels, reupholstered the seats, and painted the number 130 on the doors, engine cover, and hood.

Barris had the wrecked car towed to his shop, but as it was being loaded onto the trailer, it slipped off, trapping the mechanic underneath. When they removed the chassis, it was clear the man's leg had been broken.

Barris decided it would be better to chop up the car and sell some of the parts off. A man named Troy McHenry bought the engine while one William Eschrid bought the drivetrain. They put the components into their own cars and thought a race between the two would be a perfect display of the Porsche's repurposed engineering.

During the race, McHenry's car lost control and hit a tree. He died instantly.

Eschrid was almost killed when his own vehicle locked up and flipped during a turn.

But Barris, unconvinced of the Spyder's supposed curse, would not be deterred. He sold two unscathed tires to a new owner, who ran off the road after both of them blew out at the same time. It seemed no part of this car wanted to be separated from the whole.

Of course, owning such an infamous piece of movie history brings its own problems, and no, not of the supernatural kind. Two thieves attempted to steal pieces of the Porsche from Barris's garage. No doubt to sell for a quick buck, but it seemed the car had other plans. The thief who'd tried to remove the steering wheel sliced his arm wide open, and his cohort, who had been struggling with one of the seats, suffered a similar injury.

After all the stories of the various accidents and deaths surrounding the car got around, the only people brave enough to take possession of it were the California Highway Patrol. They wanted a striking display for their highway safety museum to scare people into being more defensive drivers, and what better example than the most famous car wreck of all time?

They carted the metal carcass off to a police garage . . . which quickly burned down after accepting it through its doors. The car, however, suffered no damage. Well, no more than it already had.

The wreck then moved to an exhibit at a local high school, where it slipped off its mount and broke a student's hip. James Dean's zippy little race car had developed a bloodlust of sorts. Having had enough of the bizarre events surrounding the car, the Highway Patrol loaded it onto a truck bound for storage.

If I were a betting man, I'd bet the truck never made it. And I'd be right. It flipped during transport and the driver was tossed from the cab. He landed somehow in the path of the Spyder, which fell from the back of the truck, crushing him.

Barris knew something had to give. He bought the car back. No one else needed to get hurt or die over it. But it was during this final transport back to his garage when the strangest thing happened: the car vanished. And no one has seen it since.

You might think the curse—if you believe in such a thing—began with James Dean's death, as though his vengeful spirit had inhabited the car, dooming all who dared to own a piece of it. But you'd be surprised if you knew the truth . . . and the other person responsible for it.

Just after he'd had the car upgraded by Barris, James Dean ran into another famous actor outside a Hollywood restaurant. He invited him to take a look at his new ride parked in front. The actor walked around the little Porsche, then turned to Dean with a sour look on his face and said, "If you get in that car, you'll be found dead in it by this time next week."

He was right, too. Dean died in that crash seven days later. And the actor who had given him the ominous warning?

None other than Obi-Wan Kenobi himself, Sir Alec Guinness.

BOTTOM OF THE NINTH

We put a lot of stock in numbers. I don't mean the ones that run our daily lives, like our 401(k)s or the stock market. I'm talking about the numbers we hold close to us, the lucky lottery numbers we play every week, and the not-so-lucky numbers we avoid because of superstition. Triskaidekaphobia—the fear of the number thirteen, for example—stems from Jesus's Last Supper with his twelve apostles just before the crucifixion, thus its cultural designation as an unlucky number. Though, many other cultures see the number as a source of good luck and fortune.

But do you know enneaphobia? You might not, as its prominence isn't nearly as widespread as the fear of the number thirteen. Enneaphobia is the fear of the number nine, and for many classical composers throughout history, they had a good reason to worry.

Over the course of his career, Ludwig van Beethoven composed five piano concertos, one violin concerto, thirty-two piano sonatas, sixteen string quartets, one mass, one opera . . . and nine symphonies. He started composing his Ninth Symphony in the fall of 1822, working tirelessly for the next two years in order to complete it for the Philharmonic Society of London. The Ninth was the last symphony he created before his death in 1827.

Anton Dvorak, born fourteen years after Beethoven's death, wrote a number of operas and chamber music pieces before his death in 1904. Among all those compositions? Nine symphonies.

Franz Schubert, Jean Sibelius, Alexander Glazunov, Kurt Atterberg, and a whole host of others met similar fates. It didn't matter how many operas, or choral pieces, or cantatas they wrote. Once they each reached their ninth symphony, the curtain fell for the last time.

The phenomenon had become so prominent in the nineteenth century that audiences and critics grew superstitious that anyone who dared to complete a ninth symphony would meet their death soon after.

German composer Gustav Mahler, however, thought he could beat the curse in an inventive way.

Mahler, born almost thirty years after Beethoven's death, composed dozens of works, including chamber music, piano suites, and yes, symphonies. He was well aware of the curse and its influence. In fact, death had weighed heavily on his mind in the years leading up to the composition of what is widely considered his greatest work, The Song of the Earth.

He had just resigned as director of the Vienna Court Opera House, his oldest daughter had passed away, and Mahler himself had been diagnosed with severe heart defects. He had gone through the worst times of his life, and those experiences fueled in him the creation of a new work. His most beautiful and inspiring to date. In 1908, Mahler began composing The Song of the Earth, his ninth symphony. Comprised of six songs, the piece was to be sung by two singers with each person taking turns singing each of the many movements.

He finished it one year later, but the Curse of the Ninth still hung over him like a fog. He worried constantly, and because of his worry, he changed the title of his latest work. Rather than numbering it the way he'd done for his eight previous symphonies, Mahler subtitled it "A Symphony for Tenor, Alto and Large Orchestra." Without a number attached, he still technically remained a composer of only eight complete symphonies. Quite the musical loophole.

This left him free to focus on what would be his *true* ninth symphony, which he started composing around the same time he was working on The Song of the Earth.

After beginning work on this ninth symphony—the real, official one, that is—he told his wife "the danger is past." He'd successfully begun ten symphonies, counting The Song of the Earth. Unfortunately, he was too quick to celebrate. Fate had seen through his ruse. Only two movements into his new work, Mahler's diagnosis had caught up with him, and he died of heart failure.

As the composer Arnold Schoenberg once wrote in an essay shortly after Mahler's death, "It seems that the Ninth is a limit. He who wants to go beyond it must pass away."

BAD OMEN

In AD 66, the Eastern Mediterranean became the site of a major conflict between the Jewish people and the Roman Empire. The Jewish people had endured enough of the Romans' excessive taxation practices, and so they revolted—and the Romans retaliated.

The fighting carried on for four long years, with the conflict reaching its climax in the city of Jerusalem. Jewish men, women, and children of fighting age took up arms against their oppressors, hoping to fend them off, but the Roman armies were too strong. They tore down the city walls and burned the temple to the ground.

In the end, Jerusalem fell to the Romans. Survivors were enslaved and their Jewish culture was almost eradicated.

Many centuries later, the Romans found themselves at the center of another battle, this time against Attila and his army of Huns. They fought in an area of eastern France known as the Catalaunian Plains. Attila's plan was to invade Gaul, a Roman territory made up of several European countries, including modern-day France, Belgium, northern Italy, and Luxembourg. However, while both sides faced casualties in the thousands, in the end it was Attila who was defeated and the Romans retained control of their land.

Then, in 1066, King Harold of England went up against William, Duke of Normandy—also known as William the Conqueror. William had brought with him armies from all over France and Belgium after King Harold had defeated the Norwegian invaders moving in on his land. And though Harold put up a valiant effort, William's forces proved too strong to overpower. The English aristocracy was destroyed. Its control of the Catholic Church fell to the Normans, who transformed England forever.

All three historical events have something in common. They involve war, death, and destruction. Each event had a winner and a loser. Power was gained and power was lost. And yet, there's something else. Something *otherworldly* that binds these seemingly disparate events together: Halley's Comet.

Even though the comet wasn't officially named until the 1700s, it had been viewed as an omen of tragedy since the beginning of time. Scholar and historian Titus Flavius Josephus had seen the comet streak by just before the fall of Jerusalem at the hands of the Romans. He described it as a "star resembling a sword."

Halley's Comet had also been spotted in 451 at the time of Attila's defeat in western Europe. And in the months leading up to King Harold's defeat at the Battle of Hastings, there it was again, a "long-haired star" as it was described at the time. A prophecy of William's impending conquest.

But perhaps the most notable coincidence tied to the comet occurred in 1835 when a child named Samuel Clemens was born in Florida, Missouri. Only two weeks prior, Halley's Comet had made its closest approach to earth.

As we all know, Samuel Clemens went on to great success under the pen name Mark Twain, writing as a commentator and storyteller. He had a knack for pointing out hypocrisy, and in some ways, he gave birth to modern observational comedy through the numerous talks he gave throughout his career.

In fact, his observational skills came in quite handy in 1909. He'd been working with noted biographer Albert Paine on his own life story when he told him that he had come in with Halley's Comet and how it would be the greatest disappointment of his life if didn't go out with it. One year later, on April 20, 1910, Halley's Comet soared through the night sky right on schedule.

And Mark Twain died of a heart attack the following day.

VERY
SUPERSTITIOUS

Athletes are no strangers to superstition. Wade Boggs famously ate chicken before each baseball game. Michael Jordan wore his UNC shorts under his Bulls uniform for all of his NBA games.

There have been stories of unwashed socks and lucky gloves and all sorts of rituals that anyone outside the locker room might find strange. These sports stars believed their traditions were what helped them play their best and win. However, superstitions are not limited only to professional sports.

The world of professional music is also home to many bizarre customs and superstitions. For example, since the 1960s, several famous rockers have joined what's known as the "27 Club," named for those who died at the age of twenty-seven. Jimi Hendrix, Janis Joplin, and Jim Morrison are all members, as is Kurt Cobain.

Even weirder is the white lighter curse. Legend has it any musician who uses a white lighter is doomed to an unpleasant fate. And wouldn't you know it, four people who were carrying white lighters when they died were Jimi Hendrix, Janis Joplin, Jim Morrison, and Kurt Cobain.

Superstition has struck singers in the Philippines as well. Karaoke bars all over the country have pulled Frank Sinatra's "My Way" from their song collections due to the high number of deaths of people who have sung the song.

But perhaps the worst case of superstition affecting a musician can be found in the case of Austrian composer Arnold Schoenberg. Born on September 13, 1874, Schoenberg changed the face of music through two world wars.

He also developed a severe case of triskaidekaphobia—the fear of the number thirteen. Schoenberg was known to avoid rooms, floors, and buildings numbered thirteen. In his compositions, he would number the measure between twelve and fourteen as 12a. He even titled his last opera *Moses and Aron,* the latter name spelled with one A instead of two, because otherwise the title would have had thirteen letters in it instead of twelve.

And if his age or birthday year happened to be a multiple of thirteen, it set him on edge like nothing else.

As his sixty-fifth birthday approached in 1939, Schoenberg consulted an astrologer regarding his horoscope for that year. Even though 1939 was not a multiple of thirteen, sixty-five certainly was. The astrologer told him it would be a dangerous year, but he would survive. The assurance calmed him. However, in all his worry about multiples of thirteen, there were other parts of his life he hadn't considered. One such area was in the digits of his age.

For example, on his seventy-sixth birth-day in 1950, another astrologer warned him to be careful. Not only was 1950 a multiple of thirteen, but when the numbers seven and six were added together, they totaled—you guessed it—thirteen. It seemed as though Schoenberg couldn't escape the cursed number no matter where he went.

On the day of his seventy-sixth birthday, a nervous and depressed Schoenberg decided to spend it in his bed. There was no party. No one paid him a visit or called to wish him well. At 11:45 that night, as he and his wife lay in bed, she looked at the clock and said to herself, "another quarter of an hour and then the worst is over."

Soon after the words left her mouth, the phone rang. It was the doctor. Her husband made a sound with his throat, then his heart stopped. Arnold Schoenberg's worst fear had come true.

He'd died at thirteen minutes to midnight on his seventy-sixth birthday.

In 1950.

On Friday the thirteenth.

FANTASTIC BEASTS

COLD-BLOODED

On June 14 of 1494, the authorities showed up to arrest her. I realize that it might have come as a shock to her, but for all of her neighbors and the community beyond them, it had only been a matter of time. Justice would eventually win the day.

Her crime was murder. Just a little over two months prior—on Easter Sunday, in fact—she had walked into the home of her neighbors, the Lenfants, and found the place empty. Well, not entirely. There was a cradle off to one side of the main room, and in it slept the family's youngest son.

I'm not sure I fully understand why she did what she did next, but some people simply make bad choices. She chose to harm the boy, as horrible as that sounds. And as a result of his injuries, the boy died. Whether that was her intent or not is irrelevant. She was guilty of murder, and so they came to arrest her.

The trial was swift. So many people came forward to testify against her that her guilt was without question. Still, witnesses were examined and cross-examined. Testimonies were heard. The judge deliberated, and then returned to the courtroom to declare his verdict.

Guilty.

Her sentence was execution, specifically by hanging. So a gallows was hastily built nearby, and preparations were made. On the appointed day, she was led to the wooden platform by strong men. Her hands and feet were bound, and a noose was slowly fitted around her neck. And then, after a pronouncement by a priest, the trap door was opened, and she fell.

I wish I could offer a happy ending to this story. That at the last minute a witness came forward to reverse the charges. Or that the noose snapped and the killer was given a second chance. But this isn't one of those stories. No, the killer was guilty, and she hanged for her crime. The end.

I suppose in that way this story isn't really anything special. Sadly, the pages of history are filled with the names of killers, and most of them met a similar fate. But this story has one small difference that deserves to be pointed out. The killer, you see, was special.

No, she wasn't a queen, or a celebrity, or even well-off. She wasn't even *human*.

She was a pig.

GETTING AHEAD

There's so much advice out there that involves our heads. Keep a level head. Don't lose your head. Do your best to get ahead in life. It's all in your head. You get the idea, I'm sure, but this focus isn't without justification. Think of all the rulers, traitors, criminals, and soldiers who have literally lost their heads over the span of history and . . . well . . . it's almost become normal.

In November of 1904, Michigan business owner Herbert Hughes was getting ready for his hotel's weekly Sunday dinner. Part of that involved slaughtering the chickens that would be part of that night's dinner. While it wasn't the most pleasant process, at least it was efficient. With a whack, he'd remove the chicken's head, and then pass the body to a maid for cleaning and gutting. Everything was going fine—that is, until she started *screaming*.

With a shriek, the maid bolted from the room, leaving Hughes alone to figure out what had frightened her. It was, as you might expect, one of the chickens that had driven her away, but not for the reasons you might assume. No, it wasn't the blood, and no, it wasn't the process of gutting the bird or cleaning the feathers off. It was something a lot less expected: one of the chickens was still walking around the room. Without its head.

I imagine there was a moment of shock for Hughes, but after he recovered, he began to see things in a more positive light. He decided to keep the hen around, and even gave her a name: Biddy. He put his new headless chicken in a cage, gave her space to walk around, and even fed her using a syringe to inject food down into her open esophagus. Biddy could do lots of normal chicken-like things, such as flap her wings and sit on a perch, and most surprising of all, she showed no signs of pain or distress.

Hughes knew a business opportunity when he saw one. Believing the notion that a living, breathing headless chicken might bring in more patrons than ever before, he put Biddy on display for his guests. And it worked, too. People flocked to his hotel—no pun intended—and enjoyed watching the show. Sadly, though, it would all come to an end less than a month after it all began. Poor headless Biddy passed away on November 30.

You might think that Biddy was a one-of-a-kind bird, but you'd be wrong. Roughly forty years later, in September of 1945, a similar thing happened. A Colorado man named Lloyd Olsen tried slaughtering one of his chickens in the same way Herbert Hughes had, and was just as surprised when his bird got back up and walked away—sans head.

Olson named his walking miracle Mike the Chicken. There didn't seem to be much the bird couldn't do, either. He would walk around the yard, flap his wings, even crow like the other birds. Except, well, without a head, it just sort of sounded like a low gurgling noise.

Maybe it was the more modern world that Mike lived in compared with Biddy, or perhaps Olsen had a better sense for publicity, but word about the headless chicken traveled far and wide. He even landed on the covers of magazines like *Life* and *Time*. Olsen took the bird on the road, too, traveling with sideshows and giving folks across the country a chance to lay eyes on the bird who lived.

Sadly, in March 1947—nearly two years after losing his head—Mike got a kernel of corn caught in his throat while out on the road. Olsen had forgotten his cleaning and feeding tools at the sideshow the day before, and so he was helpless to remove the corn. With no way of saving his beloved bird, Olsen had no choice but to say goodbye.

Even now, seventy years later, Mike's hometown of Fruita, Colorado, remembers the remarkable chicken with a special holiday held in his honor. "Mike the Headless Chicken Day" celebrates the creature's short, yet determined life with a series of events, including a 5K run, egg tosses, and live music including, of course, the Chicken Dance.

It sounds unbelievable, I know. One chicken surviving a beheading is amazing, but *two* chickens—well that almost seems too good to be true. Scientists say it has to do with the way a chicken's brain sits inside their head. Unlike our own brains, theirs rests at a 45-degree angle near the top of the skull, and basic motor functions are carried out by the brain stem. So if the head is removed in a sloppy manner at just the right angle, the brain stem might remain intact, giving the chicken a second chance at life.

Some might say chickens represent the best of us. They're caring, social creatures, they share child-raising duties, and they fiercely protect their own. But perhaps there's one new lesson that Biddy and Mike can teach us, even after all these years.

Don't lose your head. But if you do, try to make the best of it.

HORSING AROUND

We've seen them on TV. Mediums who claim they can speak to the ghosts of deceased loved ones. Perhaps it's a letter of the alphabet that triggers them, or a smell, or someone's name. Whatever it is, the person on the other side is always astounded by how much the medium claims to know. You'd think they were really talking to the dead.

We know better now, and we're able to see through a lot of the techniques mediums use to dupe their audiences. How they speak in generalities and convince the other person to give up more information without even realizing it.

But at the turn of the century, Hans had them all fooled. He wasn't a medium, but he'd convinced everyone he had all the answers. Complicated equations, difficult words to spell, musical riddles—Hans knew it all.

He traveled all over Germany with his translator, Wilhelm von Osten, right there beside him. Hans was known to gather crowds of men, women, and children who tried to push him to the limits of his expertise, and every time, he came out on top. No one could stump him.

One man, however, thought he could catch him.

Dr. Oskar Pfungst was a psychologist who wasn't convinced of Hans's talents. He saw something else going on while everyone was distracted by his big brain. Dr. Pfungst discovered Hans didn't know anything at all. I mean, he knew some things, but not as much as everyone believed. Hans, like today's TV mediums, had mastered the art of cold reading.

When he was close to an answer, he'd watch the person's body language change. If they tensed up, if their lip twitched or their hands shook, he knew he had them right where he wanted them. He'd give his answer based on that shift, and over 90 percent of the time, he was right.

Dr. Pfungst published his findings to better educate the crowds coming to see Hans perform, but Hans didn't care. Neither did the throngs of people coming to see him. He continued to travel around Germany for several years until his translator died in 1909.

But some good did arise out of Dr. Pfungst's work. He came to the conclusion that every person gave off the same body language Hans had noticed no matter how hard they tried to suppress it. There was no way to hide it.

And so his work is still used by comparative psychologists when they conduct studies today. They keep their subjects in complete isolation so they can't read each other's mannerisms and tics. In some studies, computers are used to administer questions and record the answers since they are incapable of emotion.

It's called the Clever Hans effect. Today, a common place to find it in action is in drug-sniffing dogs used by police. They're often given subconscious cues by their handlers to find drugs where they don't exist.

But that still leaves a big question unanswered about Hans and his special skill. If he was so good at it, and made so much money from it, why'd he stop? Why didn't he just hire another translator?

That's because Hans couldn't hire anyone. He couldn't talk. At least, not with his mouth. He gave all of his responses by using his foot, stomping out the answers to math questions and musical riddles, among others. He'd been taught to do simple algebra, tell time, read, spell, and calculate fractions.

All of this sounds pretty basic, like something any adult or even a child could do, so what made Hans so special? It's simple really: Hans wasn't an adult. And he wasn't a child, either.

Hans, you see, was a horse. And his translator, Wilhelm von Osten, was also his trainer.

SMALL WONDERS

Must be seen to be believed! Patronized by royalty, nobility, and clergy! The smallest performers in the world, interesting alike to old and young, rich and poor.

These kinds of proclamations graced the enchanting advertisements for one of the oldest and most lucrative sideshow exhibits, the flea circus.

Depicting cartoon insects fencing one another, or balancing on a tightrope, these inventive ads promised entertainment the likes of which had never been seen. Or at least *couldn't* be seen without the help of a magnifying glass.

If the idea of a flea circus sounds too good to be true, that's because it is. The concept of minuscule bugs swinging on the trapeze or launching themselves from a tiny cannon forces the spectator to suspend disbelief. To consider that the humble flea, once the harbinger of the Black Death that killed half of Europe in the 1300s, could also be trained to perform daring feats in a venue no larger than a Monopoly board.

The truth is much darker. Fleas only live

for a few months, so they can't be trained. Instead, most "ringmasters" thread gold wires around their necks, which are then tied to various props for them to interact with. Fleas, like ants, can lift objects much larger than themselves, so they appear to be kicking or carrying things when in reality they're just trying to find a way out.

However, most flea circus owners didn't go to that much trouble to make their circuses seem authentic. Many simply wired up their dollhouse-sized diving boards and carousels with electric mechanisms so it only *looked* like they had trained fleas to perform when in fact, no fleas were present at all.

The earliest known flea circus was said to have debuted in London in the 1820s, and since then, they've become novelties, nothing more than wholesome entertainment for nostalgic audiences. But the use of tiny insects to demonstrate their ingenuity goes back much further than the 1820s. In fact, it dates back all the way to 1578 and a man named Mark Scaliot.

Mark was a blacksmith, and a darn good one at that. His work was renowned for its intricate detail and impeccable quality. But Mark really wanted to show the world what he could do. Swords and armor and the occasional piece of jewelry were fine, but Mark was capable of so much more, so he enlisted the help of the sideshow host's favorite creepy crawly: the flea.

Mark worked day and night crafting something no one else had seen and, if he did his job right, no one else would see. He constructed a miniature lock, and to go with it, a key, all of which was constructed using only eleven pieces of iron, steel, and brass.

Strung on a chain made up of forty-three links, all of it weighed no more than a grain of gold. And these weren't just sculptures to demonstrate how small his work could get. The key he'd constructed actually did function inside the lock, and he hung it all around the neck of a flea.

Yeah. A flea . . . which had no problem moving around while wearing the necklace.

Scaliot's work is said to have given birth to the modern flea circus, though it took a while. Stories of his feat, however, made the rounds for over a hundred years after he debuted his teeny tiny necklace and paved the way for people like Oswaldus Norhingerus, who made 1,600 flea-sized dishes out of ivory. Pope Paul V was said to have counted them all by hand using a special pair of glasses.

Or Johannes Ferrarius, who built wooden cannons and carriages no bigger than a peppercorn. Or Claudius Callus, who carved miniature birds designed to sit on the tops of trees and tweet as they reacted with the water flowing through the trunks.

This was truly inventive and skilled work done without the use of laser-cut blades or the technology we take for granted today. It became the basis for entire movements of miniature artwork, dioramas, and Hollywood special effects.

And all of it, down to the molecule, hung upon the shoulders of one tiny flea. Some might call that . . . curious.

BEAR NECESSITIES

Roderick Ross MacFarlane had always loved nature. He'd grown up off the coast of Scotland in the early 1800s, where he was surrounded by a veritable zoo of birds, mammals, and sea life. His love of the outdoors eventually took him to the Hudson's Bay Company, a retail business specializing in the trapping and trading of furs. The perfect place for a budding naturalist to grow his career.

Starting as a clerk, Roderick traveled all over the world, working his way up to management. He ran the trading posts at several forts in the Northwest Territories of Canada for many years until he was put in charge of Fort Anderson farther north in 1861.

During his time there, Roderick befriended the local indigenous people who traded with him and taught him about life in the territories. He also encouraged them to bring unique specimens they found for him to send to the Smithsonian Institution in Washington, DC, where he worked on the side as a collector.

During the winter, he'd stow away eggs, hides, and other natural history items, and write letters to the museum's curators about what he'd found. Then, when the weather warmed up, he'd box it all up, and ship everything south.

Over time, Roderick and the Inuit came to respect and enjoy each other's company, which is probably why they approached him after an unexpected kill one day in 1864. Their hunters had been attacked by a bear that day and barely survived. Using a Hudson's Bay rifle, spears, and knives, they'd managed to kill the animal and drag its carcass back to the trading post where Roderick happily accepted it.

He didn't think anything of it. It looked a little different from the other bears he'd taken, but nothing extraordinary. He skinned the bear, had the hide cured, and sent everything to the Smithsonian as he'd done so many times before.

The items sat in storage for over fifty years before the dean of naturalists, a Dr. C. Hart Merriam, found them. He'd never seen anything like them. What MacFarlane had dismissed as a standard barren ground grizzly bear was actually something entirely new.

It had been found far outside the normal hunting grounds for bears of the region at the time. Its fur was yellow, not dark brown like the grizzly's, nor white like the polar bear's. Its skull was smaller and its sharp teeth had formed much differently than the teeth of the bears known to the area. Dr. Merriam concluded the objects that had been sitting in a box in the Smithsonian's archives belonged to a whole new species of bear.

Vetularctos inopinatus is what he called it. Translated, it meant "ancient unexpected bear."

Though it hadn't been entirely unexpected. Other explorers, such as journalist Caspar Whitney, noted encounters with bears like the one MacFarlane had been given. Whitney described it as "a cross between the grizzly and the polar," with rear claws as big as the front claws, a wide forehead, and ears like a dog's. Unfortunately, there was no way to verify the existence of others like it. Given the time in which it was discovered and the lack of similar specimens, the bear was declared extinct.

As our knowledge of different species and our methods of testing DNA grow, it's becoming easier to track the lineage of such rare animals. It's possible the bear really was, as Whitney described it, a hybrid grizzly-polar bear. Such animals have been spotted with strikingly similar features to the bear at the Smithsonian, including the yellow fur and enlarged skull.

It's also been suggested the bear was a species that had survived past the Ice Age and died out on that fateful day in 1864. We might never get a definitive answer as to what species it really was, though, which is disappointing, I know.

Some might even call that . . . *unbearable.*

PRINCE OF WHALES

The humble farmer. The backbone of the American way of life. They grow and harvest to provide not only for their own families, but ours as well. Everything from corn to potatoes to squash is cultivated across rural farmland from coast to coast. However, in 1849, something else was unearthed in a farmer's field. Something that didn't make sense. Something that didn't belong there.

Workers in Vermont were digging up land to build the first railroad between Burlington and Rutland. During the dig, one of the workers noticed something sticking up in the dirt. Bones. Quite a few of them in fact. He didn't think much of them, seeing as how horse skeletons had been spotted from time to time as they were pulling up the land. So they kept working, not caring too much about what happened to the former horse they'd just unearthed.

A local resident, Mr. John G. Thorp, had been passing by when he, too, saw the bones poking out from the dig site. There was something about them that struck him as odd, though. He certainly didn't think they were horse bones, so he convinced the man in charge of the railroad project to move his workers to another plot of land so he could collect and analyze the bones.

Naturalist Zadock Thompson was brought in for his expertise in identifying what kind of animal the bones had once belonged to. Thompson was a prolific author of many animal and nature guides, despite serious limitations to his situation. No one else was working in his field, and he had no access to specimens or books to further his studies.

He was charting new territory for the scientific community, but that didn't stop him from studying the various flora and fauna of his native Vermont, including the skeleton Mr. Thorpe had rescued from the railroad workers.

After some consideration and examination, Mr. Thompson identified it as having belonged to the ancient ancestor of the beluga whale. While there was no way to determine its sex, its skull and teeth indicated the twelve-foot-long specimen had been a full grown adult before its death. It was a fascinating discovery, but there were two questions the men shared, as did everyone else who came across the specimen.

First, how did a beluga whale wind up in the middle of a farmer's field in Vermont, 150 miles from the closest shore? And how had it made its way so far down from the native arctic waters of the north? Such a creature had no business being so far from its home.

Well, it took a while for technology and environmental studies to catch up, but scientists eventually learned that the Charlotte whale—named for the town where it was discovered—had been stuck in Vermont for a very long time.

The bones had been preserved under ten feet of blue clay sediment left over from the Champlain Sea, a temporary inlet that had formed when glaciers retreated at the end of the last glacial period. The sea had dried up thousands of years ago, leaving the whale, and presumably other creatures, in the middle of Vermont with no way out.

Today, the Charlotte whale is the official state marine fossil of Vermont. And while it's certainly strange to find something as large as a dead whale so far from the ocean, it happens more often than we realize. Discoveries like this teach us about how the earth changes, how oceans shift over time, and even how those changes affect the migration of wildlife around the globe.

The world around us is never constant. We may think we're fine, but if we sit still long enough, we might discover we've missed our window out.

Just like the Charlotte Whale.

PIG HEADED

As the old saying goes, "give a man a fish and he'll eat for a day. Teach a man to fish and he'll eat for a lifetime." Education, to that enlightened fisherman, was as important as life itself. To some, it's the reason they were put on this Earth in the first place. A good teacher can move us forward, make us better—make life a little more fulfilling. But a good teacher can do more than that. A good teacher can teach the unteachable and fulfill not only *their* lives, but the lives of those around them.

Samuel Bisset was just such a teacher. He was born in Perthshire, Scotland, in the early 1700s, and originally sought work as a shoemaker before trying his luck in London at a different, more lucrative career. He was reading a story about an attraction at a local fair when he was struck with an idea—an idea that might have sounded absurd to anyone else.

Bisset read of a horse that could perform odd tricks. The novelty, combined with his own stubborn refusal to settle down into one line of work, set him on a path toward becoming an animal trainer. He started by training a horse and a dog for his act, then moved up from there. He trained one monkey to dance on a tightrope while another held a lit candle and turned a barrel organ.

Not content with his small zoo of performing animals, Samuel went bigger. Well, technically smaller, but with the plan to put on a grand musical performance with cats. Not those cats, with the costumes and wigs. I mean actual cats. He purchased three kittens and worked with them for months, teaching them how to hit dulcimer strings with their paws so as to create music. The Cats Opera, he called it, ran for almost a week and made Bisset rich, which only encouraged him to add more animals to his routine.

He taught a rabbit how to play military marches on a drum with its hind legs. Small birds, such as sparrows and canaries, could spell anyone's name in the audience. And even though he already had a dog in his lineup, he taught a turtle how to play fetch. But while Bisset had proven successful in training animals with uncharacteristic talents to entertain crowds, none of his acts proved as financially successful as his Cats Opera.

He thought perhaps he had exhausted his opportunities in London, and decided to take his show on the road, moving his human family and his furry family to Ireland for a new start. It was there where he encountered a seemingly unbeatable challenge. According to some local folks, the only animal that was too stubborn to train was a pig. It couldn't be done, they said.

Bisset wanted to prove them wrong. He accepted the challenge and purchased a black suckling pig for three shillings. He immediately taught it to lay down under the stool where he worked. Unfortunately, that's about as much as the pig would learn at first. Bisset nearly gave it away until he looked at the problem from a different angle. He worked closely with the pig over the next sixteen months, turning what was originally considered an obstinate and unreasonable animal into something akin to a loyal golden retriever.

The Learned Pig, as it had come to be known, could do all sorts of amazing tricks to enthrall audiences. It could tell time down to the second. It had an impeccable talent for picking out married folks from unmarried folks. It knew how to spell out a person's name and in some cases, read a woman's mind. It could also kneel out of respect, the way you might do before the Queen.

But not everyone loved Bisset and his Learned Pig. One night, a man wielding a sword broke into his hotel room with the intent to *kill* the pig. To him, the animal was an affront to God and everything decent. The man swung the sword around the room, destroying everything in its path, before plunging the blade into the unsuspecting trainer. Bisset begged the man to leave, and showed him the permit he'd obtained from the chief magistrate for his pig to perform.

The attacker accepted the proof, but threatened to drag Bisset to jail if he ever showed his face in town again. It wouldn't matter, though—the injury he'd sustained became infected and not long after, he passed away.

The pig, however, lived on. Not only did it continue to perform under a new owner, but it inspired similar acts all throughout the nineteenth century. The image of an educated pig even became a common way for cartoonists to illustrate the greed of the rich, and the overindulgent nature of celebrities and politicians.

In a way, the Learned Pig became something all of us today might recognize: the first and longest lasting meme.

GREAT ESCAPE

Walls are meant to be protective. Four walls and a roof are part of a person's basic needs, along with food and clothing. However, walls can also be confining. The stone walls of a prison, for example, aren't seen as protective to the people inside, even if they're meant to protect those of us on the outside.

Fu didn't see walls as a shelter. He saw them as a hindrance. Something to be overcome. Fortunately, Fu was resourceful. He'd been locked up since the early 1960s, back before security cameras and sensors adorned every corner and corridor. He learned the guards' schedules. He knew when they patrolled his cell and when no one was in the vicinity.

The first time Fu escaped, he got as far as the tree line before he was captured and thrown back in. The guard in charge, Jerry Stones, was furious. He threatened to fire anyone taking shortcuts and not doing their jobs. Security was of the utmost importance. The second time Fu got out, he was captured on a nearby rooftop.

Then one day, one of the other guards noticed something odd. He watched the prisoner from a distance, taking note of his behavior. Fu produced something from his mouth. It was a piece of metal, which he jimmied into the lock on his door. The guard didn't know how he'd gotten it. More important, he had no idea how Fu was able to pick the lock by himself. But like I said, Fu was resourceful.

The authorities were at a loss for how they could keep losing track of him. They thought they were doing everything right, and technically they were. There was just one thing they hadn't counted on: animal intelligence.

Fu's full name was Fu Manchu and in 1968, he wasn't in a prison per se, but he was certainly behind bars: in the Omaha zoo. He was an orangutan and did not enjoy staying trapped in his enclosure. Fu liked climbing down the exterior of an air vent into a dry moat that led to the furnace. He would use his strength to pry the furnace door open just enough so he could slip the wire, which he kept tucked between his bottom lip and his gums, into the crack. He'd slide it upward to unhook the latch and then roam around the zoo.

The head zookeeper, Jerry Stones, couldn't believe the ape had figured out how to break out on his own. But almost twenty years later in San Diego, another male orangutan managed to do the same thing.

This one, named Ken Allen, had become very good at scaling the walls of his enclosure. Zookeepers there eventually brought in a team of professional rock climbers to find ways of keeping Ken from climbing his way to freedom—or worse, teaching the other apes to do the same.

However, to animal researchers at the time, these escapades weren't as interesting as what was going on in other zoos around the country. The famous gorilla Koko in California could communicate with American sign language. She knew over a thousand different signs and was able to convey emotions, as well as *ask* for things from the researchers.

And then there was Colo, a female gorilla at the Columbus Zoo in Ohio. Colo couldn't sign, but she had other ways of getting what she wanted. One day, zookeeper Charlene Jendry learned Colo had taken possession of something her colleagues couldn't identify, as she'd been keeping it hidden. Thinking it might be something dangerous, they'd tried to bargain with her. They offered her peanuts to try to coax it out of her hand, but she wouldn't budge.

She wanted more. Charlene added a slice of pineapple to the deal. That's when Colo showed her what she'd been hiding—a key-chain. But rather than give her the whole thing, Colo saw an opportunity to increase her earnings. She broke the keychain into pieces and only gave a new piece away when Charlene presented a new piece of pineapple.

The object in Colo's hand hadn't been anything dangerous after all, but the experience had taught Charlene something important about apes: they knew how to negotiate.

Fu Manchu, Ken Allen, Koko, and Colo had all learned how to perform different tasks once considered only teachable to humans. The ability to pick locks, outwit zookeepers, communicate via sign language, and barter for stolen goods apparently came naturally to the curious creatures.

And however scientifically inaccurate it might be for me to swap animal names in this particular story, the old adage couldn't be more relevant, given the circumstances: after all . . . money see, monkey do.

MONSTER MASS

Before the days of mechanical refrigerators, we'd place a giant block of ice in a box and then store our food there to keep it fresh. Someone had to go and get that ice to deliver it to customers.

They were called ice men and they were often farmers who worked during the winter harvesting ice from frozen lakes and rivers. They'd walk out onto a lake with at least a foot of ice on the surface and use a large handsaw to cut out the blocks. Those blocks were then stored in large buildings during warmer months so people could still refrigerate their food in the summer.

As you can imagine, it was a dangerous job. One wrong step and an ice man could be lost until spring. As a result, the men who did the work tended to be pretty tough to scare. However, in 1891, two midwestern ice men came face to . . . eye (?) with something that made their blood run cold.

It was early September, and Marshall McIntyre and Bill Gray of Crawfordsville, Indiana, were getting ready to deliver ice into town. As they were fastening harnesses around their horses, something appeared overhead. It was several hundred feet in the air, and swirling above them.

The creature measured roughly eighteen feet long by eight feet wide. It had been described by witnesses as "a great white shroud" that seemed to move through the air using large fins that ran along its sides. It had no head, but looked down upon the men and their barn with a large, flaming eye in its center and let out a plaintive wheezing sound.

As it got closer, the creature circled above the farmhouse and the barn. Bill and Marshall had no idea what it was or what it wanted, but they didn't want to risk being devoured by it. They fled to the barn and waited until it disappeared, which it eventually did. It flew toward the center of town before turning back to the farm. Bill and Marshall watched as it floated overhead for another hour until they decided enough was enough. The men darted for the ice house, mounted their horses, and departed for town.

When they returned to the farm after sunrise, the creature was gone. The ice men gave an interview to the local paper all about their bizarre encounter, telling the reporter that they'd be carrying a rifle on their deliveries from now on in the event the creature ever returned. The story was published later that day in Crawfordsville's *Daily Journal*.

A few days later, another article was published in the *Journal*, this time featuring eyewitness testimony from townsfolk who also saw the enormous white thing squirming in the air. Its mournful screeching continued, and some Crawfordsville citizens even reported feeling the creature's hot breath as it passed overhead.

The story soon spread to the *Indianapolis*

Journal, a much larger paper, before making its way across the country to outlets like the *Brooklyn Eagle* all the way in New York. But even though the story captured the imaginations of people from coast to coast, the Crawfordsville Monster had solidified itself as a local legend. In the ensuing weeks, the Crawfordsville postmaster received numerous letters about the creature. It seemed the whole town had monster fever.

That is until other two men, John Hornbeck and Abe Hernley, encountered the white, wheezing shroud terrorizing the town. They followed it for several miles before discovering the truth about its origin. It wasn't a shapeless, otherworldly mass.

It was made up of birds. Killdeer, to be exact. The gathering of birds had likely grown confused by the town's electric lights, which had recently been installed. Compounded by the damp, foggy air reducing visibility, Marshall McIntyre and Bill Gray and all the other Crawfordsville locals simply hadn't realized what they were looking at.

Whoever first thought up the old cliché had it right when they said, "Seeing is believing," but that doesn't mean we have to believe everything we read. The only thing more frightening than the Crawfordsville Monster was how quickly everyone bought into the story, without doing a bit of critical thinking.

Even though ice houses have faded into the past, our gullibility is as strong as ever.

Which might be the most *chilling* part . . . of the entire story.

THE STOWAWAY

Most people don't usually set out to be the hero. They tend to be pushed into a situation where their will and determination are put to the test. Prove yourself during a time of war, and medals and ticker-tape parades aren't far behind. That's just the way things often work.

Simon didn't choose to go to war, though. He was drafted, but his reluctance didn't stop him from helping his fellow troops, and his work following World War II cemented him as a hero of the British military for years to come.

Several years after the war had ended, the British Navy got word of a communist uprising happening in China. They sent the HMS *Amethyst,* an armed frigate, to keep an eye on things in case they got ugly. The ship docked at a port in Hong Kong where one of the younger men—a boy, really—seventeen-year-old George Hickinbottom, stumbled upon someone fending for himself. His name was Simon, and he was sick and hungry and in need of medical attention.

George snuck him aboard the ship, and then helped him get back on his feet. As Simon recovered, he started getting to know the crew. When he was well enough to stand, they allowed him to remain on the ship, and gave him a job. He was put in charge of pest control, a task he handled with gusto. After all, the alternative was ending up back in Hong Kong, alone and hungry.

Captain Ian Griffiths took quite a liking to Simon, as had the rest of the crew, and he became their moral support when times got tough. They shared their food with him, and allowed him to sleep where he liked. Later, when Griffiths was promoted and replaced, folks on board the ship worried that Simon might have to go, but the new commander was just as friendly toward him.

Soon after, the crew given a new order: to travel to Nanjing and replace the ship that had been on duty there. But during their journey, the *Amethyst* was attacked. A field gun battery operated by the People's Liberation Army had opened fire on the ship. The new commander took one of the first hits while he was in his cabin, and died shortly after. Simon happened to be with him at the time.

Simon, too, had been badly burned, and had sustained shrapnel injuries as well. But he managed to crawl across the deck while the shelling continued, escaping to the medical bay with a small group of crew members, where they waited out the sounds of explosions outside. Death was almost a certainty, but the crew took care of Simon's wounds as best they could.

For ten days, the ship took fire while the crew struggled to stay alive—and afloat. They packed the holes below the waterline with hammocks and bedding. Meanwhile, Simon fought to recover. He distracted himself—and the other crew—by doing what he did best: catching rats. After the *Amethyst* was able to get away, more than a week after shelling had begun, news of Simon's efforts made its way to England.

The public was enamored of this unexpected hero, one who had never asked to be a part of something so dangerous. But he'd handled it all with grace, not once succumbing to fear or panic. People sent him letters from all over—so many, in fact, that the Navy hired someone just to answer his mail for him. He even received *awards* for his bravery, including the Dickin Medal.

For those who don't know, the Dickin Medal is the highest award given to animals in the British military. You see, Simon, who had hunted rats and kept up morale aboard the HMS *Amethyst* . . . wasn't a man.

No man would've been able to nap inside the captain's hat or go wherever he pleased on board a military ship.

Simon . . . was a cat.

GOOD BOY

They say dogs in the workplace lead to less stress for employees. This results in more productivity, fewer sick days taken, and higher morale. But the idea of taking your pet to work didn't originate with big companies like Google or Amazon. In fact, as far back as the 1800s, canine companions were a common sight at certain workplaces.

One such pooch was named Owney. He was a terrier, and the unofficial mascot of the Albany, New York, post office back in the late 1800s. Owney liked to hang around and sleep on the mailbags while his owner worked. And even after his owner quit the post office, Owney stayed behind to keep watch over the letters and packages that came through.

The dog was very protective of the mailbags, and when one was moved, he would follow it to the train that it was eventually loaded onto. Riding the rails from Albany to another location, Owney stayed with the mail and made sure only mail clerks ever handled the bags. And since none of the trains he rode on ever derailed or crashed, they started to view him as a good luck charm.

Over the years, Owney traveled all over the United States protecting the mail. The New York Central Railroad system was able to go just about anywhere from the Albany station, taking Owney to places like Boston, Cleveland, Chicago, and even farther out. And no matter where he went, the little terrier from New York always had someone to look out for him. Mail carriers across the country loved Owney like he was one of their own. And in a way, he was. He was kind of an honorary postal employee.

While the Postal Service unofficially adopted him as a mascot for the whole organization, they also treated him much like a parcel. Wherever he went, they tagged him, stickered him, and then sent him along to the next destination. The only difference was that he got to eat and drink before the trip.

At every stop along the way, Owney would have another tag added to his collar, and as his trips grew longer, that collar grew heavier. It would jingle as he walked, and when it got to be too much for him to carry, the Postmaster General had a coat made to display them instead.

Over time, even *that* became too cumbersome for him. He was just a little terrier, after all. It's believed that over time, Owney had accumulated more than a thousand medals and tags during his time on the rails, which was a lot for that tiny pooch to carry.

He certainly earned each one, though. On one trip, a mail pouch had fallen off a delivery wagon, and Owney jumped out to stay behind and protect it. After all the deliveries had been made, the clerks noticed the missing bag—and the missing dog. They retraced their route until they eventually found the bag . . . and there was Owney, lying on top of it waiting for them.

But the dog's greatest journey was still ahead. In 1895, Owney went international. He rode on trains and steamships, protecting the mail as it traveled through Asia, Africa, Europe, and the Middle East—and he did this for an entire year. According to one report, he even received passports and medals directly from the Emperor of Japan. And when he finally returned to America on December 23, Owney's feat was publicized by newspapers all over the country, turning him into a pint-sized celebrity.

But all that travel would eventually take its toll on the beloved mascot. After accumulating more than 143,000 miles throughout his time at the Postal Service, he'd had enough. It hadn't helped that his health was failing, and he'd grown a bit aggressive in his old age.

Two years following his famous trip around the world, Owney was put down. He'd apparently attacked a postal clerk and a US Marshal, though it's believed he'd been mistreated prior to the attack.

Regardless, Owney left an indelible mark on both the Postal Service and the country as a whole. The clerks who had been ordered to bury the dog refused to do it, claiming he deserved better. Instead of being buried, Owney was preserved and his remains are on display to this day at the Smithsonian National Postal Museum in Washington, DC.

It's a fitting tribute for the dog who managed to turn a famous stereotype on its head: rather than chasing the mailman, Owney *became* one.

Now that's what I'd call . . . a good boy.

RAT RACE

Despite their intelligence and friendly nature, rats are often hated by the public. Their role in spreading bubonic plague has been greatly exaggerated—it was the *fleas* on the rats that actually carried the disease—and they've been considered a nuisance for probably longer. Vermin to be exterminated with prejudice.

But did you know rats can detect gunpowder residue? That's how they're used in the Netherlands, because they're cheaper and easier to train than dogs. Even more amazing, the Gambian pouched rat of Africa has been trained to detect landmines and tuberculosis, all thanks to their incredible sense of smell.

Regardless of their occupations or contributions to society, though, rats are still animals. They have basic needs like all of us, like food and shelter. In the wild, they scavenge for food wherever they can find it, often going to places where they aren't welcome . . . in search of their next meal. But in 1500s France, their disregard for farmers' crops gave the people of Autun so much trouble, the town went to unbelievable lengths to remove them.

All manner of exterminations were exacted on the rat population at the time, but no matter what they did, they always kept coming back. They destroyed plants and infested homes and businesses. It was an epidemic. Even the Catholic Church got involved and decried them as creatures of the devil. The Pope attempted to exorcise them while a bishop officially excommunicated them out of the country. But it didn't stick. The rats kept coming and the crops continued to get eaten.

So the town turned to more medieval methods. Rats were subjected to all kinds of torture and abuse simply for existing within the borders of Autun. But there was one method the people hadn't tried. It didn't require burning, or stretching them out on the rack, or drowning them. Instead, the town served the rats with a summons to appear before the court.

Their crime? Destroying the local barley crops.

The trial was to be conducted within the cathedral, but for a proper trial there needed to be two sides. The town represented the plaintiffs, tired of fighting an unwinnable problem, while the rats were the defendants. And any defendant, no matter their crime, deserved proper representation. Autun turned to a local pro bono lawyer named Barthélemy de Chasseneuz to argue on behalf of the rats.

Yes, the rats were given their own lawyer—and a particularly clever one, too.

Chasseneuz had studied under the finest legal minds of the day, and performed work for major figures at the time. He had already served the Duchy of Milan and Pope Julius II, and now he had been tasked with representing the unrepresentable: a group of feral, disliked rodents causing havoc for farmers all over Autun, France.

Unsurprisingly, on the day they were supposed to appear, the rats didn't show up. Chasseneuz argued that the original summons could not be honored because rats were not pack animals. They were solitary creatures and each rodent would need to be served individually.

The court actually complied, and reissued one new summons per rat. It didn't help, though, and they failed to appear on the second scheduled day. Chasseneuz pointed out that the roads leading to the courthouse were hazardous for the rats, given the presence of larger creatures like cats and dogs along the route.

Once again, the lawyer had made a valid argument to the court. According to the law, if a defendant could not travel to court with a guarantee of safety, they were not obligated to attend the hearing and the summons could be ignored.

No one knows what the final outcome of the trial was, but it's probably safe to say that all charges against the rats were dropped. Barthélemy de Chasseneuz had won his case—and inadvertently become the first ever legal defender . . . of animals.

UNBELIEVABLE STUNTS

ON STRIKE

Sometime around 1914, Walter traveled across the Atlantic with thousands of other brave Canadians to join the fight at the start of World War I. For many, it would be a one-way trip, but Walter managed to stay alive for four straight years. In fact, no bullet or land mine would send him home in 1918. No, that would be blamed on something far more strange.

He was on patrol in the area of Belgium known as Flanders Fields when a bolt of lightning flashed out of the sky and struck him off his horse. When his fellow soldiers found him, he was lying in the mud beside his dead horse, and half his body had been paralyzed. As a result, he was put on the next ship back to Canada to begin his recovery process.

It would take Major Walter Summerford many years to become self-sufficient, eventually learning to walk with the help of a cane. But he was still young, still drawn to adventure, and still full of life. So when a group of his friends decided in 1924 to hike into the mountains to fish in a nearby lake, Walter happily joined them.

I imagine the steep hike was grueling for him, but he kept up. Walter was a fighter,

after all. But when they arrived at the lake, he decided to take a seat while his friends unloaded their gear and set up camp. Right near the water's edge was a tall tree, so he sat himself down against it under the shade of the branches. But the sun quickly faded away as a storm rolled in.

When Walter's friends found him, he was lying on his side at the base of the tree, trembling and in pain. The tree itself told them everything they needed to know. A dark, smoldering streak ran down the bark, from high above all the way to the ground. It had been a lightning strike, and Walter—against all odds—had been struck by it. Again.

Just like the first time, Walter seemed to have been paralyzed by it, and as a result, spent a long while in the hospital, doing his best to recover. It took him two years before he could walk again, but he did it. He was a fighter, and giving up wasn't an option. So he pressed onward in life.

As the story goes, Walter took a trip to the park in Vancouver in the summer of 1930. He was probably there with family, or maybe those same fishing buddies. We don't really know. But I have a feeling you could guess what happened next, right? Against all the laws of probability, Walter Summerford was struck by lightning for the third time in his life.

They say this one was the worst. Or perhaps it was just so devastating because it was the third time in twelve years that it had happened. Whatever the reason, Walter never walked again, and spent the last two years of his life in a wheelchair. When he passed away in 1932—still very much a young man—he went to the grave as a member of a very special club. Lightning rarely strikes twice, but for Walter Summerford it did that and more.

You would expect the story to end there, wouldn't you? No more Walter, no more lightning, right? Well, not exactly. Because in 1934, just two years after he passed away, lightning *did* strike again in his hometown. Now, I know what you're thinking—without Walter, where could it possibly strike? The answer, though, might be more obvious than you were expecting.

It struck his gravestone, naturally.

OUTLASTED

When the trapdoor of the gallows was opened, the entire crowd held its breath. They were about to watch an innocent man die, and there was nothing they could do to stop it.

It was February of 1894. The person on the platform was a young man named Will Purvis, who had been sentenced to death by hanging for the murder of a local farmer named Will Buckley. The trouble, was, Purvis claimed he was innocent. He swore to it.

Thanks to a bit of circumstantial evidence, though, the jury ruled unanimously against him. Purvis was stunned. He hadn't committed the crime, and yet no one had believed him. Angry and bitter, he lashed out in the courtroom. "I'll live longer than the lot of you!" he shouted.

Regardless, on a cold February day in Mississippi, Will Purvis was escorted to the gallows for his execution. He was led up the stairs, where a noose was lowered over his neck and tightened, and then a black sack was slipped over his face. Finally, the trap door was triggered, and Will Purvis dropped to his death.

Sort of. He actually fell a few feet and landed on the soft grass below the platform.

The crowd glanced back up at the rope and immediately spotted the reason why: the noose had come untied. Sure, Purvis had a bit of rope burn around his throat, but he was alive and breathing. So the crowd went wild.

The executioners tried to rebound from the failed attempt. They rushed down and scooped Purvis up, and then hauled him back up to the platform where they reset the trap door. After a moment, though, they gave up. Maybe it was the nervousness of retying a noose in front of thousands of angry onlookers. Perhaps it was a desire to do things on their terms, at their pace. Or maybe they could hear his words to the jury echoing in the backs of their minds.

Somehow, despite the odds, he had survived.

So they tossed Will Purvis back in jail. He had already spent two years in prison awaiting his trial, and now he was back. He made an appeal for a new trial, but it was denied. He made another appeal, and received yet another denial. This went on for two long years, all while Purvis had to endure

hard labor alongside the other prisoners. But finally, in January of 1896, something changed.

Actually, it was some*one*.

Mississippi had elected a new governor, and when the new man—Anselm McLaurin—took office, he changed Purvis's sentence. The executioner's noose no longer loomed in his future. Two years after that, enough evidence and public outcry had flowed in that he was actually pardoned. Roughly six years after his life fell apart, Will Purvis was a free man. Two decades later, the true killer of Will Buckley came forward and confessed, closing the case for good.

Purvis went on to live another four decades. He never found himself back inside the courthouse or at the center of another murder trial. He eventually received a large payment from the state as restitution for his time in prison, and lived a full, normal life.

Will Purvis passed away in 1938—forty-four years after his failed execution, and just three days after the death of the final member of his jury.

He was a man of his word.

ROUGH LANDING

On average, there are fewer than one hundred airplane crashes each year. Your chance of dying in one is one in eleven million. In fact, since your odds of dying in a car accident are higher, at one in five thousand, you're better off in the *air* than on the *ground*.

Still, no matter how low the chances are, we hear the stories. Small aircraft and jumbo jets do go down and people die without ever reaching their destinations. It's a sad truth about air travel, and nobody knows this better than the pilots and flight attendants who work on these planes every day.

One such attendant was Vesna Vulović. Born in Belgrade in 1950, Vesna loved to travel. It was her love for the Beatles that took her to London, where she happened to see a friend of hers wearing a flight attendant's uniform and thought, *That's what I want to do.* Traveling to distant lands, seeing new places, and meeting new people—it was the life she'd dreamed of.

To satisfy her wanderlust, Vesna returned to Serbia in the early 1970s and joined JAT Airways, where she was hired as a flight attendant. It was a dangerous time for Yugoslavian travel, as Croatian nationalists had been carrying out terrorist attacks across the country.

None of that bothered Vesna, though. She had her crisp, new uniform and a ticket to adventure. And things were fine for the first year as she settled into her new life, but this would not be the fairy tale she'd imagined. On the morning of January 25, 1972, Vesna was called in to work Flight 367, which would be landing in Copenhagen the next day to pick her and the rest of the crew up before flying to her hometown of Belgrade.

She'd made trips like this before, but this one seemed different. There was something in the air—no pun intended, I swear. The rest of the crew could feel it, too. Dread. Hopelessness. Despair.

Vesna had planned to do a little sightseeing before takeoff, but decided to join the other crew members in a shopping trip instead. All of them seemed sad, like they knew what was about to happen. The captain had gone as far as to lock himself in his hotel room the previous day, not coming out until a few hours before the flight. Even the passengers felt it.

As they deplaned at Copenhagen Airport, one man in particular was so frustrated, he refused to get back on the plane, leaving his baggage behind. When Flight 367 took off a few hours later, there were twenty-eight passengers and crew aboard, including Vesna.

She handed out drinks and snacks and attended to passengers' needs as the airplane climbed higher and higher. About an hour into the trip, once the plane had reached its maximum altitude, it happened. The vague, ominous threat that had been hanging over their heads had finally found them.

An explosion, which began in the baggage compartment, ripped through the plane, tearing it in half like a napkin. Vesna and the twenty-seven other people on board fell more than thirty-three thousand feet into a small Czech village below. Authorities determined the explosion had been caused by a briefcase bomb, allegedly left behind by that frustrated man who'd refused to board the plane back in Copenhagen.

At least, that's who Vesna pointed out when they questioned her.

You see, a villager heard screaming from inside the wreckage not too far from his home. Peering inside, he saw a woman in a flight attendant's uniform covered in blood. It was Vesna. And despite her six-mile fall to earth, she had *lived*.

Vesna Vulović spent months in the hospital recovering from her wounds, which included a fractured skull and temporary paralysis, but she didn't let her injuries stop her. When she'd finally healed, she got back on with her life—including her job JAT Airlines, albeit in a less exciting role: negotiating freight contracts from the safety of the ground.

Many people don't bounce back after a serious injury. Athletes leave the field. Riders never get back on the horse. Shark attack victims don't get back in the water. But once in a while, a person like Vesna Vulović manages to fall out of the sky . . . and land on her feet.

WEST SIDE STORY

Variety may be the spice of life, but I like to think there's something comforting about routine. Routine is familiar. It keeps us on track. Focused, even. Routine can be the difference between exercising daily and gaining ten pounds in a month. Routine can also be the difference between life and death.

For the choir members of the West Side Baptist Church in Beatrice, Nebraska, routine was key to their daily lives. Every Wednesday afternoon at 4:30, Reverend Walter Klempel would light the furnace so the church would be warm enough when practice started. He'd go home, enjoy dinner with his family, and then he, his wife, and his daughter would go back to the church at 7:15 for choir rehearsal.

And every Wednesday at 7:25 p.m., Mrs. F. E. Paul, the director of the West Side Baptist choir, would begin practice for the fourteen other members who had arrived at 7:20. This had been their routine every single week until the Wednesday of March 1, 1950.

On that day, Reverend Klempel lit the

furnace just as he'd done every Wednesday afternoon prior. Furnaces don't always stay on, however. They run for a time and fill a space with heat until the desired temperature is reached. Then they shut off and wait until the chill returns and begin the process all over again.

But when Reverend Klempel turned on the furnace that afternoon, he was not aware of the broken gas pipe behind the church. He had no idea that when he turned on the furnace, he was filling the church with natural gas rather than heat.

The Reverend went home as usual. He relaxed for a little while before he, his wife, and their daughter enjoyed their supper together. Afterward, their daughter changed out of her school clothes and into a dress her mother had ironed earlier. Then all three Klempels bundled up against the chilly pre-spring air for a walk to their weekly choir practice.

At 7:25, the furnace started up once more. The gas had been building up inside for hours, working its way into every nook and cranny of the modest church.

The gas ignited in a fiery blast that shattered every window in the building and sent the walls flying outward. The roof collapsed straight down over where the choir stood during practice. The explosion even took out a local radio station.

Firefighters quickly arrived to put out the blaze and once the fire had been extinguished, there was the task of recovering remains. Except there weren't any.

Reverend Klempel's daughter had spilled something on her dress that evening. Her mother ironed a new one for her to wear, which kept the family home much later than anticipated. They were still at home when the church exploded.

Choir member Ladona Vandergrift always arrived to practice early, but on that night the high school sophomore had been stuck on a particularly tricky math problem as part of her homework. Rather than give up and head to rehearsal, she decided to stay home and finish the problem first.

The choir's pianist, Marilyn Paul, was supposed to be at the church by 6:45, but she'd fallen asleep after dinner. Her mother, also a choir member, woke her up at 7:15 and the two of them never made it to practice.

Every member of the West Side Baptist Church choir had had a reason for being late that night, from car troubles to feeling under the weather. Not a single one was in the church when the explosion happened.

The choir had never experienced such a night. I don't mean the explosion, which was definitely a first, but an evening when each person had been running late. A once in a lifetime occurrence. Definitely a break in the routine.

Call it a miracle, or divine intervention, or even the luckiest of coincidences, but you have to admit this may be the only occasion of a choir performing at its best because it couldn't keep proper time.

CRADLE
WILL FALL

There's a reason so many people are afraid of heights. Except it's not the height they're afraid of, rather the risk of *falling*. The World Health Organization has estimated that each year, about 646,000 people die from some kind of fall, from simple stumbles to Christmas-light disasters on the roof. Humans just can't seem to stay on their feet . . . or land on them.

Well, most of the time, that is. Because many of us have heard stories of people who've fallen from airplanes and lived to tell the tale. In fact, between 1940 and 2008, 157 people fell from airplanes during crashes and survived.

A fall from a great height isn't always a death sentence . . . as long as you have somewhere nice and comfy to land. Water works well, as does snow. However, in the case of one man in 1930s Detroit, a safe landing meant using whoever was available. Yes, you heard what I said: *who*ever.

Joseph Figlock probably didn't expect to be involved in a freak accident that day. He'd been sweeping up an alley when it hap-

pened. It had fallen from above. No, not a meteor, nor an airplane. Not even a rogue satellite thrown from its orbit.

It was a baby. And it lived four stories above him. Whoever had been watching the child, perhaps the mother or a nanny, had lost track of him when he found the open window. Seeing a new space to explore, the baby crawled toward it and—once at the precipice—kept going.

It's a good thing Joseph had decided to do a little cleaning that day, otherwise things might have gone much differently. The baby landed right on top of his head and shoulders. Both suffered minor injuries, but the baby survived the ordeal. It was probably more traumatic for the mother who wondered where her child might have gone, only to panic at the sight of the open window.

And Joseph Figlock was a hero, albeit an unintentional one. But he didn't let his accidental hero status go to his . . . um . . . head. He carried on his life as usual, sweeping out the alley each day, expecting what anyone else might have expected: that what had happened to him would be a onetime occurrence.

Except the following year, another child, this one a bit older than the first, decided an open window would be the perfect place to play. He drifted too close and lost his footing, falling four stories toward his impending death below.

Well, he would have, except a certain person happened to be standing between the boy and the pavement. Joseph Figlock had once again found himself in the precarious position of catching a falling child.

Neither Joseph nor the toddler were

seriously injured in the fall, though I'm sure Joseph kept his eyes to the sky while sweeping the alley from that point forward. It must have been surprising to learn that while lightning may not strike the same spot twice, babies certainly do.

OVER A BARREL

Like most of us, Annie had big plans for her life, but plans don't always work out, do they? In upstate New York in the 1850s, Annie's prospects were slim. She came from a *big* family with *big* needs, and after her father's death in 1850, Annie struck out on her own.

She sought an education to become a schoolteacher. It was during this time when she met David. The two fell in love and eventually married, but like I said before: plans don't always work out.

The couple had a child who didn't survive past infancy. David died a short time later. And poor Annie spent the next several decades floating from one odd job to the next. She opened her own dance studio in Michigan, then left to teach music up north, eventually making her way to San Antonio, Texas, and Mexico City before finally settling back in Michigan.

Times were changing, America had entered the twentieth century, and Annie was getting older. She had no long-term financial solution to fall back on, and retirement was out of the question. Most women at the time would have looked for simple ways of keeping their situation, but not Annie. She needed to make a splash to stay afloat—literally.

Her idea was simple. On October 24 of 1901—her sixty-third birthday, in fact—she would pack herself into an oak pickle barrel and launch herself over Niagara Falls. Like I said: simple, right?

Understandably, she had trouble finding people to help her, though. Few people wanted to be responsible for a woman killing herself in the most ostentatious way possible. Yet she continued with her plan, and even did a test run a few days before the main event. Not with herself, mind you. She used a cat.

And don't worry—the cat *survived,* and forty-eight hours after it had emerged from the barrel, Annie stepped inside her own. It was lined with a mattress to absorb some of the impact, and a rescue team was established at the base of the falls to retrieve her once the barrel reached the bottom. She planned for everything, it seems.

Annie and the barrel rowed out toward Goat Island—situated at the top of the falls—along with some of her friends. She tossed the barrel overboard and climbed inside while her associates screwed the lid down tight. They then used a bicycle pump to compress the air inside the barrel, which they sealed off with a cork.

And that was it. The time had come for Annie to make good on her promise, and hopefully make a little money at the same time.

The current carried the barrel down the river and over the falls, where it plummeted to the waters below. The team of rescuers found her and, fearing the worst, pried the barrel open. They peered inside. There was Annie, her head smeared with blood. A little worse for wear, but still alive. She'd done it. Annie Edson Taylor had become the first person to go over Niagara Falls in a barrel, and had lived to tell the tale—which she did often, of course.

Not long after her stunt, Annie went on a brief speaking tour. When asked whether she'd ever try it again, she was quoted as saying, "I would sooner walk up to the mouth of a cannon, knowing it was going to blow me to pieces, than make another trip over the Fall." Still, her speaking engagements didn't garner her the financial security she'd hoped for. She took to posing for pictures with tourists, and planned on doing another plunge several years later, but nothing ever came of it.

She spent her final years once again bouncing around from job to job, at one time finding herself conducting séances as a medium, before passing away in 1921 in relative obscurity. Since her stunt, Annie's life and experiences have inspired numerous stories, television specials, and even a stage musical. However, they have inspired rumors as well.

One such rumor involved a stowaway inside her barrel. According to reports at the time, the cat that went over the falls days before Annie's stunt hadn't been the only feline involved. Apparently, a black cat had been placed *beside* Annie before she was sealed inside the barrel.

And when that barrel was recovered and opened, they say, the cat emerged unharmed . . . except for one small change: All its black fur . . . had turned white.

ONE-TRICK PENNY

John Trickett had no intention of sitting out the Great War. Not while his two older brothers were out there fighting for queen and country. He was built for it, too—he was tall, stocky, and he loved horses. A gentle giant, some might have called him. He also looked much older than he was, which was probably why no one questioned him when he enlisted.

He left his home in Lincolnshire, England, to follow in the footsteps of his brothers who had been shipped out earlier. Along with his clothes and toiletries, John packed important things to remind him of home when he was on the battlefield. One of those items was a penny from 1889. On one side, it featured a bust of Queen Victoria. On the other, the figure of Britannia seated upon a rock with a shield to her right and a trident in her left hand. It wasn't special outside of John's sentimental longing for the simple things back in Lincolnshire.

Sadly, before the war ended in 1918, John's brothers had been killed in battle, leaving him the only Trickett left. He came home at the end of the war having left a piece of himself back on the Western Front where he'd been stationed. He was now deaf in one ear, and had trouble with his left hand.

However, it didn't take long for him to settle in at home and build a new life for himself. John took up a job as a postmaster and as a switchboard operator. He fell in love with a girl named Clementine and the two got married. They had eight children together. Grandchildren eventually followed, but it's not known whether John got to spend much time with them, as he passed away in 1962 when he was only sixty-three years old.

He'd held on to almost all of his belongings from the war, including his medals, a pocket watch, some photographs, and the penny he'd kept tucked in his breast pocket under his uniform. When his grandchildren discovered his collection of memorabilia, however, it wasn't the medals or the photographs that captured their imagination. It was the coin.

There was something about it, how part of Queen Victoria's face seemed to rise up from underneath. When John's granddaughter, Maureen, inspected the other side, she saw why the late Queen's nose had exploded outward.

The penny had been hit by a bullet.

On the other side, right beside Britannia, Maureen and her siblings saw the round divot where a bullet had been stopped. They ran their fingers over the attempted hole and suddenly had a visual representation of the stories they'd been told so many years ago.

How their grandfather had clashed with a German soldier who had tried to shoot him in the chest, but instead hit the penny, which deflected the bullet upward and through John's left ear. It had deafened him for the rest of his life and caused permanent nerve damage.

John had been one of many soldiers who had packed objects in their pockets. Doing so was common practice as a way to prevent bullets from getting through. This was a time before Kevlar vests, after all. It just so happened that on that day, at that time, that particular German soldier had aimed . . . and fired at the exact spot where John's penny happened to be hiding.

It's hard to blame John for being worried about what awaited him on the front lines. And no one can fault him for how he handled it—by holding on to a small memento that reminded him of home. It was a good idea for many reasons. If it hadn't been for that little metal disc, after all, Maureen and her siblings might not be here today.

Looking back, he could have kept that coin anywhere. His pants. His rucksack. Even his hat. But no, John placed his favorite coin in his breast pocket, close to the heart that was full of so much emotion.

He had planned ahead, and those plans—as they say—were right on the money.

COLD TRUTH

The human body is not meant to handle the extreme cold. Scores of aspiring hikers have perished trying to scale the deadly Mount Everest. Fifteen hundred souls were lost when the *Titanic* sank in 1912, many of whom froze to death in the frigid North Atlantic.

When our internal body temperature drops below ninety-five degrees, hypothermia begins to set in. Our breathing slows down. The pulse weakens. The brain starts to lose function, and words become slurred while our motor control falters.

You don't want to get caught in the cold, especially with no warmth or shelter nearby. Aside from hypothermia, frostbite can claim fingers, toes, and entire limbs without proper treatment. Folks in places like Minnesota know all about handling harsh winters and sub-zero temperatures. If only they had been nearby when Jean Hilliard needed them.

It was a winter's night in 1980 when Jean lost control of her car and ended up in a ditch. The snow and ice prevented her from getting the car back on the road. The temperature had reached minus twenty-two and the area was pretty rural. She caught sight of

a farmhouse not far from her position and decided to trudge through the snow toward it. They'd have a phone and she could call someone to come pick her up. Except once she got there, she learned it was empty.

She tried the next door neighbor's house. Same result—nobody was home. Being farm country in Minnesota, neighbors weren't easy to come by and there wasn't another house anywhere in the area, but Jean remembered one about two miles back. With no other option than to freeze in her car until daybreak, she started walking back the way she'd come.

The next day, the owner of that house, Wally Nelson, stepped outside and noticed something in the snow. It was big and it wasn't moving, so he inched forward for a closer look.

It was a girl—Jean, in fact. She'd collapsed fifteen feet from Wally's front door. Her body had frozen solid and her skin had been hardened by the cold. It was clear she had died overnight, but Wally was at a loss for what to do about her. He could call the authorities, but they wouldn't be able to get to him for some time, and he couldn't just leave her there in the snow.

Then he heard something. Faint, like a whisper. Jean moaned at his feet. He carried her to his car and placed her in the back seat while he turned on the heat. He drove her to the nearest hospital hoping doctors might be able to save her.

Her joints refused to bend. The thermometers they used were useless on someone so cold. They couldn't remove her boots either, as her feet had frozen to their shape. And her pulse was practically nonexistent at only twelve beats per minute. By all measures, Jean was essentially dead and not expected to survive the next twenty-four hours.

The doctor on duty, Dr. George Sather, heard the same faint moan as Wally had, and knew he couldn't let her go just yet. He wrapped her in an electric blanket and gave her oxygen. Two hours later, her temperature had returned to 98 degrees. She burst back to life with a seizure before calming down and getting her bearings.

Despite her brief confusion as to what had happened to her, Jean was fine. Her brain was still fully functional and she didn't require physical therapy once she got back on her feet. In fact, doctors had thought that even if she *did* survive, they'd have to amputate her legs from the severe frostbite they'd sustained, but that wasn't the case. The frostbite started to fade away and her skin slowly returned to normal.

It was a miracle, they thought. Until her tests came back. They revealed the simple explanation as to why Jean had survived overnight. It wasn't just because Wally had found her in time, nor had there been any divine intervention. She'd merely had a few drinks in her system when her car broke down. The alcohol had prevented her organs from freezing, meaning her skin had taken the brunt of the cold.

Jean had gotten a second chance at life— and I think it would be fair to say that anyone would consider that . . . a sobering experience.

UNBALANCED

When the stresses of life are getting you down, it's normal to want to find a quiet place to decompress. Somewhere far from the hustle and bustle, where your troubles just sort of fade off into the distance. Charles Blondin had a place like that—and nothing could get to him while he was there.

Charles was born in northern France in 1824 and took up gymnastics when he was five. Unlike other boys at the time who studied to become doctors or bankers or went on to do manual labor, Charles dreamt of becoming a performer. He trained as an acrobat, and eventually debuted to the world as "The Little Wonder," a graceful performer who enthralled crowds with feats of agility.

As he got older, though, his dreams of stardom grew bigger—and France was honestly just too small to contain them. He got married, had three children, and took his show on the road—well, overseas. In 1855, Charles traveled to New York City to join a family of French circus performers. They'd been entertaining audiences for four generations, and often took on outsiders to flesh out their act.

Now that he was part of a large group, however, Charles needed a way to stand out. More important, he had to earn his keep. Then it came to him: a way to put his skills to the ultimate test, to draw the largest crowds he'd ever seen.

Charles . . . would cross Niagara Gorge . . . on a tightrope.

The hemp tightrope he'd walk across would measure 1,300 feet long, and be about three inches in diameter—which is smaller than one of the credit cards in your wallet. It would be suspended 160 feet over the gorge, with the Niagara River churning beneath him. And he refused to use a net, claiming that preparing for disaster often invited it. Thankfully, that stubbornness worked to his advantage by further entertaining the audience.

One thing was true about performances such as his: as much as people wanted to see him cross the gorge safely, they also wanted to see him *fail*. It was something he got a kick out of, too. He loved when people bet on the odds of him falling to his death.

On the morning of June 30, 1859, twenty-five thousand cheering spectators gathered to watch Charles attempt to cross the gorge. Among them were congressmen, judges, generals, and reporters. Anyone who was anyone was at Niagara Falls watching Charles put his life on the line—literally.

Unfortunately, for all his preparation, Charles couldn't predict the deep sag in the middle of the rope. Everyone said the dip would throw off his balance and that the rope itself wouldn't support him. One person said he "deserved to be dashed to atoms for his desperate fool-hardiness." Charles ignored them all, though.

At five o'clock that afternoon, he took his first step on the American side. He carried a twenty-six-foot balancing pole in his hands to steady himself. The crowd grew silent. Some averted their eyes, unable to watch in case he didn't make it. After several minutes, roughly one-third of the way across, something unbelievable happened: Charles . . . took a seat.

Yeah, he sat down on the rope and invited the tourist boat, the *Maid of the Mist,* to stop just below him. Using a separate line, he pulled up a bottle of wine from the boat and drank as everyone stared in awe. When he'd finished, he tossed the bottle and began his walk again, at one point even running.

He'd done it. Charles Blondin had successfully crossed the Niagara Gorge on a tightrope—and enjoyed a tasty beverage along the way. But his show wasn't over yet. After a brief rest, he set out again—this time with something strapped to his back. About two hundred feet from the Canadian side he stopped and fastened his balancing pole to the rope. Then, untying the load on his back, set up a Daguerreotype camera on a stand and took a photograph of the crowd before packing up and finishing the journey back to the American side.

He repeated his feat again a few days later on July 4th of that year, and several more times after that, varying the different tricks he performed. He once walked half the rope facing forward and the other half backward. On another attempt he pushed a wheelbarrow all the way across.

And during what was perhaps his most daring performance, he stopped in the middle of the rope, unpacked a camp stove he'd been carrying on his back, and cooked himself an omelet.

Now that's what I'd call . . . a well-balanced breakfast.

THE OLD MAN AND THE PLANES

It's said that cats have nine lives. Humans, on the other hand . . . We have to make do with one. At least, that's *usually* how it works. But Ernie—the man at the center of today's story—was special.

In 1953, Ernie gave his wife, Mary, an incredible Christmas present: He'd planned a couple's trip to Uganda, where they would visit Murchison Falls. A part of the Victoria Nile, the waterfall was home to hippos, crocodiles, elephants, and lions—not to mention the lush natural forests that surrounded the river.

The area was extremely isolated and difficult to access, but that only made Ernie and Mary more excited. They were both from the American Midwest, and both in their fifties, so a trip like this would put them completely out of their element. It was the vacation of a lifetime.

The following year, they packed up and flew to Uganda. Once they got to the country's main airport, they chartered a small Cessna plane to take them northwest toward Murchison Falls.

But their dream vacation quickly took a nightmarish turn. As the Cessna approached the falls, a flock of birds flew in front of the window, blocking the pilot's view. The pilot swerved and accidentally hit a telegraph wire. All of a sudden, the tiny plane was careening downward. It crashed into the Nile River.

Ernie crawled out of the wreckage with a sprained shoulder. Mary emerged with a number of cracked ribs. The pilot seemed unhurt; he helped the couple set up camp for the night on the shores of the Nile. They slept among the wildlife, barely sheltered from the threat of lions and crocodiles.

In the morning, a tourist boat floated down the river and found them. The three survivors jumped on board and rode to the nearest town. There, they boarded another plane—this one headed *out* of Uganda.

The plane took off . . . and almost immediately caught on fire. As flames overtook the aircraft, it, too, careened to the ground. The pilot—a different one this time—ran into the cabin to open an emergency escape window. He climbed through the window, then pulled Mary out to safety.

But Ernie was too big to fit. Terrified of the growing blaze, he slammed his body against the plane's exit door until it finally opened, and he tumbled to the ground outside.

In addition to her cracked ribs from the *first* crash, Mary had now sustained several severe burns. Ernie was burned, likely suffering from smoke inhalation, and had given

himself a concussion and a fractured skull shoving the door open.

The couple, once bright-eyed and optimistic about their vacation, was in horrible shape—and, after back-to-back disasters, they weren't in a hurry to get on another private plane. Instead, they took a car back to Uganda's main airport, where a commercial airline brought them back home.

But when Ernie arrived, he was met with some startling news. In the wake of not one, but two near-fatal plane crashes, reporters apparently believed Ernie and his wife were dead. Newspapers published their obituaries under dramatic headlines, declaring the Hemingways deceased.

That's right—the Hemingways. You see, Ernie was just the nickname his friends called him. His full name was *Ernest*—as in, Ernest Hemingway, the famous American author. So you can see why his double brush with death was big news.

In the following months, Hemingway wrote a letter to his lawyer, detailing his and his wife's various injuries. One section said, and I quote:

> *Couldn't write letters much on account of right arm which was burned to the bone third degree and it would cramp up on me . . . But fingers burned and left hand third degree too so couldn't type . . . The trouble is inside where right kidney was ruptured and liver and spleen injured . . . I am weak from so much internal bleeding.*

Which is honestly difficult to read. I mean, this was a horrible tragedy for the couple. But over the years, this handwritten letter became something of a collector's item. It recently sold at auction for a whopping $237,000.

But here's the most curious part: While the double plane crash was awful, it was far from the only time Hemingway became gravely injured. By one estimate, he suffered at least *nine major concussions* during his life.

So, forget cats. Ernest Hemingway was the one with nine lives.

BIZARRE
EVENTS

DARKNESS FALLS

Turn on the news today and outside of the latest political turmoil, you'll probably see Mother Nature terrorizing a part of the world. Volcanoes in Indonesia triggering devastating tsunamis, tornadoes in the Midwest reducing homes to nothing but splinters and rubble, and perhaps the most destructive of all, catastrophic forest fires in California that have burned entire neighborhoods to ash. And let's not forget the Category 5 hurricanes that have all but wiped entire islands off the map.

It's enough to make you think the end of the world is close at hand. Well, such assumptions are nothing new, and if you lived in New England in 1780, you might have thought the same thing.

The skies from Maine to New Jersey had been yellow in the days leading up to the bizarre event that occurred on May 19. The region had just emerged from one of the coldest winters ever recorded and warmth was still hard to come by, even as Spring had begun to bloom. But instead of a bright, golden sun up above, it shone red during the day, giving way to a pinkish moon at night.

Down below, rivers and lakes were blackened with soot, and signs of smoke were all around. Given that we were still hundreds of years away from social media and twenty-four-hour news coverage, people came up with all sorts of reasons as to what was happening, and many jumped to the same conclusion: that the end of days was nigh.

Then, on May 19, the symptoms that had plagued New England for the last several days culminated in a strange and extraordinary phenomenon. The sky went completely dark. A thick fog enveloped the northeastern United States and parts of Canada for more than a day. Reports came in from upstate New York where the sun wasn't rising. In parts of Massachusetts and Connecticut, candles were required from 2:00 p.m. onward.

And it wasn't just the people who were affected. Roosters also had no idea what time it was, and crowed in the middle of the afternoon. Crickets chirped as though night had fallen early. Cows retired to their stalls believing the day to be over. And farmers couldn't tell the difference between manure and the ash that had fallen, inches thick in some places.

Clergy believed the Day of Judgement had arrived, and people flooded churches to confess their sins. Some of the less religious men fled to taverns where they filled their bellies with drink, and cavorted with women as they tried to forget that tomorrow might not come.

All manner of explanations were tossed around as to the cause of the darkness—everything from planetary movements and meteor strikes, to God's anger toward the Revolutionary War. No one at the time had any real insight into why the skies had suddenly turned black.

But we know better today. Based on the records of the event and the eyewitness reports at the time, we can make more informed assumptions as to what transpired on that fateful day. But we also have trees.

Yeah, trees. You see, trees can tell us a lot about history, thanks to their growth rings. Researchers examining the growth rings on trees in Ontario, Canada, noticed extensive scar damage on some of the inner rings from when the trees were young. From those scars, they were able to deduce that an enormous forest fire in the area may have caused the darkness that fell upon New England back in 1780.

Today, our forest fires are certainly dangerous, and they have been known to cause miles and miles of destruction. Thanks to news networks and social media, we know just how horrific they can be to live through, and many of us have friends or family who have been touched by those events.

Which puts the Dark Day of May 1780 into real perspective. A fire so massive that it left inches of ash all over New England, and blotted out the sun for an entire day. Combine that with those eerie red sunsets that led up to the darkness, it's frightening to imagine just how bad that blaze must have been to have left such destruction and chaos in its wake.

And thanks to the unpredictability of the world we live in, it also leaves us with a chilling thought: what if something that massive happened again?

Let's hope we never find out.

WHAT
ALES YOU

The Industrial Revolution brought significant advancements to Britain in the eighteenth and nineteenth centuries, including chemical manufacturing, the steam engine, and machine tools—what we would call "power tools" today. As new industries arose, existing industries were also upgraded. One of the most significant—and the oldest—was *beer*.

The actual method of brewing and storing beer hadn't changed much over the past few hundred years, but as with any period of change, competition bred growth. Literally. London breweries started building their cisterns and vats larger and larger. Capacities quickly grew from 2,400 barrels' worth of beer all the way up to nearly ten times that amount, large enough for one crafty brewery to actually host a dinner party for a hundred guests inside an empty one.

Of course, revolutions don't just happen. They build up over long periods of trial and error, and when you're racing competitors to build the largest beer vats in the city, errors are bound to crop up.

It was a Monday evening in October of 1814 when it happened. A leak had sprung at the Henry Meux and Company brewery in central London. Well, leak might be an understatement. A vat holding 3,500 barrels, or 135,000 liters, of beer burst wide open. The deluge was so powerful that it also knocked over a number of casks of porter, resulting in an ocean of ale totaling over 1.47 million liters.

The flood ripped through one of the brewery's twenty-five-foot walls like it was paper and collapsed part of the roof. Streets became rivers and nearby houses were obliterated. On the first floor of one such house, a mother and her young daughter were at tea when a wave of beer swept them away, killing them instantly.

Others in the vicinity were either carried off in the flood or crushed to death by debris. One major problem contributing to the higher death toll and complicated rescue efforts was the town's flatness, which prevented the beer from draining away. Instead, it simply poured into basements and washed out roadways.

The current of the flood was so strong that it dragged debris from the homes it had destroyed, which created obstacles for rescuers trying to reach the victims. By the time rescuers were able to reach the areas hit hardest, it was too late.

Bodies began floating up from the ruins around midnight, including that of a woman who had been in her backyard at the time and had been buried under the wreck of her home. All told, eight people had perished in the flood.

As you should know by now, the story

doesn't end there. A week after the disaster, the brewery was taken to court to determine the cause of the accident. A brewery employee by the name of George Crick came forward with his account of what had caused the flood. George had noticed one of the iron hoops holding the vat together had fallen off.

I know what you're thinking. Why didn't George just pick the hoop back up, grab some tools, and put it back where it belonged, right? Well, these weren't the usual metal hoops you might find around pickle barrels. Each of these weighed roughly one metric ton.

George and the owners had determined that the rivets holding the hoop to the barrel had simply worn out over time and, like the button on a pair of pants two sizes too small, they popped out. The weight of the liquid inside proved too much for the vat to handle and the rest, as they say, is history.

History, but also a *tragedy*. Lives were lost. Homes were destroyed. Businesses were closed. And most tragic of all, even though the accident was a product of human error, the brewery got off without a hitch. In fact, a year later, they managed to get the Crown to give them back the tax money they'd paid on the lost beer.

The court might have called it an "act of God," but looking back, I think a larger, more universal truth needs pointing out, however obvious it might be.

Some people just can't hold their liquor.

MAKE IT RAIN

Charlie was tired of selling sewing machines. Charlie wanted to get rich, and walking door to door in the hot summer sun—fingers crossed for a sale every few days—was not going to get it done. Charlie wanted to make it rain—so he did.

He'd been born in Kansas in 1875, but his Quaker family packed up and moved to southern California five years later. They settled in on their dusty ranch about thirty-five miles north of San Diego, and then life just sort of kept going.

By 1904, Charlie was a twenty-nine-year-old sewing machine salesman who was frustrated with his lot in life. He still lived with his parents, and judging by how hard they had both worked just to stay afloat all these years, Charlie's own future was far from bright and sunny.

Charlie was a smart guy, though. He'd been paying attention, and he'd noticed something about the weather. As far as he could tell, rain storms had a way of following big battles that involved cannons and rifles. He wondered if there was a chemical reason why, and started to dig into the field of *pluviculture*—literally, the science of rainmaking.

Charlie got busy testing out his ideas. He began to experiment with different chemicals, mixing them inside a large wooden tub. When he was sure he had the recipe right, he covered it and let it sit for a while before carefully pushing the lid off from a distance with a long pole. The resulting steam drifted up into the sky—and then caused rain to fall on his father's bone-dry ranch. He'd done it.

The first place he took his services was north to Los Angeles. They agreed to pay Charlie $1,000 if he could give them eighteen inches of rain, and that was a lot of money to a poor sewing machine salesman—close to $30,000 in modern currency, in fact. So Charlie built himself a small tower near Rubio Canyon, put his big wooden vat on top of it, and let the chemicals get to work.

And it worked. Charlie gave Los Angeles more than eighteen inches of rain, and took home a big fat check. With success under his belt, and the testimony of a happy city, he started going elsewhere. In the decade between 1905 and 1915, Charlie worked on as many as seventeen contract jobs. Sometimes they were cities, others times they were groups of farmers looking for a little help. And then San Diego called.

They were in the middle of a big drought, and after hearing about Charlie's services, they decided to give the rainmaker a try. They asked him to fill their depleted reservoir, and he agreed. The city council met and voted on the project, and agreed to pay him $10,000—*if* he could deliver on his promise.

The first thing he did was build another of his towers about sixty miles to the east of the city, on the edge of the Morena River. I'm not sure how moving his chemicals twenty feet higher was supposed to help a process that involved sending fumes into the clouds to agitate them and create rain, but Charlie insisted on it.

That was January 1, 1916. Four days later, the rain arrived. The local newspaper reported on a "light sprinkle" that day, although it was certainly not enough to fill the local reservoir. But it rained the next day as well, and the next after that. In fact, it wasn't stopping. The rain just seemed to keep coming, pouring from the sky day and night.

In those first five days, the city recorded at least seventeen inches of rain. It was wonderful, but also a bit troubling. The rain had filled the San Diego River, and it was beginning to spill over into the land around it. Reports of flooding and mudslides began to pour in, as did the news that homes were being swept away.

It was still raining on January 27 when the reservoir's dam broke. A torrent of water at least forty feet high crashed down from the hills toward the city, destroying buildings and taking lives along the way. It was pure and utter devastation. All because of the rain.

The January 1916 rainstorm brought thirty inches of rain into San Diego, but it was also a disaster for Charlie. The city was so upset over the destruction his rain had caused that they refused to pay him. The resulting legal battle took two decades to fizzle out, but Charlie never saw a dime for it.

He did well elsewhere for a while. He apparently signed a contract in 1921 up in Canada, and received offers from Cuba. But when the Great Depression arrived, cities no longer had the funds to pay for something as frivolous as rainmaking. He eventually closed up shop and went back to selling sewing machines.

Charlie Hatfield never wrote his recipe down. He repeated it dozens and dozens of times, and we have accounts from witnesses about what he did with his mixture, or what it smelled like, but never what the ingredients were. So when Charlie died in 1958, he took his secret formula with him to the grave.

His recipe might be forgotten, but the catastrophe he delivered certainly hasn't been. San Diego still remembers Hatfield's Flood, although folks are still divided on how it all really happened. Either Charlie Hatfield was the miracle worker he claimed to be, or he simply managed to arrive at the perfect time for an extraordinary act of God.

I'll let you decide which option to believe.

ASCENSION

When Catherine the Great, the longest reigning Empress of Russia, passed away in 1796, her son Paul I ascended to the throne. That's how things are done in a monarchy, after all. But that doesn't mean the people had to like it.

Granted, the people of Russia had gotten used to Catherine, so Paul seemed like a small, cheap replacement for something so powerful and irreplaceable. Which might explain why the conspiracies began almost immediately. Five years later, he was assassinated, and his son Alexander I took the throne.

Now, there's been debate for decades about that situation, about whether or not Alexander had a part to play in his father's death. Certainly, there isn't enough proof to make a solid case for it, but there's wiggle room in there, for sure. Most of the reports from Alexander's life say that he was very emotional about his father's death.

Maybe it was guilt, or perhaps it was just grief. We'll never know. But it's important to keep that in mind when I tell you the rest of the story. Because the next twenty-four years were a roller-coaster ride for him, and it didn't end well.

There were victories, such as the 1812 defeat of Napoleon, who had tried to invade Russia and march to Moscow, only to be turned back. But he was plagued by attempts on his life, and even a botched kidnapping plot. By the end of his life, he was incredibly distrusting of the people around him, and wanted to escape it all.

In the fall of 1825, he had his chance. His wife had been ill for some time, and they decided to take a journey to the southern city of Taganrog, on the coast of the Sea of Azov. Along the way he caught a cold, and eventually died of typhus. His wife passed away while his body was being returned, and the throne passed on to his brother Nicholas.

That's the story we're all told, but there are rumors of something more bizarre. It's said that Alexander—haunted by remorse for his father's assassination and driven by a desire to get out of the spotlight—hadn't died after all, but had actually stepped down from his position as emperor so he could remove himself from society.

It would mean two things, though. First, that his coffin in Saint Petersburg was empty, and second, that the real Alexander lived on for many years elsewhere in Russia. It's a fantastic tale, but there might actually be some truth to it.

In 1836, someone in the mountains outside of Perm claimed to have seen a man who looked exactly like the former emperor. He lived as a hermit in the area, and locals referred to him as Father Kuzmich. One tale in particular spoke of how a student of this monk had the chance to visit the city, where she had the opportunity to see a portrait of Emperor Alexander. Upon returning to her teacher, she told him that he was the spitting image of the dead ruler.

Was Father Kuzmich really Alexander I in a sort of self-imposed exile? We'll never know for sure, but it's certainly fun to imagine it being true. That a ruler as powerful as Alexander could simply step aside, fabricate his own death, and then live out the rest of his life helping others in the mountains as a monk . . . well, it's intriguing at the very least.

Father Kuzmich passed away in 1864, after a long life of serving and teaching. More than a century later, in 1984, he was canonized by the Russian Orthodox Church. Whether he was an emperor or a hermit, the people of Russia have refused to forget him.

And the coffin of Alexander? Well, it seems that it's been opened back up on more than one occasion. The most significant of those events took place in 1921. It's said that the Soviet authorities were looking for valuables, and had opened up a number of tombs to see what they could find.

When they reached the tomb of Alexander, they found the royal seals on his coffin still intact. Breaking it open, they peered inside, hoping for some lost treasure or priceless jewelry that might be used to raise money. Instead, they found something much less precious: lumps of lead weights.

Alexander's body, assuming it had been there in the first place, was nowhere to be found.

BOMB'S AWAY

In 1945, as World War II was coming to an end, US forces were making plans to invade the Japanese mainland. On August 6, after months of air raids conducted against the Japanese people, the United States dropped the atom bomb over Hiroshima, followed by another bomb over Nagasaki a few days later. Hundreds of thousands of civilians were killed. Those who survived were subjected to horrible side effects, such as cancer and severe burns, while children born in the aftermath had numerous complications and birth defects.

And while those two bombs remain the only times nuclear force has been used during war, countries all over the world continue to threaten mass destruction with similar weapons to this day. In fact, in 1958, a nuclear incident occurred in a very unexpected location—South Carolina—and most people have never heard of it.

In March of that year, a Boeing B-47 bomber departed Hunter Air Force Base in Savannah, Georgia, bound for the United Kingdom. Safely tucked inside its cargo bay was a Mark 6 nuclear bomb, a nuclear explosive based on the original bomb that had leveled Nagasaki thirteen years earlier.

The bomber's mission was simple: fly over Great Britain, deliver the payload, and continue on to a base in North Africa for refueling and debriefing. During the flight, Air Force Captain Bruce Kulka was called by the pilot of the plane, Captain Earl Koehler. Earl noticed a light in the cockpit indicating the bomb harness locking pin hadn't engaged, meaning the bomb could roll about the cabin freely in the event the plane suddenly shifted too hard in one direction.

He sent Bruce to the cargo area to fix the pin. With no easy way to reengage the pin, Bruce took hold of the straps keeping the bomb in place. As he pulled himself up, he accidentally triggered the emergency release pin. The bomb fell out of its harness and down to the bomb bay doors below. Thankfully, it didn't detonate, but the impact, combined with the object's massive weight, forced the bomb bay doors open.

The bomb plummeted toward the earth from fifteen thousand feet above. Meanwhile, in Mars Bluff, South Carolina, two young girls were playing with their cousin near a playhouse their father had built for them in the woods next to their home. The bomb hit the playhouse, and when it went off, it disintegrated the structure. Both girls were thrown back, and their father—a former World War II paratrooper—was also injured, as were his wife and son. Seven buildings within the vicinity saw significant damage as well.

A nuclear blast is capable of decimating anything within sixteen square miles, and yet not a single person died. The only structure that fell was the playhouse in the woods. How could this be? Simple: the bomb hadn't been loaded with its nuclear core, which was still on the plane.

The B-47's mission hadn't been to eradicate the United Kingdom, but to use it as a testing site. Despite our differences, we haven't been at war with England in many, many years. During the 1950s, the United States and the UK worked out a deal which would allow the US Air Force to test nuclear bombs on British soil in order to record the accuracy of the drops.

The plane hadn't left United States air space when the problem was noticed, nor had its dangerous cargo been primed for a full-scale nuclear assault. Instead, when the Mark 6 landed on the South Carolina playhouse, the regular explosives inside detonated, which obliterated the playhouse and left an impressive seventy-foot crater in the family's backyard.

No one was killed, though the injuries the family endured earned them roughly $54,000 from the United States government, close to $600,000 today. The crater is still there, too, indicated by a historical marker and access sign.

So, even though the United States hasn't dropped a nuclear bomb on another country in almost eighty years, it was responsible for the first—and *last*—nuclear attack on its own soil.

STEAMY DREAMS

The 1860s was not a good era for transatlantic travel. The most advanced passenger ships were steam-powered, but even with that technology the average journey from England to America took nearly two weeks. That's a long time to be in the middle of the ocean, considering how often weather can change over a two-week period.

In October of 1863, two ships departed Liverpool on their way to America. One of them, the *Africa,* encountered horrible weather, and reportedly sank as a result. The second ship, called the *City of Limerick,* wasn't doing much better, either. They had been moving through rough seas and dark storms for nearly a week, and there didn't seem to be an end in sight.

On board was a man named Mr. Wilmot, who was returning to the United States, where his wife awaited him at home in Connecticut. Wilmot was sharing a stateroom with a friend, a man named Mr. Tait. The two men slept on bunks in the room, Wilmot on the bottom and Tait up above, but for at least a few days, Wilmot had barely moved from his bed due to seasickness from the choppy waves.

One stormy night, Wilmot was asleep in his bunk when he had the most vivid dream. In it, he could see the door to the tiny stateroom slowly open, and there, dressed in a white nightgown, was his wife. It was a logical vision; he missed her terribly, and the growing anticipation of being reunited with her hadn't helped. Even if it was just a dream, it was good to see her again.

When she stepped into the room, Wilmot noticed a nervous look on her face. She cast a worried glance in his direction, but higher up, as if she were looking at the bunk where Tait slept. Then, carefully, she crept over to Wilmot's bed, stooped down low, and kissed him. A moment later, she stood back up, slipped out of the room, and the dream was over.

The next morning, Wilmot awoke to find Tait standing beside his bed, starring down at him with a frown. "You're a pretty fellow," Tait said sarcastically, "to have a lady come and visit you here."

Wilmot was confused, and asked his friend to explain himself. Tait went on to describe, in incredible detail, the visit of a woman in a white dressing gown, who had approached the bunk and kissed Wilmot. Naturally, Wilmot was stunned. It was exactly how he had dreamt it, but that wasn't possible. How could two men have the same dream, let alone doing so inside the same *room*?

This would be an amazing tale if it ended right there—but there's actually more. About a week after the shared dream, the steamship docked in New York and Wilmot caught a train north to Connecticut. His entire family had gathered to welcome him home, and it was probably a very happy occasion. But the moment he and his wife had a second alone, she surprised him with a very unusual question.

"Did you receive a visit from me a week ago?" she asked.

Stunned, Wilmot nodded, but also noted that it would have been impossible. How could she had boarded his ship and found him in his quarters?

Her answer was chilling. Apparently, after hearing the news of the sinking of the *Africa*, she had spent days suffering from deep anxiety, worried for the safety of her husband. One night about a week before his return, she found herself still awake late into the night, and was so overcome with fear that she imagined visiting her husband as he traveled.

She described entering the room, and how she could see Tait, awake in his own bed, watching her as she looked around. She described the kiss, the gentle caress, and then her silent exit. Then, as if to prove it had all really happened, she described every detail of the room, right down to the structure of the bunks the two men slept on.

If the story of Mr. and Mrs. Wilmot is any indication, love is a powerful, mysterious force that binds us to each other. Sometimes we love someone so deeply that we can't shake the feeling that they're right there *with* us, even when they're far away.

And perhaps there's a good reason why.

LOOKING UP

On November 17 of 1896, the night sky above Sacramento, California, was a source of fear and dread. It had already been a miserable night, with the skies filled with dark clouds and a steady wind. But as some of the more observant residents looked up, they were startled to see something else. There were lights in the sky, and they were moving.

Now, before you jump straight to assuming this was a UFO, let me give you more of the details. When you hear the whole story, it feels a lot less like an episode of *The X-Files*, and a lot more like something out of a Jules Verne novel. And we have a man named George Scott to that for that.

He was an assistant to Lewis H. Brown, California's secretary of state at the time. With access to the capitol building there in Sacramento, he and a few friends climbed up to the roof for a better look, and discovered something more mysterious than lights.

It was, according to him, a set of three lights. They seemed to bob slightly as they moved, almost like a ship on the water. Above the lights, all of the observers could make out the dark shape of something long and curved.

Another local claims he heard people up above him where the lights were, calling out orders for guiding the vessel. He said he could make out the full shape of the object above the lights, calling it "cigar-shaped" balloon with "wheels at the side" like a steamboat. But let's step back a moment and soak that in. This man was claiming to see a paddlewheel boat in the sky over his community. More than unlikely, this theory seemed practically impossible.

For context, hot air balloons had been around for a while. The first aerial photos of Boston were taken by a photographer by the name of James Wallace Black. In 1860, he climbed into the basket of a balloon owned by Samuel King and let it take him more than a thousand feet into the sky above the city, where he took his photos. It was a new use for a technology that had been around since the 1780s.

No one had managed to find a way to power and control those flights. Remember, though, the reported hot air balloon steamboat contraption over Sacramento happened in 1896—a whole seven years prior to the first recorded powered flight by the Wright brothers. So if the reports were true, and this was a powered flight, it would rewrite the history books.

Over the months that followed, the unidentified aircraft was seen hundreds of times. For a while it seemed to stick to the Pacific coast, flying down to San Francisco before heading north to Washington State. It vanished again for a while before reappearing near Omaha, Nebraska, in February of 1897, which seems to have been part of a larger journey eastward.

On April 11, witnesses reported that the airship had finally reached Chicago. There's an old photo of it, like a dark cigar against the pale white cloudy sky, but most historians think it's a fake. Still, people saw it, and just like in Sacramento, they wondered what it could be. Even though later reports claimed the mysterious airship had crashed, rumors about it continued to fly all over the country for some time—no pun intended, I swear.

Whatever it was, we may never know. In a culture that was deeply in love with the idea of Jules Verne's Captain Nemo, who sailed the oceans in a highly advanced submarine, anything was possible. And it spoke to the deep hunger most people have for answers to the mysteries of this world we call home. If anything, perhaps the story should serve as a lesson to all of us today.

Keep your eyes on the sky. You never know what you might be missing.

ALL SHOOK UP

Don't shoot the messenger. It's a common saying with a simple meaning—don't blame the person bearing the bad news for doing their job. Unfortunately, that's exactly what happened to two American scientists working in Peru back in 1962. They weren't shot, though, don't worry. They just wanted someone to listen to their advice.

They were working in the Ancash region of Peru, on the western edge of the country. Within that area is a town called Yungay, nestled in among the mountains. Although small, the town boasts a population of over ten thousand, and it holds a place in history as the site of a major battle during the War of Confederation in 1839. Also, thanks to an American archaeologist named Thomas Lynch, we're aware of evidence from ten thousand years ago that Yungay was one of the original locations where American agriculture began.

But the town's history hides a darkness beneath the surface, one that had gone unspoken for eight years before the unthinkable happened. David Bernays and Charles Sawyer were American geologists studying the nearby mountains there. Specifically, they were focused on Huascaran, the highest peak in Peru, which towered over Yungay from less than ten miles away.

While they were there, they noticed something concerning about the mountain. Specifically one section of it. If the vertical slab on the north side ever collapsed, it would crush the town beneath it. So the scientists took their findings to the local newspaper, which published their report.

Now, you would think *that* might have sparked some kind of investigation, or even an evacuation. The number of potential casualties was unthinkable. Somebody had to listen, except nobody did. They never got the chance.

The Peruvian government got wind of the geologists' research and ordered them to print a retraction. What they'd proposed was impossible. It would cause mass panic and chaotic riots. And if the two men wouldn't listen, they'd be arrested. So rather than face jail, Bernays and Sawyer fled the country, never to speak of their findings to anyone again. Even the town's own citizens were prevented from mentioning the possible collapse.

And that was it. For years, the town of Yungay went on about its business without fear. Maybe those scientists had been wrong. After all, Huascaran was an enormous mountain peak that had been there for eons. It wasn't going anywhere anytime soon.

Then in May of 1970, eight years after Bernays and Sawyer published their predictions, an earthquake occurred around three o'clock in the afternoon. It started off the coast of Peru, and devastated the entire Ancash region, including the town of Yungay. Roads collapsed, buildings were reduced to rubble, and all communications were destroyed. But perhaps worst of all was what happened to the northern wall of Huascaran.

That vertical slab the geologists had warned everyone about *did* fall. The resulting avalanche sent more than fifty million cubic meters of glacial ice, rock, and snow down the mountain, an unstoppable deluge that buried Yungay. Over twenty thousand souls were lost that day. Most of the bodies were never recovered. The government declared the town a national cemetery, and prohibited workers from excavating the area. Eventually, a new Yungay was established about a mile north of the original.

We may never know what might have happened if the government had actually listened, or how many lives might have been spared if the town had been evacuated earlier. Rather than a mass grave, the demise of the city could have just been an interesting footnote to one of the worst natural disasters to ever strike the region.

But it sadly turned out to be much more than that, due to the inaction and denial from the people at the top who could have helped the most.

Instead, it will go down as perhaps the greatest preventable disaster in history, predicted by two men who just wanted to help.

A COOL DREAM

It's been said that beauty is fleeting. This is often interpreted as meaning our good looks won't last as we age. What once was beautiful will eventually wither.

But there's another meaning, a deeper one. That something is beautiful not because it lasts, but because it is temporary. We have it only for a short time and therefore should cherish it, because one day it will all be gone. People, animals, flowers—all have limited time on this planet and are therefore beautiful.

Maybe that's what Anna Ivanovna, the empress of Russia, had in mind when she ordered the construction of a new palace in Saint Petersburg. Her forces had just defeated the Ottomans in a war that spanned four years, and Empress Anna wanted to do something big to celebrate. A party would not last long enough, and a statue was too small. She needed a true monument to their success built in order to honor their victory and the scores of soldiers lost on the battlefield.

She hired renowned architect Pyotr Yeropkin to design the impromptu castle. Yeropkin had been responsible for redesigning Saint Petersburg after the death of Peter the Great, as well as palaces for chancellors and princes all over the country. If you were building a grand structure in Russia, Pyotr Yeropkin was the man with the plan.

The palace was designed to be more than 65 feet tall and 164 feet wide. The giant bricks the builders used, however, weren't held together with mortar. Instead, Georg Krafft, who was overseeing the construction, put his scientific background to the test and instructed workers to use plain water as a binding agent. An odd choice for something as massive as a palace, but a wise decision in the end.

When completed, the palace featured a garden lush with trees and wildlife, such as birds. An elephant was also brought in to entertain guests. Sculptures of all kinds adorned the walls, as well as artillery similar to that used during the war. Elaborate furniture pieces filled each room and a tall wooden fence was erected around the perimeter of the building—to keep commoners out, naturally.

Once completed, the palace became a setting for ceremonies and amusing performances, including a mock wedding between two jesters.

Years earlier, Empress Anna had taken offense at the marriage between a prince and a Catholic woman. After his new wife passed away, the prince was forced to become a jester for the empress. At the start of the wedding, Empress Anna chose one of her poor servants to become his new bride, someone she knew the prince would find unattractive.

The reluctant couple rode atop the elephant, both of them dressed as clowns while a menagerie of creatures and circus performers trailed behind them. After the wedding, they were stripped of their clothing and tossed into a freezing honeymoon suite with nothing to keep them warm but their own body heat—and a sheepskin coat the servant had bartered for with one of the guards.

Books about the palace were published almost a hundred years later with films hitting screens a century after that. The unique and charming castle had captured the imaginations of everyone who heard about it. If only Empress Anna had lived long enough to enjoy it more. She passed away one year after construction was completed, leaving behind her glorious creation for all to enjoy . . . until the following summer.

You see, there was one problem with the structure, something the architect or the builders couldn't have fixed regardless of the level of engineering that went into its construction: it couldn't handle the heat. By the following fall, Empress Anna's palace had disappeared entirely.

It had melted. You see, the palace was never intended to exist beyond Russia's famous winter. The sculptures, the furniture, the trees, the birds, and even the elephant . . . had all been carved . . . out of ice.

DEAD WEIGHT

Some athletes become legends for a reason. Olympic gold medalist Usain Bolt is widely considered to be the fastest man alive. Tennis icon Serena Williams is the winner of twenty-three major singles titles, an Open Era record. And Jim Thorpe, born in 1887, was the first Native American to win a gold medal for the United States when he competed in the 1912 Olympics. He's also considered the greatest athlete of the first half of the twentieth century.

They poured their lives into their passions. Their hard work and determination earned them worldwide fame. Children look up to them. Aspiring Olympians idolize them. However, not all legends are born out of sweat and gold. Some don't work as hard as the others. Some stumble onto the pages of history without doing anything at all.

Frank Hayes was born in Brooklyn in 1888—one year after Jim Thorpe—and got his start working around horses. He'd tried his hand at jockeying to no success, eventually becoming a stable hand for a local horse breeder. Work was work, after all, and he wasn't about to look a gift horse in the mouth.

Frank's boss saw potential in him, though, but not as a jockey. Instead, he wanted Frank to train his thoroughbreds to race. And Frank was a natural. Despite never winning a race of his own, he went on to train several champion steeds, earning him respect from all over the sport of horse racing.

Still, Frank never forgot about his first passion. He was a jockey at heart and he dreamed of the day when he would once again mount up and ride one of his trained horses to victory. And that day eventually arrived in June of 1923.

He'd been training a particular horse named Sweet Kiss for a steeplechase at New York's Belmont Park. A steeplechase is different from a regular horse race, in that it involves jumping over obstacles, such as fences and ditches. Unfortunately, with the event only days away, Frank found that riders were in short supply.

He was only too happy to volunteer his services for the event—and hopefully the horse's owner would agree. The owner, however, didn't want him to compete, claiming his weight would slow down the horse.

But time was running out and there were no other jockeys. If Sweet Kiss was going to compete at Belmont, they had to rely on Frank to do the job. He went on a severe diet to lose the weight needed to qualify, and on the day of the race, Frank Hayes got his wish.

He was thrilled, of course. Finally, someone had taken a chance on the thirty-five-year-old stableman, and he *wasn't* going to throw it away. Even the other jockeys could see how excited he was to compete.

It didn't matter that the odds were against him—literally, at 20–1. Frank climbed atop Sweet Kiss at the starting line and waited for the signal. The starter waved the flag, and the race was begun. Frank and Sweet Kiss took off like a rocket, jumping over hurdles around two miles of track leaving the other horses in the dust.

As they pulled into the final turn, it was just the two of them galloping toward the finish line. Frank hunkered down, leaning into Sweet Kiss, the wind whipping overhead. The audience roared. They stood to watch the underdogs, this horse and its jockey who'd had no chance of winning minutes before, about to win the competition.

They crossed the finish line to deafening cheers, and Sweet Kiss gradually slowed to a stop over another hundred yards. Frank Hayes had won his first race after years of staying off the track. The horse's owners and the people in the stands all ran down to meet him, to congratulate him for what he'd accomplished. It was joyful chaos.

But as they got closer, it was clear something had gone wrong. Frank fell off the horse and landed face down in the dirt. Almost immediately, Dr. John Voorhees, the track physician, hurried over to see what had happened. And the news he delivered to the others was bad.

Apparently Frank's excitement got the better of him. During the race, he had suffered a heart attack, but somehow managed to hold on. By the time the horse finally crossed the finish line, Frank was nothing more than cargo, hitching a ride on its back.

It's ironic, I know. Frank Hayes had wanted to be a jockey. But in the end, he turned out to be nothing more than dead weight.

HOLD ON

Under the best circumstances, the odds of dying in a plane crash are one in eleven million. You're more likely to be struck by lightning or die in a car accident than you are to perish in a malfunctioning airplane. However, no matter how unlikely the scenario, the fear of falling out of the sky from thirty thousand feet up is very real and it's only amplified by stories like that of Tim Lancaster.

Tim Lancaster was a forty-two-year-old British Airways pilot. With more than eleven thousand flight hours under his belt, he was more than capable of handling a simple flight from Birmingham, England, to Spain. On June 10, 1990, Tim and his copilot, Alastair Atchison, took British Airways Flight 5390 into the clouds along with eighty-seven precious souls.

Takeoff was perfect. The plane soared skyward for twenty minutes as it worked its way to its target altitude. It was only when the plane reached twenty-three-thousand feet that everyone started to realize this was a one-in-eleven-million flight. An explosion in the cockpit startled the passengers and blew the door to the flight deck clean off. They saw everything: the open window, the debris and paperwork being sucked out the front of the plane, and that the pilot had gone missing.

The windscreen—basically, the plane's windshield—had come loose and flown away, completely depressurizing the cabin. And the pilot, Tim Lancaster, had been sucked out through the opening in a matter of seconds.

Another crew member bravely ran into the cabin and took a position in the pilot's seat while Atchison, the copilot, got his bearings. He strapped on an oxygen mask and told the passengers to hold tight. They were about to make an emergency landing.

He got on the radio to signal to the closest airport that he needed a place to land, but the wind whipping through the plane made hearing anyone at air traffic control almost impossible. Without their confirmation, Atchison couldn't begin the emergency landing procedures. After some time, however, a message from Southampton Airport came through and Atchison began his descent toward the runway.

He landed the plane without incident, saving the lives of every single person onboard. But you might be wondering what happened to the pilot, Tim Lancaster. After all, authorities eventually found the windshield and were able to deduce what had caused it to separate from the rest of the plane. An investigation revealed the use of bolts of varying sizes in securing the windshield to the flight deck, none of which had been strong enough to handle the changes between the cabin and the outside air pressure.

And Lancaster? Well, they didn't have to go far to find him—because he'd never *left*. The seasoned pilot *had* been sucked out the window, but Atchison, thinking on his feet, had grabbed his colleague's ankles and held on with all his strength until more crew members were able to come and help him.

Being exposed to such strong winds at that high an altitude should have killed him, especially as his body continued to slide further outside the cockpit. According to flight attendant Nigel Ogden, the first crew member to take over holding the pilot's ankles, Lancaster kept hitting his head on the fuselage, but letting him go risked his body being sucked into one of the engines, thus bringing down the plane even faster and killing everyone onboard.

So they held on, Ogden withstanding frostbite and exhaustion until Atchison was able to bring Flight 5390 safely to the ground. Not a single passenger or crew member died in the incident, thanks to some quick thinking by everyone involved.

And although Lancaster *also* suffered from frostbite and minor injuries, he was back on the job six months later . . . with a heck of a story to tell. I can't help but wonder, though, if he warned the people he shared it with.

"This one will give you chills," he must have said, "so hold on tight."

STRANGE
LITERATURE

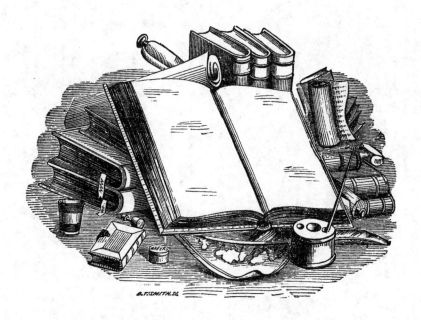

DREAMS OF PARADISE

Dante Alighieri spent nearly two decades writing his most famous work, what we now call the *Divine Comedy*. I say "now" because for the first two centuries after his death, it was simply called *Comedia*, and the *Divina* was added around 1555. It's seen as the most significant work of Italian literature, and is still studied by scholars and woven into popular culture today.

If you've heard the phrase "the circles of Hell," you have Dante to thank for that. Most recently, the author Dan Brown—known for his book *The Da Vinci Code*—published a novel called *Inferno*. As you might imagine, Dante features heavily in the story. It's amazing to see a work of literature still be so influential after over five hundred years in print.

But it almost didn't happen.

As I said, Dante spent nearly two decades writing his masterpiece. Everyone around him had plenty of time to learn about his project. His two sons, Jacopo and Pietro, were most likely allowed to read along as he wrote it. I guess my point is that people were aware of the book; it was the center of his existence for so long, after all.

And then, in 1321—just a year after he had completed the whole thing but before he had a chance to publish it—Dante died. His family went through the same sort of grieving process we would experience today, wrapping up his affairs and making sure his burial was taken care of properly. But within weeks, life would have moved on. Except, his sons couldn't forget that manuscript—and who could blame them.

Now, the *Divine Comedy* is a collection of a hundred parts, called cantos. Going through his papers after his death, Dante's sons discovered that there were thirteen cantos missing. That's 13 percent of the book, one-eighth of the completed work. And not just any 13 percent, either. They were missing the final chapters of the entire story. It was maddening.

According to an early Dante biographer, the sons searched the family home for months. They went through every scrap of paper they could find, dug through drawers and boxes, and looked for any clue that might tell them where the missing pages had gone. But nothing worked, and they were left empty-handed.

Friends recommended that the two men simply complete the story themselves. They knew how it was supposed to end, and they were familiar with their father's work, so why couldn't they just piece together the final parts and call it a day? And that was certainly *possible*—but it was far from *ideal*. They, like a lot of people, wanted their father's *official* ending.

As the story goes, one the sons—Jacopo—

went to sleep one night after another frustrating day of searching for the papers, and a short while later, he began to have a dream. In it, he saw the figure of his father, dressed in white and glowing in that Renaissance painting sort of way. Still fixated on the missing papers, Jacopo asked his father about them, and the older man nodded before walking over to a particular spot along his chamber wall. And then he pointed.

The next morning, Jacopo called for a lawyer to watch as he searched the room. There, right in the spot his father's ghost had told him about, he found a hidden compartment, with stacks of paper inside. They were covered in mold and had begun to rot on the edges, but they were legible. After reading through them for a moment, he smiled. The missing pages had been found.

It's crazy to imagine, but one of the most significant works of literature of all time almost didn't happen. The *Divine Comedy* is responsible for providing us with vivid images of the world beyond our own, from hopeful visions of Paradise to the nightmarish trials of Hell. The fact that they even exist at all today feels like a random victory for Dante.

For his sons, though, it was nothing short of a dream come true.

OPEN MIND

Charlie grew up with an eye for the other world. As a child, his favorite nanny would entertain him for hours with eerie, dramatic tales of ghosts and monsters and things that go bump in the night. And these stories left their mark on him—a mark that would be visible for the rest of his life.

Later on, as an adult, he would profess no interest in the supernatural world, and yet those ghosts seemed to follow him around and haunt him. Once, on New Year's Eve in 1863, he came face-to-face with those forces during a game with his children. They had built an elaborate set of wooden rods and black fabric, but something about it troubled Charlie.

A few days before, he had been at the funeral of a dear friend, and maybe it was all that black cloth, or the shape of the shadows on the wall, but something about the game reminded him of that somber gathering. Then again, perhaps Charlie was ignoring the spirit world he had grown up so aware of, because the following month, terrible news reached his home.

Charlie's son Walter, it seems, had passed away while serving with the British military in India. It had taken a long while for the news to reach him, though. The date of his son's death was New Year's Eve, 1863.

There were other moments that brought the world beyond the veil a little closer to Charlie's life. Once, in 1851, he stood nearby as his father was operated on to remove kidney stones. The procedure failed, and Charlie's father died soon after. A short while later, Charlie awoke in the middle of the night, and swore he saw the figure of his father sitting at the foot of his bed.

He once claimed that the spirit of his wife's sister—a woman he had loved deeply before she died at a young age—actually followed him around for a while. Charlie claimed that she would be fully visible to him, but no one else could see her. The spirit world, it seems, was a tricky realm—few had the experiences that Charlie claimed. And while he might not have sought it out, he seems to have had an open mind about it all.

It's true, Charlie did grow out of his passion for the otherworld, but the spirits never really gave up on him. His adulthood was filled with great success, and punctu-

ated from time to time with these ghostly moments. From what I can tell, they did much to influence everything he went on to create.

Charlie was a writer, you see—and a writer who frequently allowed ghost stories to slip into his creations. While he's mostly known for the tales without them, he wrote at least twenty ghostly tales during his four decades behind the desk. And we're grateful for them all, because Charlie's ability to see through the veil and into the world beyond our own has brought us wonderful moments of entertainment that are still with us, more than a century and a half later.

Just who was this writer born with a knack for seeing the things that most of us are completely blind to? He was a literary giant, a champion of serial publication, and the creator of some of the most beloved characters in English literature. Without him, we wouldn't have one of the most famous ghosts of all—the Ghost of Christmas Past.

Let's all be thankful that Charles Dickens had an open mind.

TRIFLES

Joseph Bell was born in 1837 in the beautiful city of Edinburgh, Scotland. From the moment he took his first breath, he was part of something larger than himself. He had a destiny to fulfill, a purpose that seemed to be part of who he was. There was no other path for him.

His great-grandfather, Dr. Benjamin Bell, is considered to be the first truly scientific surgeon in Scotland. In the late eighteenth century, you see, Edinburgh became one of the leading centers of medical education, and many think that this explosion of influence and progress would never have happened without Dr. Bell. His illustrious career helped all of Europe move forward, medically speaking.

His son Joseph also became a surgeon, as did his son Benjamin. And it was that Benjamin who, along with wife Cecilia, welcomed young Joseph into their lives. Obviously, the boy grew up to become a doctor. How could he not, being surrounded by so much of that world? And apparently, he was amazing at it. Possibly the most talented physician the Bell dynasty had ever known.

All of that brilliance was apparently on full display when Bell taught at the University of Edinburgh. His reputation as a diagnostician was practically legendary by the end of the nineteenth century. Bell believed that medical doctors could better serve their patients if they were more observant. As he said himself, he believed in "the vast importance of little distinctions, the endless significance of trifles."

The trouble, according to Bell, was that people saw things without really observing. They needed to be able to look past the obvious and see the important details. And he proved this time after time in his lectures by bringing in strangers and telling the students all about the person's occupation, history, and medical needs . . . all before the person spoke a word. And he was almost always correct.

Hundreds of students learned from Dr. Bell over the years that he taught at the university. Most of them went on to be physicians, just like their professor, but a few of them went into other careers. In fact, a good number of authors came out of his classroom.

James M. Barrie was one of them. He would later go on to create the story of *Peter Pan*. Robert Louis Stevenson, author of many popular novels including *The Strange Case of Dr. Jekyll and Mr. Hyde,* was also among them. But it was another student who turned his memories of Dr. Joseph Bell into the central character of a series of novels and short stories that he published for decades.

They were wildly popular tales about a man with an amazing sense of observation, an ability to see things that others ignored, and the true value of paying attention to all of the little trifles and distinctions around him. Of course, the world would never know this character as the great Dr. Joseph Bell, because that's not the name this author used when he wrote about him.

No, this author—Sir Arthur Ignatius Conan Doyle—made up an entirely fictional name for the character his medical professor had inspired.

Sherlock Holmes.

RED LIKE BLOOD

Henry worked on the same ship as his brother Sam because that's what older brothers do, right? They walk a little ahead and hold the door open for the people they love. And boy, did Sam love Henry.

They were young—Sam was twenty-three, just three years older than Henry—and they were adventurous. They had managed to get work on a ship, and Sam had worked his way up to steersman. Their work took them all over, and they had a lot of fun meeting new people and learning new things. But there were also moments of trouble.

One of their coworkers was a man named Brown, and Brown apparently had a checkered past as a troublemaker. In the course of their daily work, Henry discovered that Brown didn't care for him much, but he did his best to avoid the man. Which he did until one day, while Sam was at the helm guiding the ship. That was when Brown lost control and punched young Henry.

And that wasn't a good idea. Not only did Sam love his brother, but he was protective of him. When he heard what had happened, Sam walked away from the helm and left the ship on its own, located Brown, and then laid him out cold with a powerful punch. It solved one problem, but it created another: Sam and Brown couldn't stay on the same ship any longer.

So when the ship docked for the night in the same town as Sam's older sister, he left the crew and spent the night in town. I imagine they had dinner that evening, caught up on everything that had happened since they last spoke, and shared some laughs. Eventually, though, Sam went to bed, but when he did, he fell into a dark, tense dream.

In it, he was standing in the living room downstairs. All of the furniture had been pushed out of the way, and in the middle of the room was a coffin resting on a pair of chairs. The coffin was the sort that'd been covered in a sheet of glossy metal, and the top half was open for viewing. So Sam crept closer.

Inside he found his brother Henry. He looked peaceful, and a small bouquet of white flowers rested on his chest. At the center of that white bouquet was a single red flower. Red like blood.

Sam awoke in a panic. He rushed to his sister's room, shook her awake, and then told her what he had seen. It was just a dream, she told him. It was nothing to worry about. But of course, dreams like that don't go away easily or quickly.

The following day, Sam watched as the ship he had worked on for so long with his brother pulled out of port. He boarded a different one a short time later, and followed

Henry's ship from a distance. The plan was to wait until the captain could find a replacement for Brown, and then it would be safe for Sam to rejoin Henry on the ship.

Except that never happened. On June 13, an explosion rocked the lead ship, and 250 passengers and crew were instantly killed. One of the survivors, however, was young Henry. He had been thrown high into the air by the explosion, and then landed in the water far from the ship. But he was brave, and even though he was injured and burned horribly, he swam back to save others.

By the time Sam's ship arrived, Henry had been found and removed to a hospital for emergency care. His lungs had been scorched by steam, and his body was broken to pieces inside. But he had saved so many others, and as a result, a number of crew had gathered to hold vigil around him as he slowly died before their eyes. And that's the scene Sam walked in on when he finally arrived.

When Sam showed up the next day for the crew funeral, he walked into a large room filled with a dozen coffins, all made of pale wood. All except one. In the middle of the room, resting on two chairs, was a metal coffin. Inside it, Sam found Henry. It turns out, so many crew members thought of Henry as a hero that they all pitched in and upgraded his coffin.

As Sam stood over his brother's body, people milled in and out of the rows of coffins paying their respect. It was a somber moment, and the air was heavy with pain and grief. But in the middle of that, an elderly woman stepped through the crowd and approached Henry's coffin. Then, she placed a bouquet of white flowers on his chest, and walked away.

Sam glanced at them. Sure enough, right in the middle of the white flowers was a single red one. Red like blood.

The experience altered Sam's life completely. He wouldn't be content to work as a steersman for much longer. Instead, he wanted to leave his mark on the world, to create something beautiful by telling stories. And he did.

I can't help but wonder if the loss of his brother fueled the lifetime of writing that he left behind for future generations to enjoy. Writings that included reflections of his time on the ship with his brother, dressed up in fictional characters, of course. Yes, that loss was painful, but it helped to create a man now known as a legend of American literature.

Sam, you see, was Samuel *Clemens*, but most of us would more easily recognize his pen name.

Mark Twain.

THE PLOT

On a cold December night, Mary vanished. She had left a note describing a last-minute trip north, and then seemed to have fallen off the edge of the world.

Mary's friends and family began asking around, but no one had seen any sign of her. Her own husband, a retired colonel, tried pulling a few strings, but she still remained undiscovered. It wasn't until a couple of days later, when her car was found, that people really began to worry.

The car had been abandoned, along with clothing and her ID, on a small country road. Those with overactive imaginations began to suspect something more than a simple mistake, or even a practical joke. They believed Mary had been kidnapped, possibly even killed. And they knew just who had committed the crime: Mary's husband.

You see, he was already in a bit of hot water, so to speak. A few months earlier, he had requested a divorce from Mary, and in the weeks since, they had been fighting constantly. He had found another woman, and Mary was standing in their way of happiness. If you'd asked, some of them might have even suggested that he was a bit resentful of that. It was easy to connect the dots and label him a suspect.

Which is what the police did. They questioned him, and his mistress, but in the end they didn't think he had committed a crime. And in the meantime, search parties were expanding their reach. At one point, at least a thousand law enforcement officials and fifteen thousand civilian volunteers painstakingly examined the region Mary had disappeared from, all while being shadowed by a number of airplanes.

Her disappearance was covered by *The New York Times*. Celebrity mystery writers even got involved, spinning their own theories. And one man hired a medium to examine one of Mary's gloves in hopes that it would lead them in the right direction, but it didn't work.

Don't worry, though, this story does have a happy ending. That's because eleven days after she vanished, Mary was found over 230 miles to the north. She'd checked in to a hotel under a different name, and claimed she had no memory of the entire ordeal.

Some people believed Mary was telling the truth—that yes, she had somehow lost touch with reality for a week and a half. Psychologists call it a "fugue state," in which a person going through a traumatic experience subconsciously creates an entirely new reality where the stress no longer exists.

But others thought there was something more going on. They believe Mary actually knew what she was doing, and that the purpose behind the whole ordeal was to have her husband charged with her murder. People who believe this theory claim that once he had been executed for her murder, she would have strolled back out of the darkness and claimed amnesia.

They believe, in a sense, that Mary was a master of deception and planning, something pulled straight out of the pages of a dime-store novel. But like a lot of things in life, we'll never know for sure, because she never talked about it or explained herself. It was all just one big mystery.

Whatever the truth was, she recovered nicely enough. She went on to marry an archaeologist, which I find rather ironic, because archaeologists—at the basic level—are really just people who dig around for clues that tell a story. And Mary's life was built around clues.

In fact, without her, popular literature wouldn't be what it is today. She's still the best-selling author in history, ahead of J. K. Rowling, Stephen King, and even William Shakespeare with more than 2 billion books sold. Nearly everything she wrote has been adapted in some form or another. And you've heard about her your entire life, just not as Mary.

That's because she has been, still is, and always will be the queen of the mystery novel. Agatha *Mary* Christie.

EXPELLED

He was failing all of his classes, and that meant his plan was working. Before long, he would be expelled, and everything would be okay.

That probably doesn't make a lot of sense right now, so perhaps we need to take a step backward. Ed didn't always have the best of luck, no matter how he tried. And it started young, too. By the age of three, both of his parents were gone, leaving him an orphan. Thankfully, some friends of the family took Ed in and raised him as their own.

Even that was riddled with trouble, though. As he grew older, Ed started to fall out with his adoptive parents. They fought constantly, and not all of it could be chalked up to the headbutting between strict parents and an angst-ridden teen. The fact was, his father was a bit of a jerk. The guy was rich, you see, but he refused to share that wealth with his family.

Which is why it was ironic when Ed's father sent him to college to get him out of the house and end the quarreling, because he didn't send the young man away with any cash. Ed was a smart guy, and he did well during his first term, but those classes were expensive, and since he was broke, the debt just sort of added up.

When Ed asked his father for the money to pay off his school debts, the man pulled him out of college instead. With one door closed to him, the young man had to find a different path. A few weeks later, he enlisted in the army, which came with a little pay and a lot of commitment, but nothing close to a college education. He stuck with it for two years before begging his father to help him go back to school.

And it worked. Ed's dad helped the young man get into West Point, of all places, and for a while it seemed that everything was going to be all right. But again, he did all of this without his father's money, so of course the debts returned. At one point a creditor sent him a letter asking for payment, and Ed replied that he kept trying to ask his father for the cash, but the man was drunk a bit too often.

So the creditor did something sneaky: they forwarded Ed's letter to his father. Naturally, the man was embarrassed and upset, but he also paid the debt off. Oh, and then he disowned Ed and cut off all communication with him—which was unfortunate, because Ed needed his father's permission to withdraw his enrollment from the school.

So there you go. That's why Ed was purposefully failing his classes at West Point. He didn't want to stick around. In fact, he couldn't afford to. So he needed to do everything in his power to get out and go get a job of his own. He stopped going to class, he stopped going to the required chapel gatherings, he even stopped eating. But after a while the school caught on and—because West Point is a military college—they arrested him and then dismissed him for negligence of duty.

Ed did all right, though. Life would continue to tough for him, but he poured that pain and suffering into his true passion: writing. Over the next eighteen years he would build a name for himself, and while he would never again be on good terms with his father, John Allan, he would carry the man's name with him for the rest of his short life.

Ed, you see, was one of America's first literary celebrities, and we still read his work today. So be thankful that his father disowned him, and that West Point kicked him out. Because without those failures, the world might never have met . . . Edgar Allan Poe.

APRIL FOOL

Some people get *really* into certain holidays. You've seen them around your neighborhood—the folks who decorate their homes at Halloween and Christmas with lights and animatronic characters. They wait all year, often prepping months in advance in order to make the most of the short time they have to celebrate.

And then there are the holidays we enjoy, but don't really think too much about, like April Fools' Day. The one day a year when no one and nothing can be trusted. One historical figure who loved April Fools' Day the way many of us love Halloween and Christmas was Isaac Bickerstaff.

Toward the end of 1707, Isaac had taken issue with the 1708 edition of the *Merlinus Almanac*. It was a periodical, like most almanacs, filled with facts and figures to help people navigate their daily lives for the following year. But it was one particular sentiment that rubbed Isaac the wrong way.

The almanac's writer, astrologer John Partridge, had made a sarcastic remark about the Church of England, referring to it as the "infallible Church." Isaac was a devout follower and could not let a statement like that stand. So he concocted a unique plan of retaliation: he would predict John's "infallible" death over the next year by writing several letters and one eulogy about his demise to be published months apart until April 1: All Fools' Day.

Bickerstaff published his first letter, the prediction of John Partridge's death by "raging fever," in January of that year. The second letter, written not as Bickerstaff, but as a government employee, came out that March to "confirm" that Bickerstaff's prediction had come to pass. An elegy quickly followed suit—more a poem than a letter—but it put the blame of Partridge's death on both Partridge himself and anyone who bought his almanacs.

The hoax took off like a rocket. Mourners gathered outside Partridge's home, crying all night and keeping him awake. No matter what he said, they wouldn't believe he hadn't died. After all, the letters had been printed for the public as a matter of fact.

An undertaker even came to his house to arrange the drapes for a wake while a stonemason carved his gravestone. By that point, though, John Partridge had seen enough, and published a letter of his own to dispel the silly hoax once and for all.

It didn't work. No one believed him, especially after Bickerstaff responded, writing, "They were sure no man alive ever to writ such damned stuff as this." I know. A real jerk move.

Finally, All Fools' Day had arrived and Isaac Bickerstaff gave up the ghost, so to speak. He published one last piece titled "A Vindication of Isaac Bickerstaff," in which he came clean about the whole charade. John Partridge hadn't died. There had been no fever. The undertaker and the gravestone and the mourning people outside his home had all been in vain. John Partridge was alive and well and probably pretty angry.

Bickerstaff's shenanigans didn't go unnoticed, though. The founder of the British literary journal *The Tatler* named Bickerstaff his new editor, which wasn't surprising as Isaac had been a contributor to the publication in the past. In fact, Bickerstaff went on to publish numerous works throughout his life, such as essays, pamphlets, periodicals, and even fiction. Mostly satire, of course.

Isaac Bickerstaff made his living from writing satire directed at the rich, the irreligious, and other groups he thought needed taking down a notch. His work is still read and taught in classrooms all over the world. He was prolific, and yet, you probably have never heard of him. At least, not as "Isaac Bickerstaff."

But you certainly know his essay *A Modest Proposal,* in which he suggests impoverished Irish families sell their children to the rich as a food supply. Or his travel journal parody *Gulliver's Travels.*

That's right. Isaac Bickerstaff, the man who convinced the world of one man's untimely death, was actually none other than Jonathan Swift.

OH MY

William Porter was a man of many skills. Born in Greensboro, North Carolina, in 1862, he spent much of his younger years under his aunt's tutelage. It was his family who helped him develop his love of reading and learning. As he got older, William's aptitude extended to painting, playing the guitar, writing, and singing, skills that would come in handy when times got tough.

After he graduated high school, William put his education to great use at his uncle's drugstore where he became a licensed pharmacist. In his spare time, he explored other creative endeavors, such as drawing and writing. But Greensboro had gotten a bit small for William, and the climate was even affecting his health. Over the years, he'd developed a bad cough that refused to heal.

A family friend, Dr. James Hall, had an idea to help him get better. Together they traveled down to Austin, Texas, where William took a job working as a ranch hand for Dr. Hall's son. Being outdoors and exercising daily improved his health, but he quickly realized that ranch hands barely made enough money to survive. He went back to his old ways, gaining a job as a pharmacist and writing short stories in his spare time.

His stories became the talk of the town, and William found himself invited to gatherings all over Austin. It was at one gathering in 1885 where he met Athol Estes, the woman he would eventually marry. Four years later, Athol gave birth to a daughter, Margaret.

Being a new parent came with new responsibilities, and those responsibilities cost money. Luckily, William's relationship with his former employer, Richard Hall, had survived over the years. When Richard became Texas Land Commissioner, he gave his old buddy William a cushy gig at the Texas General Land Office drafting maps. The starting salary was $100 a month—about $3,500 monthly, or $42,000 per year, today. Nothing extravagant, but enough to live on and support a family in turn-of-the century Austin.

Through it all, though, William never gave up on his writing. He contributed stories to newspapers and magazines whenever he could, and when he wasn't drawing maps, he was working on novels with characters based on the people he worked with.

Unfortunately, his position within the General Land Office had been a political appointment, and once his friend Richard Hall was voted out in 1891, William had to resign. He started working as a teller at the First National Bank of Austin, where he focused more on his writing than the money he was handling each day. William was a creative soul, after all, and staring at numbers all day was so much less interesting than concocting new plots for his short stories.

He didn't pay close attention to the records he kept, and when the bank found out, they fired him. Out of steady employment, William depended on writing full-time to make ends meet. He wrote for a weekly publication called *The Rolling Stone,* and when that fizzled out, he moved his family to Houston where he became a journalist for *The Houston Post* newspaper.

Things started looking up for William, who had gone through several jobs in only a few years. His work at *The Houston Post* was even getting his name out there, as were his published fiction stories. However, unbeknownst to William, his name was also on the lips of investigators back in Austin. Federal auditors had discovered the lost funds that had gotten him fired. It didn't take long for them to officially charge him with embezzlement.

William tried to run, but his wife's health had taken a sharp turn, and with her death looming, he decided to turn himself in. He was sentenced to five years in the Ohio State Penitentiary, where his background as a pharmacist came in handy. He got a job within the prison as the night druggist, while he continued to publish his writing from his cell.

Now, no prison was going to allow one of their inmates to have short fiction published while that inmate was serving out a sentence for embezzlement. But where there was a Will, there was a way—pun *intended.* He sent his stories to a friend in New Orleans, who would then forward them on to publishers, to hide their author's current situation.

If the warden had ever found out about William's use of prison resources to further his writing career, he would've been in a lot of trouble, and the privileges he'd earned thus far would've been revoked. As a foolproof way to distance himself from his work, William always authored his stories under one of many pseudonyms, but there was one that really took off during his stay at Ohio State.

According to an interview he gave *The New York Times* later in his life, he found the name while reading a story in the newspaper about notable guests at a fancy ball.

But that anecdote lacks the pizazz we've come to expect from great historical figures. In a book about William Porter from 1973, the author claimed William's pen name was born the same way all of his characters were: by using the people around him to influence his work.

This time, it was a prison guard by the name of Orrin. Orrin Henry. William Porter chopped off most of his first name except for the initial letter, giving him a name we still remember today. There's even a short story award named in his honor.

O. Henry.

BURNING MAD

When I look back on my middle and high school English classes, certain authors come to mind immediately. Hemingway, of course, and also Jack London, J. D. Salinger, and one other writer in particular. His tale of pirates, buried treasure, and tropical islands is taught in schools all over the world, and has been translated into countless languages.

But it's his other story, the gothic tale about dual personalities, that's really stuck with me over the years. And it stuck with its author, Robert Louis Stevenson, too. *Strange Case of Dr. Jekyll and Mr. Hyde* was first published in 1886, though parts of it were published in plays and short stories before then. Stevenson had searched for years for a way to tell the perfect good versus evil story until the idea came to him in a dream.

Suddenly inspired one night, he toiled for days, maybe even weeks, on the novella, oftentimes coming downstairs from his bedroom to read portions aloud to his wife and stepson. Stevenson called it his greatest work yet. And while the story may have begun in a dream, he'd almost certainly pulled details from his life.

Some of those details were in the news.

Wealthy cabinetmaker Deacon William Brodie had been caught and convicted for multiple charges of theft. He had led a secret double life involving hidden rooms and a costume for his nocturnal crime spree, and it was certainly an inspiring tale. But other details came to Stevenson from people he was close to.

One of his friends, a French teacher named Eugene Chantrelle, had been accused of poisoning his wife. Stevenson sat in the gallery during the trial. He recalled the looks of horror and disgust on his friend's face as the prosecution went through the details of the murder, as though it had been committed by someone else entirely. The jury didn't agree, though, and Eugene was executed a short while later.

Stevenson used this courtroom experience as inspiration for the story, and after the novella's completion, he did what he always did with his first drafts—he gave it to his wife, Fanny. In fact, we wouldn't have Robert Louis Stevenson at all if it weren't for her. Fanny's opinion was of the utmost importance. She knew what made for a great story, and often wrote her comments in the margins of the pages for her husband's benefit.

You might call her his number one editor. You might also call her his greatest critic. On this occasion, Fanny's criticisms were not exactly . . . constructive.

She referred to her husband's seminal work, a story that has been adapted for the stage and screen more than 120 times since its publication, as "a quire full of utter nonsense." She knew it could be better, but her husband needed a bit of motivation. In a letter she wrote to a friend shortly after she'd read the draft, Fanny said she planned on burning it before it ever reached readers' hands.

But she never got the chance. Robert read through his wife's marginal note, and in a fit of rage over his wasted time and effort, tossed the pile of pages into the fireplace himself, watching the flames reduce it to ashes.

Upon realizing what he'd done, he spent the next three days feverishly re-creating the draft while sitting up in bed. According to some biographers, Robert had been sick for weeks, and was hopped up on cocaine the entire time he wrote it, adding a bit of real-life inspiration to Dr. Jekyll's ingestion of a serum to become a completely different person.

Strange Case of Dr. Jekyll and Mr. Hyde became a great success almost immediately. It made Robert Louis Stevenson a household name, but we might not be teaching it in classrooms today if it weren't for his wife, who saw its potential even at its *worst*.

She said as much in that letter written to a Mr. William Henley. Henley was a poet and editor in his own right, but also a longtime friend to both Fanny and Robert—and for good reason. Robert saw something in him, a cleverness and a joy that warmed everyone around him. But he also saw something else. Well, not exactly. According to him, there was something about William Henley that *wasn't* visible.

Years before he'd completed that rewrite of Dr. Jekyll's tale of transformation, Robert Louis Stevenson had worked on *another* story. It was a novel that needed an antagonist. Now, Henley wasn't a mean guy. Everyone who knew him thought only the best of him and his jovial nature.

But Henley had suffered from tuberculosis at the age of twelve. The complications from the disease had cost him dearly, and doctors amputated his left leg below the knee. And that was the key detail Robert borrowed, just as he'd done so many times before, for one of the most famous villains in all of English literature.

The legendary pirate himself, Long John Silver.

IT'S ALIVE

Giovanni Aldini was a scientist like his uncle, Luigi Galvani. If that name sounds familiar, that's because it's where we get the term "Galvanism." Galvanism is the contraction of a muscle when exposed to an electrical current. If you've ever seen someone get tased, you've seen galvanism in action.

Toward the end of the eighteenth century, Aldini traveled extensively, performing grotesque experiments before captivated—and disgusted—audiences. He would lop the head off an animal, then hook it up to a battery and demonstrate how its jaw would open and close, or how its eyes would move about in their sockets. To many, the animal looked like it was somehow alive again.

Aldini took his research further and began experimenting on humans. He was one of the first doctors to practice electroshock therapy on the brain, claiming it could be used to cure a number of mental illnesses. However, his greatest experiment was yet to come, and it would change the world in an unexpected way.

A London man named George Forster had been convicted of murdering his wife and child. The trial was scheduled quickly and witnesses called in to testify. During the trial, Forster's mother-in-law explained how her daughter and grandchild had gone to see him one Saturday afternoon in December of 1802. Apparently, he and his wife did not live together, despite her insistence that they share a home as a family. She and the child left on Sunday morning. On Monday, their bodies were found in the Paddington Canal.

It took almost no time for the jury to find Forster guilty. The court sentenced him to hang, followed by a dissection of the body shortly after. Forster was despondent. Not only had he lost his family, but hanging was not a wholly effective method of execution. Death row inmates had been known to lose consciousness, giving them the appearance of having died, before being dissected alive on the exam table afterward.

And *that* was Forster's greatest fear, so he fashioned a knife out of what he could find in his cell and attempted to kill himself before his hanging. It didn't work. With all other options dried up, Forster decided to come clean. He confessed to his family's murder, and to how he hated his wife and had brought her to the canal twice before, but couldn't find the nerve to end her life until that third visit.

The hanging proceeded as planned, and Forster's body was quickly sent off to be examined. The pace of the trial, hanging, and dissection of the victim's body were considered hasty, even by the standards of the time. It was thought that Forster's confession had been coerced out of him, and that an officer named Mr. Pass had rushed the trial simply to acquire a fresh corpse for a wealthy benefactor.

That benefactor's name? None other than Giovanni Aldini. He had big plans for the late Mr. Forster, which he demonstrated at London's Royal College of Surgeons in 1803. The audience was packed with doctors and civilians, all craning their necks to get a better look at the spectacle in the operating room below.

With the victim laid out on the table, Dr. Aldini proceeded to take two conducting rods connected to a battery and press them against various parts of Forster's body. He would apply them to his face and watch as the jaw moved and the muscles underneath contracted. The left eye even opened. When touched to his backside, Forster's entire body tensed up and his legs moved as though he was coming back to life.

That's what some in the audience believed to be happening right before their eyes—a man was being electrocuted back to life. Mr. Pass, the official who had allegedly obtained the corpse for the scientist, was so disturbed by what he saw that he died of shock soon after leaving the theater.

The fascination around galvanism and Aldini's experiments never really subsided, even as medical science continued to progress throughout the nineteenth century. English poet Samuel Taylor Coleridge often discussed with friends how electricity could be used to regenerate life.

Among those friends were a family of writers known as the Godwins. Their daughter, Mary, fascinated by these perverted tales of "mad science," eventually channeled her obsession into a story of her own. In fact, Mary Godwin and her story have come to define an entire genre of literature.

But you might know her better as Mary Shelley.

HEAD SPACE

The greatest minds in history left behind legacies of legendary proportions. Albert Einstein's theories and research have contributed to some of the most important scientific discoveries of the last sixty years. Leonardo da Vinci's art has influenced not just other artists all over the world, but inventors as well. And William Shakespeare's impact on literature and theatre continues to inspire new generations of writers everywhere.

However, their work is only part of their genius. We'll never know their hopes and dreams, the passing thoughts that might have changed the world if they'd been explored further. If only there had been some way to peek inside their minds. Well, one man may have done exactly that in 1794, kicking off over two hundred years of rumors about what happened to one of the most important historical figures of all time.

His name was Dr. Frank Chambers. For years, he kept a diary of his day to day life, and it was in this record that he wrote some entries about a bold endeavor he'd undertaken. You see, he *wanted* something. Something that belonged to a famous literary figure—the aforementioned Bard of Stratford-upon-Avon, William Shakespeare.

Shakespeare had died almost two centuries prior, in 1616, and his body had been buried in the Church of the Holy Trinity, about a hundred miles northwest of London. So Dr. Chambers led a team of grave robbers into the church one night with a plan to dig up Shakespeare's body.

They weren't after jewels, or even a quill pen he might have been buried with. No, they wanted something else: a piece of the man himself—specifically his skull. And according to the stories, Chambers was *successful* in his pursuit, and reportedly later sold the skull for three hundred British pounds.

But something about those stories has never added up.

To a lot of historians, it just seemed too outlandish to be true. Shakespeare's grave had been unmarked, so successfully finding it in the dark seemed like a fool's errand. There was also the inscription meant to warn away potential robbers: "Blest be the man that spares these stones, and curst be he that moves my bones." That should have been enough to give *anyone* pause.

But not Dr. Chambers. Allegedly, of course. In his explanation of his exploits, the intrepid thief made note of several specific details. For example, he claimed Shakespeare was not buried in a coffin, but wrapped in cloth and placed in a shallow grave. That only lessened the credibility of his story. After all, why would someone as famous and brilliant as William Shakespeare have been buried in such a common and unfitting way?

Unfortunately, there's no way to be sure. The church would not let anyone exhume the body for verification, heeding the Bard's final request that no one disturb his grave. And so for centuries, the rumors of Dr. Chambers's exploits persisted, although no one took them too seriously. Scholars and theatre aficionados alike just couldn't accept that such a great mind might be resting in such a mundane grave.

That was, until 2016—four hundred years after Shakespeare's death. That's when archaeologists found another way to get the answers they needed. Using ground-penetrating radar, the scientists scanned Shakespeare's grave to get a more accurate picture of what was inside—and what they found shocked them.

Dr. Chambers, who had sworn the truth about his outrageous claims regarding the writer's grave . . . had been right all along. William Shakespeare had, in fact, been wrapped in cloth before his burial, in a shallow grave only three feet deep.

What's more, perhaps the boldest and strangest claim of all hadn't been so strange: the head really *was* missing. No one knows where it is today, or who might have it, but I like to imagine it's being used in a very special performance of Hamlet.

Dr. Frank Chambers confused the literary world for centuries with his amazing claim, but in the end it was proven true.

He might have been our predecessor, but he certainly got a head of us.

LIVING A DREAM

Sleep is a vulnerable state. While we slumber, any number of things can happen. We might not hear the pop of a pipe as it fills the basement with water. Or the subtle steps of a burglar hunting for whatever is within reach. Some of us might even raid the fridge in a half-conscious state, hunting for a snack that will satisfy our midnight cravings.

And then there's Ansel. He was a man with a complicated relationship with sleep.

In the late nineteenth century, Ansel worked as both a carpenter and an evangelical preacher in Rhode Island. He had a wife and two adult daughters with families of their own. He was well-known around town, too, but not for his woodworking skills, or even his sermons. No, Ansel was prone to certain . . . episodes. Ones where he would briefly forget who or where he was. It was a form of temporary amnesia known as dissociative fugue, or sleepwalking.

Some at the time might have called it "somnambulism," which was a scary word. Those who suffered often fell down stairs or hurt themselves due to their semiconsciousness.

But Ansel usually came back to himself after a short time. That is, until one day in March of 1887, when locals noticed the preacher had disappeared.

He'd just up and vanished. Meanwhile, 250 miles away, the small town of Norristown, Pennsylvania, was trying to solve a mystery of its own. It seemed an older gentleman named A. J. Brown had been running a stationery and confectionery shop—and he was a bit confused. He'd taken to showing up on his landlord's door asking him questions like "Who am I?" and "How did I get here?"

It just so happened that Mr. Brown had woken up in the middle of ringing up a customer in his store, and he couldn't remember how he got there. In fact, his situation was so unusual and frightening to him that he called a local doctor for help, a man by the name of Louis Read. And soon enough, they got to work looking for answers.

The story Mr. Brown told him was a wild one. It was the story of a man who had gone into a fugue state and traveled south from Rhode Island to Pennsylvania, where he ran his own store for two months as a completely different person.

Dr. Read then asked him about the last thing he remembered before he woke up. It had been January 18 and he had taken a horse and carriage to a bank in Providence. He'd been on his way to visit his son. He remembered the ride to the bank, withdrawing the money, even the street signs he passed on the way, but after a brief visit with a nephew it was all a blank. The next thing Ansel knew, two months had gone by, and he'd become the owner of a new business.

Ansel's amnesia was obviously worse than he'd known. So his nephew was called to collect him, and not long after returning home he was able to learn more about his condition. Because it just so happened that William James, often called the father of American psychology, was teaching at Harvard University. He heard about Ansel's incident and traveled from Massachusetts to Rhode Island to study him.

Using hypnosis, Dr. James was able to draw out either Ansel or Mr. Brown from the poor man's consciousness—and neither personality had any recollection of what the other had done. It was as if Ansel had a whole other person living a completely separate life right inside his mind.

But there's something else. Ansel's story was so interesting that other people started to take notice outside of academic circles. One of those people was an author with an idea for a character suffering from amnesia. A character who, upon waking on board a fishing boat with no memory of what happened to him, would end up traveling the world to learn who he really was.

Oh, and if I told you that Ansel's last name was Bourne, you might be able to guess the name of the writer. But if your memory has failed you, you're not alone.

That writer was none other than Robert Ludlum, author of *The Bourne Identity*.

REMARKABLE INVENTIONS

INTEL INSIDE

They built a machine that could play chess. Now, I understand that's not exactly earth-shattering news. We live in an era when Deep Blue from IBM and AlphaZero from DeepMind can beat just about any opponent placed in front of them. Clearly, artificial intelligence has grown by leaps and bounds, allowing us to pack more and more power into the devices we use each day.

But this wasn't a sleek, modern processor-fueled brain; it was a wooden box and a mechanical dummy. They called it the Turk, and it was built in Vienna in 1770. Think of it like a large wooden chest, four feet long, two feet wide, and about three feet tall. Hefty, for sure, but it served as a desk upon which a chessboard sat. And behind that desk stood the Turk himself.

Well, "him" might be stretching it. The Turk was a mechanical man, an *automaton* if you want to be technical about it. And this eighteenth-century robot could play chess. The man who invented it was Baron Wolfgang von Kempelen, an inventor from Hungary who was born in 1734. Armed with this amazing device, he traveled all across Europe pitting his invention against the best chess players he could find.

He would begin each match by opening all of the cabinet doors beneath the desktop, so everyone gathered could see his brilliant mechanical engineering firsthand. Gears and cogs and drums and levers . . . all of it served to power the Turk as it picked up chess pieces and made move after move against the humans who chose to play it.

And most of the time, the robot won. It's said that the Turk defeated Napoleon, Benjamin Franklin, even Empress Catherine I of Russia. It was so popular that after von Kempelen died in 1804, the Turk was sold to a Bavarian musician who carried on the constant touring. In the 1820s, that tour included America.

In fact, the author Edgar Allan Poe watched one of these demonstrations himself in 1836, and he wrote an article about it in a periodical called the *Southern Literary Messenger*. Which is ironic, because just a few years later, the Turk would be purchased by Poe's own physician, John Kearsley Mitchell.

All told, the Turk was a source of entertainment and delight for nearly seventy years. It inspired a lot of questions and a lot of wonder, which I have to admit is still pretty attractive today. The fact that someone built a mechanical device more than 250 years ago that could play chess and beat humans . . . well, it sounds like something out of a Jules Verne novel. And yet it happened.

Well, sort of. You see, there are enough drawings and firsthand accounts of how the device operated to hint at the true power of the robot. Thanks to magnets in the base of each chess piece, and corresponding metal balls in the inside surface of the chess board, it was possible for a person to watch the game unfold and then operate the robot like a puppet as each game moved along.

Sadly, the Turk was destroyed in a museum fire in July of 1854, and when that happened, the physical proof of its trickery *literally* went up in smoke. Still, it's hard not to see our modern world reflected in that eighteenth-century invention. In the pursuit of progress and entertainment, we still try our best to cram as much power as possible into our devices.

At least we've stopped using live humans to do it.

DRESSED DOWN

It's amazing how the threat of imminent danger can add such clarity to our daily lives. When faced with a serious threat, we're able to see what's truly important and what can be disregarded to ensure our safety. Oftentimes war is the catalyst for such realizations, and for the people who participated in World War I, that danger didn't just add clarity—it also added a little ingenuity.

It was called the Great War for a reason. The conflict lasted for four years and stretched across almost all of Europe. But its effects were especially felt in Great Britain.

It wasn't just that almost nine million British soldiers fought in the trenches. If you were an average citizen in the United Kingdom in 1915, then you likely witnessed firsthand the terrifying creation of Count von Zeppelin. This new weapon of mass destruction, as you can probably guess, was an enormous, hydrogen-filled aircraft, appropriately called . . . the zeppelin.

It floated above the streets of England late at night, its engines thrumming in the ears of sleepy and frightened families below. While the zeppelins did drop bombs and cause quite a bit of damage, that wasn't their intention. Their primary mission was to instill fear in the British in order to break their morale and make them pull out of the war.

And it almost worked. People jumped out of their beds with the clothes on their backs and dashed into smoke-filled streets littered with rubble. Buildings collapsed. Homes were destroyed. Survivors of the zeppelin raids recalled not knowing where the danger ever really was, and whether they were running toward it or away from it.

Functioning on little sleep and a sudden jolt of adrenaline, British citizens often found themselves shivering in the street wondering if and when the big one would hit them next. Or whether they'd have a home to return to when it was all over.

As the raids grew more frequent and people began to expect them, fear quickly turned to embarrassment. After all, folks were standing in public in their nightgowns and underwear, something only their significant others were supposed to see. Women began preparing the night before by hanging cloaks and scarves by the door. Bald men even had "emergency toupees" at the ready.

This was Britain in the early 1900s, and social status was everything. What would the neighbors think if one was caught looking less than their best, even when the war was doing its worst? But there were other problems with their choices in nighttime fashion. First, and most important, they weren't that fashionable. A cloak was just a big, wearable blanket and nobody wanted to look frumpy in front of their friends. Second, running from explosions proved incredibly difficult when one's legs were being restricted by long, bulky coats.

So they turned to the French, who had been known to lounge around in comfortable, luxurious clothing when they were waiting for the bombs to strike. It was a solution that was breathable and stylish. So stylish, in fact, that a British fashion editor at the time stated she actually looked forward to the evening raids just so she could show off her new black threads.

Funnily enough, this new fashion trend quickly eschewed function for form. Rather than keeping the colors dark so that targets were harder to spot during the night, colors lightened up from blacks and dark blues to pinks and reds. Sure, friends and neighbors could get a good look at them, but the British didn't mind. And eventually the raids subsided as German resources were needed elsewhere during the war.

But their hot new nighttime clothing only grew in popularity—and we still wear them today, though thankfully not for bombing raids. We just wear them to relax in bed or in front of the television while we binge our favorite shows. So I guess we can thank the French and the British for a lot of the things we still love today:

Sherlock Holmes, a good glass of wine, and of course, pajamas.

HAPPY ACCIDENT

World War II took its toll on the lives of soldiers and civilians in many ways, though not all of them violent. Women became combat nurses, military pilots, and expert welders to support the war effort. Men who couldn't fight would volunteer in other ways, helping to sell war bonds or collect scrap metal.

As the war progressed, the use of certain materials increased exponentially, including tin, paper, and rubber. The military needed tin cans for rations, paper for packing materials, and rubber for things like tires, pontoon bridges, and boots. While fighting was going on overseas, folks back home held scrap drives. They encouraged people to donate old pots and pans, tin toys, rubber boots, and anything else they had lying around that could be melted down and turned into supplies for the troops. Every little bit helped.

Rubber became especially hard to find as Japan took over much of the Pacific Rim, including the majority of rubber-producing countries. Its forces cut off supply access to the United States, so things like rafts and gas masks couldn't be made or repaired. The US government couldn't stand to wait around for supply routes to open up again. Rations were running low and something had to be done, so they turned to science to pick up the slack.

Scientists had already begun looking for alternatives to natural rubber. Unfortunately, nothing that had been invented came close to being as versatile and resilient as the real thing. James Wright, however, had already been on the case. He'd been working as a researcher at General Electric in Connecticut when he was tasked with finding a cheap substitute for rubber, both natural and synthetic. It had to be tough, it had to be pliable, and it had to do everything *real* rubber was capable of doing.

After some experimentation with certain chemicals, he dropped boric acid into silicone oil. The reaction left him with something new and different. Something he thought might be exactly what the government was looking for.

It looked like rubber. It smelled like rubber. But it bounced higher and stretched farther than rubber. It would never mold, and melted only at extremely high temperatures, much higher than natural rubber. He brought his new creation to his superiors, who didn't see much of a use for it. To them, it was no different than the synthetic rubber they'd already been using. Dr. Wright went back to the drawing board, but sadly never came up with the alternative everyone had been looking for.

After his failure, he put his fake rubber concoction on the shelf, where it sat dormant for years. Then, sometime after the war, it bounced into the hands of small business owner Ruth Fallgatter. She immediately saw plenty of uses for it, and so did the marketing executive she consulted, Peter Hodgson. The two of them began selling Wright's magical rubber in 1950—to very little acclaim. After it appeared in an article in *The New Yorker,* however, sales boomed.

It quickly became a worldwide success, and as more people bought it, they found even more ways to incorporate it into their daily lives. The substance has been known to be a terrific lint remover, as well as a physical therapy tool for people recovering from hand injuries. NASA astronauts used it so their tools wouldn't float away in zero gravity. It seemed the sky was the limit—*literally*—for the failure the army never wanted.

But people all over the world certainly wanted it, especially *children*—and they've been playing with it for more than seventy years. Whether squishing it into a ball and bouncing it off the ceiling, or pressing it over the Sunday comics and pulling up their own printed copies, kids everywhere have had a lot of fun with Dr. Wright's failed rubber substitute.

It probably helped that Peter Hodgson packaged and marketed it as the perfect Easter basket item. He just popped a dollop of the stuff into a little plastic egg, and then gave it the perfect name—if maybe a little silly.

Silly *Putty,* that is.

EVENING READING

At the start of the nineteenth century, Napoleon Bonaparte's reign was just hitting its stride. Within the span of four years, he would sell Louisiana to the United States, avoid an assassination attempt, go to war with Great Britain, and declare himself emperor of France in front of the Pope. Some might say he was a man of action, always looking for the competitive edge that would help him gain victory over his opponents. Others would just chalk it up to ego.

But despite his ego, Napoleon prided himself on being a forward thinker. As his armies moved across Europe and engaged with hostile forces, he noticed where his strategy was lacking. He just didn't quite know how to fix it. The problems presented themselves at night, when the candles and lamps the soldiers used to illuminate their maps made them sitting ducks for enemy snipers.

Napoleon knew the best time to attack was during the night, but if the men couldn't see where they were going or read their orders, then those plans wouldn't matter.

They'd all be dead before sunrise. So Napoleon posed his predicament to an officer in his ranks who also happened to be a former classmate of his growing up. His name was Charles Barbier and he was given a mission: find a way for the troops to read in the dark without the need for any kind of light.

Barbier was a bit of a history buff and knew of a system of message transmission invented by the ancient Greeks. The Polybius Square was a grid of five rows and five columns with a different letter of the Greek alphabet in each square, the last one left blank. If two people had the same grid, they could send each other messages using the row and column location to signify the chosen letter.

Unfortunately, this system relied on the use of torches held high in the night. The number of torches raised in a particular order indicated which row and column the letter was located in. Napoleon had told his man no light—but it did give Barbier an idea, a way to modify the system so that light wasn't required.

He created his own grid of letters that soldiers would memorize. Messages would be encoded using special symbols that could be read in the dark simply by touching them. Barbier developed his system using six rows and six columns to accommodate the numerous letter combinations the French commonly used.

It sounded great to Napoleon, who quickly put it to use in the field. The soldiers, however, thought differently. The grid was too hard to memorize and recall in the heat of battle. Decoding a secret message proved impossible when no one could figure out what letter they were touching, nor did they have the time to really think about it.

Barbier's system was abandoned almost as quickly as it was adopted, but its inventor wasn't discouraged. Years later, while speaking on behalf of the French Royal Academy of Sciences, he introduced his grid to a classroom of children who also had struggled with reading. The old system the children had been using was far inferior, as it relied on embossed Latin letters which were harder to trace quickly with their fingertips. Among those students was a young man who took great interest in Barbier's work.

He gave Barbier feedback on how to make it better. One suggested change was to shrink the number of rows and symbols to make them easier to distinguish by touch. Barbier scoffed. There was no way some child was going to tell a wealthy, educated veteran of Napoleon Bonaparte's army how to do his job.

So the boy made the changes himself, and introduced the new system to his classmates. It worked, and as a result, his contribution changed the way the blind read forever. And this child's name?

Louis Braille.

CALCULATED DISCOVERY

It's easy to take computers for granted these days. They do so much for us. They allow us to break barriers and create new forms of art and expression and take selfies with birds flying around our heads. Important stuff, clearly . . . but they haven't always been so small.

Take the Apollo Guidance Computer. It was built by MIT and used by NASA in 1969 for their Apollo 11 mission. That's the one that put the first humans on the moon. Each one weighed fifty pounds and was the size of a piece of carry-on luggage. But they worked. We landed people on the freaking *moon*, after all.

As crazy as it might sound, though, the mobile phone in your pocket is more powerful than that NASA computer. Thirty-two thousand times faster, in fact. You see, computers have a tendency to get smaller and more powerful over time. Go back far enough and some of the earliest electrical computers were massive and slow. ENIAC was a great example; it filled up an entire room, but in 1946, it was a *super*-computer.

There's another old computer worth mentioning, though. It's not electrical, but by definition, computers are nothing more than machines that can be programmed to carry out specific tasks. Calendars, calculators, counting devices, that sort of thing. Charles Babbage is the big name in that field, thanks to the calculator he built in 1822. It was all gears and levers, but it did its job nicely. And so did this other one.

Like a lot of old computers, it's not in the best of shape. But when it was brand spanking new, it focused on astronomy. Want to know when the next eclipse is going to be? This computer would tell you. The lunar cycle? You're covered. People could even program it to track the time between special, regularly occurring social events. It was brilliant.

But here's where it gets weird: this computer is older than Babbage's 1822 device, yet smaller than NASA's Apollo Guidance Computers—which seems to fly in the face of how useful and advanced it really was for its time.

You see, this computer wasn't crafted in the workshop of a English mechanic or in an MIT lab. It was built so long ago that we forgot about it in the first place. But in 1900, some men found it and handed it over to people who might know what to do with such a powerful device.

Those men were sponge divers. They found the computer underwater, just off the coast of the Greek island of Antikythera. And it hadn't been there since the 1800s, or even the 1700s. According to the archaeologists who've studied it over the course of the past century, this computer is much older.

It was built over two thousand years ago.

KID ICARUS

Desperation can be quite a motivator. In the original *Thousand and One Nights,* a king finds out his wife has been unfaithful and has her killed. He then marries a series of women and orders the same fate the morning after their wedding night so they never get a chance to commit the same infidelity. Once there are no more women left in the kingdom, his advisor's daughter, Scheherazade, volunteers to become his next bride. The advisor is hesitant, but allows her to sacrifice herself.

On their wedding night, she begins to tell a story to the king, but doesn't finish it. He refuses to kill Scheherazade until she can complete her story, which she does the following night. As soon as she's done, however, she begins another tale and the cycle starts over.

Her desperation to stay alive gives birth to a collection of stories that have influenced cultures and literature all over the world. Her desperation didn't just allow her to keep her head—it gave her security. She became too important to discard, much like a young Italian scientist in Scotland around AD 1500.

His name was John Damian, and he arrived promising great big things to King James IV. King James allowed Damian to set up a laboratory inside Stirling Castle in order to carry out his experiments under a watchful eye. The king was in search of something important, something that had eluded rulers and explorers for thousands of years.

Every culture had a different name for it: the elixir of life, the elixir of immortality, and occasionally the philosopher's stone. And yes, for British fans of a certain boy wizard, it's *that* philosopher's stone. The king gave Damian everything he needed—money, time, resources—all in the pursuit of a substance that would not only bring eternal life, but turn any other material into gold.

And Damien certainly took advantage of his benefactor's generosity. Records from the time denote the purchase of all sorts of scientific equipment, including cauldrons, glass flasks, and other materials. He spared no expense and bought whatever he needed whenever he needed it—including copious amounts of whiskey.

Like many rulers throughout history, King James sought to control and maintain his wealth by any means necessary. This often involved research into the supernatural when realistic solutions proved too time consuming or unsuccessful. Unfortunately, after about seven years, it didn't look like Damian was any closer to eternal youth than he had been when he'd started.

Instead, he turned his eyes toward the heavens. Specifically, he wanted to get as close to them as possible. Dreams of wealth and immortality were set aside as the alchemist became obsessed with making man fly.

He watched birds, how their wings caught the wind and propelled themselves up higher and higher, how they could glide on a current of air for seconds before needing to flap again.

Damian studied the mechanics until he thought he'd figured it out. He began designing wings for himself based on his observations, even going so far as to include feathers in the final product. He had ordered eagle feathers, but could only get hen feathers at the time. No matter. Feathers were feathers, and these would have to do.

There was only one problem—Damian worked alone. He had no one to test his theory or his newfangled contraption, which left only one other possibility: he'd have to test it himself. So, at the end of September 1507, he strapped his feathered wings to his back and climbed to the top of Stirling Castle. And then he jumped.

Onlookers applauded as Damian took to the skies. He was a man of conviction who bravely tested his scientific advancements on himself when no one else would. If only his conviction was enough to keep him airborne.

You see, gluing feathers together and flapping his arms didn't have the intended effect. He fell like a stone just after takeoff. He managed to survive, though, thanks to a well-placed pile of dung waiting below.

A bruised and smelly Damian blamed his failure on his choice in feathers, claiming hen's feathers were more attracted to the ground than eagle feathers would have been. That didn't sound very scientific, though. Perhaps he should have sought some advice from a good friend of his back in Italy who had also been sketching plans for his own flying machines.

Together, they might have had more success, or at least brought more of their drawings to life.

That friend, by the way . . . was Leonardo da Vinci.

NO-MAN BAND

Most inventions arise in order to fulfill a need. Perhaps there's something tedious that can be done more efficiently, or a job too difficult for our bare hands that a machine can do for us. Inventions have the power to improve upon the world.

The automobile got us from point A to point B faster and more safely than horses ever did. The printing press allowed for the mass production of books, as well as increased literacy across the world. Books were no longer handwritten artworks meant only for the wealthy.

And then there's the Phonoliszt. Dubbed the "eighth wonder of the world" when it was unveiled in 1910, the concept behind it wasn't entirely new. It was created in Germany by Ludwig Hupfeld, a manufacturer of player pianos and orchestrions. Orchestrions were automatic music players designed to sound like full bands. Hiring live musicians to play at parties and in hotel lobbies was expensive, but a business could invest in an orchestrion and provide customers with a live performance at any time.

Many orchestrions combined pianos, drums, xylophones, and pipe organs to get a complete sound. A roll of paper with precisely punched holes was spun beneath a metal bar that would trigger a series of pneumatic bellows, activating a specific tone from one of the instruments—or several of them at once.

The Phonoliszt, however, was different. Rather than including only percussive instruments like pianos and drums, Hupfeld's creation added something *extraordinary*: violins. Three of them, to be exact. But it wasn't a simple thing to add them in.

First, a violin wasn't played like a piano. There were no keys to press. The note was made by pressing a finger against the string in a certain spot and then dragging a bow across it. In order to achieve this without the use of a human hand, each of the three violins was reduced to only one active string, then mounted vertically above a player piano.

As the paper roll was fed across the reader bar, pneumatic bellows acted like violinists' fingers, pressing each string in the right place so the correct note could be played.

And finally, a circular bow made of 1,300 horse hairs rotated around the violins, eliciting either one note at a time or full chords while the piano played underneath.

The result was a feast for the eyes *and* the ears. No one had ever built something that so accurately replicated an orchestral sound before. And no one at the 1910 World's Fair in Brussels had ever heard anything like it, either. A home or business with one of these on display didn't need to hire a band or a string quartet to liven up the place—it could do it all for them.

Stores often had coin-operated models that would play any one of several songs on demand. Occasionally, additional performers would accompany the machine, providing a live component to the automated sound. Customers would flock to watch the Phonoliszt's mechanisms move while they listened to the sweet music being played.

All told, nearly a thousand paper music rolls were made for it, though sadly its popularity didn't last too long. By the 1920s, as phonographs and radios became the norm, the Phonoliszt fell into obscurity. They were big, loud, and very expensive, and nobody wanted to hear a fake band when the real thing was one drop of the needle away.

Out of the thousands that were made, only sixty-three still exist today—and they're not cheap. One recently sold for almost $900,000.

And I've got to say, at that price, a live band doesn't sound like a bad idea after all.

SHOCKING

Most of us grew up with the story of Benjamin Franklin and his kite. It's that stereotypical eureka moment, practically an American legend at this point. Franklin tied a key to the kite and let the whole contraption fly up into the stormy sky. The string was wet with rain, the key was made of metal, and the lightning . . . well, it sent some sparks and a tingle down to Franklin's hand.

It's a lovely story, and might very well be true. If the modern world has a beating heart, we might be able to point to electricity as the force that powers it. After Benjamin Franklin's experiment, the wheels of science spun quickly.

Luigi Galvani experimented with the power of electricity to cause dead bodies to twitch. Alessandro Volta, one of Galvani's competitors, invented the voltaic pile in 1800, which was essentially a battery. Twenty years later, Michael Faraday invented the electric motor, and in the decades that followed, those same forces powered the invention of the telephone, the lightbulb, and eventually the modern personal computer.

It's shocking, I know, but we owe a lot of thanks to electricity. Still, electricity isn't a complex or challenging technology, when you boil it down to its basic elements. Back in 1978, a German named Arne Eggebrecht managed to prove just that.

He built a battery out of nothing more than a small jar, a copper tube, and an iron rod. When filled with an acidic liquid like vinegar or lemon juice, the copper and iron react to produce an electric current. Like I said, it's pretty simple, with very few ingredients.

It wasn't his idea, though; Eggebrecht had an earlier example to follow. Not something built by Galvani or Volta. Not something drawn up by Franklin or even Thomas Edison. No, his template was a bit older, and came from a land far, far away from Europe or America.

It was a battery, discovered in Iraq, from a time well outside of our modern expectations.

Two thousand years ago.

TOGETHER FOREVER

In grocery store aisles chock full of crunchy, salty snacks, one stands out above the rest: Pringles. Where other chips are shoved into bags, the Pringle stands tall in its unique, cylindrical container.

It's a great packaging design. It keeps all the chips in a neat line, stops them from getting crushed or broken, and—best of all—it keeps you from buying a bag that's 30 percent chips, 70 percent air.

The man who engineered the Pringles can was proud of it. And I mean *really* proud.

His name was Fredric Baur, and his résumé was highly impressive. Born in Ohio in 1918, he served as an aviation physiologist in the navy, then earned his Ph.D. in organic chemistry at Ohio State University. With a wife and kids to support, he soon got a job at Procter & Gamble as a chemist specializing in research and development for new methods of food storage.

He first designed the tube-shaped Pringles packaging in 1966. And, in Fredric's own words:

The Pringles can was a revolution within the realm of snack foods.

This was because, in the era of 1960s individualism, Pringles represented conformity. They weren't like your average potato chip, with varying sizes, shapes, and degrees of crispiness. Every Pringle was the same, stacked up one after another in their nice little tube.

And . . . a lot of people didn't like that. Surprisingly, Pringles weren't a smash hit—it took some years for people to appreciate what author Eric Spitznagel calls, quote:

. . . the inherent beauty and power of uniformity.

By the seventies and eighties, though, Pringles had become a grocery store staple. The iconic can was Fredric Baur's greatest legacy. You see, he'd invented a number of other food items in his day—like specialized frying oils and a freeze-dried ice cream product—but nothing had caught on quite like Pringles.

Around the mid-1980s, when Fredric was retiring, he approached his children with a bit of a weird request: He was so passionate about his invention that when he died, he wanted to be buried . . . inside a Pringles can.

At first, Fredric's oldest son, Larry, laughed. Fredric's obsession with his own packaging design actually became a bit of a running joke among his children.

Fast-forward to 2008. After a long battle with Alzheimer's, Fredric Baur passed away at the age of eighty-nine. His children reviewed his will, and were shocked to find that the burial request he'd made at least twenty years earlier was written there, in black-and-white. Fredric had never been kidding.

His will provided some more details. Seeing as a human body was unlikely to fit into a single Pringles can, Fredric's will stipulated that he be cremated, and a portion of his ashes be secured inside the snack container. Curious as it was, his kids agreed there was only one thing they could do: honor their father's last wish.

As Larry and his siblings rode together to a Cincinnati funeral home, they pulled off the road and into a Walgreens parking lot. Inside the store, they stared at a shelf full of Pringles, suddenly faced with a question that no child ever anticipates having to answer:

What flavor Pringles can should dad's ashes go in? Well, after a brief debate, they settled on Original. Because as they say, you can't go wrong with a classic.

With the chips in tow, Fredric's kids got back into the car, drove to the mortuary, and took care of the more . . . well, *normal* parts of the funeral proceedings. Fredric's kids agreed that a portion of his ashes should be put in an urn and kept with the family. The rest would go in the snack container.

In May of 2008, the Pringles can containing Fredric's ashes was buried at Arlington Memorial Gardens in Cincinnati, Ohio, next to his wife, Elaine. And I guess this could be considered a happy ending for Fredric.

Personally, though, I'll never be able to look at a Pringles can the same way again.

EERIE
MYSTERIES

FLIGHT OF FANCY

The model was meant to be a glider; the committee was certain of that. They were a collection of aeronautical engineers and experts in flight, so for them to look at the small wooden model and see its potential was a huge breakthrough.

There are certain elements that help an airplane fly through the air, and this model glider seemed to have nailed all of them. The wings had that perfect curve built into them for generating lift—what engineers refer to as the cambering. Those wings also bent downward toward the tips, another key element of aeronautical design.

And the shape of the entire model craft was exactly what you might expect: a pair of main wings that extended away from the body, and a raised tail fin with two protruding stabilizer wings. The committee could immediately see the usefulness of the design. With a small engine at the rear, they suggested, this glider might be perfect for low-speed flight. Maybe even cargo transport. It was brilliant.

And that was that problem. You see, this model was brought to the committee in 1961, after having been found in storage, where it had been for decades. In fact, it had first been discovered five years before the Wright brothers made their historic flight at Kitty Hawk in North Carolina. It was a problem because it predated powered flight, something modern men and women had taken a lot of pride in.

The box it had been rediscovered *in* was part of a collection of artifacts removed from a tomb in Saqqara, which had been the burial ground for the ancient Egyptian capital of Memphis. A tomb that had been opened in 1898, and dated back more than two thousand years. And the glider model wasn't a one-off, either. Archaeologists have found over a dozen others just like it, all of which are brilliantly designed for powered flight.

We tend to view history as a never-ending slope upward, where each new century places us further up the technological ladder. We believe we're always gaining altitude, climbing to new heights, and soaring over our ancestors. It turns out, we might be wrong.

In the end, our pride might be nothing more than a flight of fancy.

THE SHAWL

Dr. Silas Weir Mitchell was an American physician with a career that straddled the Civil War and the decades beyond it. During his own lifetime, he was known for his focus on what they called "nervous disease," what we would refer to today as neurological disorders. Basically, if it had to do with the nervous system, he took care of it.

But that's not all he pioneered. We've all bumped into his discoveries and ideas in our modern world. The concept known as the "phantom limb"? That was a Mitchell discovery. Headaches being caused by excessive eye strain? That was Mitchell, too. Bed rest? Yep, Mitchell again. He had an intuitive understanding of medicine that transcended the textbook and moved right into everyday life, and people respected him for it.

But one of his most memorable encounters happened after office hours. As the story goes, Dr. Mitchell had come home after a long day at work, had himself a bit of food and then sat down in front of the fire to read before bed. It was one of those quiet winter nights where the snow is falling and every sound seems to be muffled by it. I imagine it didn't take long for his exhaustion to catch up with him, and before long, he was asleep right there in his chair.

It was his doorbell that ended the brief nap, though. Dr. Mitchell found his way to the door and opened it to find a young girl standing in the snow. She was thin and pale, and had nothing warmer on than a well-worn shawl pulled around her narrow shoulders. Without pausing, the girl motioned toward the street.

"My mother," she said. "She's not well. Can you come and help her, please?"

Before Mitchell could answer, the girl was off, heading down the steps of his house and into the snow-covered streets of Philadelphia. Mitchell grabbed his coat and bag, and quickly followed her. Maybe it was the excitement of the moment, or perhaps it was just the chill of the winter air, but all of a sudden, he no longer felt tired.

She led him to a worn-down tenement house, up a set of stairs, and then through the mazelike hallways to her own door. Inside, Mitchell was greeted by a familiar face. The girl's mother, it turned out, was a former housekeeper of his, although she was in much worse health than he had ever seen her before. Feeling a sense of urgency, Mitchell got to work.

Soon enough, he determined that the woman was suffering from pneumonia, and found the necessary medication to administer. After rounding the critical corner, Mitchell sat back with relief, glad for a break, but also glad for the girl's quick timing. So he said as much, letting the woman know her daughter most likely saved her life.

"That can't be," she replied. "My daughter died more than a month ago."

Shocked, Mitchell described the girl who had led him there, and the tattered shawl she had worn against the winter chill. The woman nodded in recognition.

"Yes," she replied. "That sounds like my daughter. But her things are put away over there in that cupboard." Then she pointed to a small cabinet in the room.

Mitchell approached it, and then slowly opened the door. Inside, he found a small pair of shoes and a perfectly folded shawl. The fabric was very worn—with carefully mended holes and faded colors—but it was also dry and warm.

Confused, the good doctor quickly looked in the other rooms of the home, glancing around for the familiar face. Try as he might, he wasn't able to find her; the mysterious girl who had guided him to the woman's rescue that night was no longer in the house.

She was gone.

THIN AIR

When he checked into the hotel on Long Island, he did so under a false name. It was April 17, 1938, and the man listed as Albert C. White was very much not who he claimed he was. He was actually the 28-year-old nephew of legendary steel magnate Andrew Carnegie, and even shared his name: he was Andrew Carnegie Whitfield.

He paid in advance—four dollars for a single night, if you're curious what hotel rates were like in 1938—and deposited his belongings in the room before taking a car to the nearby Roosevelt Field airport, where he had a plane waiting for him. It was silver and red, very flashy, and he planned to take it for a quick flight. His destination, he claimed, was an airfield in Brentwood, New York—about twenty-two miles away.

He had plenty of fuel, perfect weather, a heavily populated landscape to fly over, and hundreds of hours of flight time under his belt. He was happily married, was enjoying success as an executive for a large company, and was even planning to relocate the family to a better home at the end of the month. He had everything going for him—on land *and* in the air.

And then he *vanished*.

When they searched his hotel room, they found a lot of things to raise questions. There were records of a phone call to his own home. His clothing was still there in the room, along with his monogrammed cuff links. Oddly, he had even brought along two life insurance policies and several stock and bond certificates that had his name on them.

But Andrew Whitfield was nowhere to be found. It didn't make sense, and no matter how hard they tried, the authorities couldn't locate him or his red-and-silver airplane. They had simply vanished into thin air.

One other thing, though: remember that phone call he made to his home from the hotel room? Well, it was unusual for two reasons. First, when no one answered, the operator who was trying to connect their call overheard him mutter, "Well, I'm going to carry out my plan."

Weird, right?

Not as weird as the second detail. That call, it seems, took place while his family was out of the house. They were out of the house because they had gone to join the search party looking for him.

The call, you see, didn't happen *before* his flight. It was placed *hours* after he vanished.

PLUMBING HISTORY

Harry arrived at the old English mansion with work on his mind, but he left with something else entirely.

He had been called upon to take care of a fairly simple task: much like the mansion itself there in York, the pipes in the basement were really old, and a few of them needed to be replaced. As a plumber's apprentice, this was the sort of task he could handle on his own, so he was sent out to get the job done.

As he worked at the top of a ladder, his neck bent to study the pipe above him, he was startled by a sudden noise. He later told others that it sounded like a trumpet, with one long, steady blast. It seemed to come out of nowhere, and took him by such surprise that he actually fell off the ladder to the stone below.

As he was returning to his feet, the sound stopped, and something entered the basement through a far wall. Well, "entered" is a misleading term; this figure seemed to step out of the wall itself, as if the stone there was nothing more than a mirage. At the sight of this figure, Harry lost his cool and rushed into a dark corner to watch it from a distance.

He claimed it was the figure of a Roman soldier, complete with weapons, armor, and a plumed helmet. After the soldier had passed all the way through the basement wall, it was followed by more. They walked in pairs, side by side, in front of horses that were pulling carts. Harry was terrified, but he watched it all nonetheless.

Each of the soldiers, he claimed, was wearing a short sword on its right hip and carrying a round metal and wood shield. Beneath their armor, Harry could see green tunics, and their feet were clad in leather sandals with straps that wound all the way to their knees.

He watched this ghostly parade for a few moments as they exited the wall on one side of the basement, and then vanished in the same manner on the opposite side. And then they were gone. Harry, though, had a choice: keep working, or run out of the basement as quickly as he could. I can't find a record of which option he picked.

What I do know, though, is that he told others about what he saw. It was a fantastic story full of suspense and drama, but it earned him a lot of criticism. It was all fantasy, some said. The Roman soldiers in his vision weren't historically accurate, because Romans wore red, not green, and they carried rectangular shields, with their swords on their left hip, not the right. Every historian in 1953 was certain of this.

It turns out, Harry wasn't the only person to have seen the ghostly soldiers. Decades before, a guest of the previous owner of the mansion claimed to have seem them

as well, but just like Harry he was laughed at and ridiculed. Not that Frank Green, the man who owned the place, ever doubted a Roman connection to the mansion—in fact, quite the opposite.

Green knew for a fact that his mansion had been built right on top of an old Roman road. He had even uncovered a number of Roman columns on the property, and placed one of them upstairs in the main house. The Romans were real, as everyone knew, but ghosts? Well, that was just fantasy.

All of that changed years later. Archaeologists digging near the mansion discovered the graves of Roman soldiers that dated to a period after the Romans had left England and gone back to Rome. They were, in fact, Roman-trained reserve soldiers, given the task of watching over Rome's investment in the area. And there was something *unexpected* about them.

Each skeleton had a sword beside it, located not on the left hip as expected, but on the right. The shields in the grave site were also unusual, since they were round, and not the typical rectangular shape. But the biggest shock of all was the discovery of small scraps of fabric, which hinted at the true color of their tunics. You can probably guess what color they were, too. That's right: green.

Our old plumber friend, Harry, took a lot of flak for his bizarre encounter that day in the basement of the mansion. He was mocked and shamed and told he was wrong. But over the years, he stuck to his story and never wavered, and I think it's safe to say that that was a good thing.

Because time—and a bit of digging— eventually proved him right.

UP IN SMOKE

Don worked as a meter reader for the gas company in a small Pennsylvania town in the mid-1960s. It was one of those idyllic jobs you imagine seeing in old black-and-white television shows like *Leave It to Beaver*. He would show up each morning bright and early in his smart, tidy uniform, and begin walking through town and knocking on doors.

Of course, it was December when this story took place, so I imagine it was slightly less idyllic with all the snow and ice around. But still, Don got to spend time outside in the sunshine and fresh air. Well, most of the time. He still had to step inside to read the meters.

On December 5, his first stop was at the home of a retired doctor named John Bentley. Dr. John was ninety-two years old, so Don made it a point to check on the man each month and see how he was doing. But when he knocked on the door on December 5, no one answered. It was, however, unlocked, which wasn't very unusual.

Don stepped in out of the cold and called out for Dr. John, but no one answered. Assuming the older man was out for the morning, Don descended the basement stairs and headed toward the gas meter. On his way across the basement floor, though, he encountered something odd: it was a pile of ash.

Don later described it as a circle of dark powder about a foot in diameter, standing maybe five inches high. He gently kicked the toe of his shoe into the ash, which scattered a bit, but then moved on to the meter. When he had recorded the number on his pad of paper, he headed back up. That's when he noticed the smoke.

It wasn't thick, but the sunlight coming in one of the living room windows highlighted a few wisps of smoke that still hung in the air. More concerned now, Don began to shout for Dr. John and walk around the house, checking all of the rooms for signs of a fire. That search eventually led him to the downstairs bathroom, and a bizarre, unsettling scene.

It was a human leg, lying beside a large, charred hole in the bathroom floor. Dr. John's old metal walker had partially fallen in the hole and was leaning against the bathtub where an tattered robe had been thrown. Stepping in and peering down into the hole, Don was surprised to see the pile of ash on the basement floor, his shoe marks still visible on its gray surface.

The coroner would later try to put the pieces together. No pun intended, of course, because there was only a leg. They searched the house for signs of foul play but found nothing out of the ordinary. They tossed around theories about Dr. John lighting his pipe and catching himself on fire, but there were no signs of burning anywhere in the house except for the bathroom floor where his walker had been found.

And that was the oddest thing about it all. The plastic parts on Dr. John's walker were still intact, as if the fire had somehow limited itself to a very small space. So small, the coroner suggested, that when the victim's leg fell out of the blaze, it failed to burn up. There was even a shiny black loafer still fitted to the foot, untouched by fire.

When it was all said and done, the authorities simply had no way of explaining what had happened to poor old Dr. John Bentley. Without clear evidence to point at, his cause of death was officially listed as "asphyxiation and 90 percent burning," which honestly sounds more like a description of the results, rather than an explanation for the cause.

Some, however, think Dr. John's death is a rare example of something almost supernatural: spontaneous human combustion.

Was his death really the result of some unnatural internal fire, or was he simply the victim of an accident that left no evidence for people to find?

And that, of course, is the burning question, isn't it?

MAKING WAVES

The march of progress is a ruthless one. In its wake, it leaves the antiquated and inefficient behind while the demands for newer, faster, and better get louder and louder.

Player pianos gave way to phonographs, which were eventually put out to pasture by 8-track players. Those lost the war against cassette tape and CD players, which eventually led to the rise of streaming music over the internet. But one thing is certain about the past, and technology in particular: it doesn't always go away forever, and it tends to repeat itself.

Vinyl records have made a triumphant return, though in a way, they never really left. Analog technology doesn't die. It just goes underground, often dug up later by hobbyists and the nostalgic. We have cell phones that allow us to talk to people anywhere in the world, yet there are still roughly three million ham radio operators.

Amateur radio operators often begin transmissions with their call signs, a combination of numbers and letters rattled off using the NATO phonetic alphabet. It's as easy as Alfa Bravo Charlie. What they expect to hear back is usually the same thing from the other person—letters and numbers identifying the party on the other end of the line. They don't expect music.

However, beginning in the 1970s, music is exactly what they got. A jaunty electronic tune like something played by a passing ice cream truck, followed by a creepy recording of a woman reading a series of numbers. They're called "numbers stations," and while their origins aren't definitive, an initiative known as the Conet Project has been cataloguing these recordings for decades.

Shortwave radio transmissions utilize the earth's atmosphere to propagate all over the world. With the help of an unlicensed station to maintain anonymity, these numbers stations became the perfect vessels for one-way communications.

The original numbers stations are thought to have been started back in World War I as a way to transmit encoded messages. The person listening to the message would often have a paper or small pamphlet with a key of random numbers or letters by which to decode the messages. Once they'd been deciphered, the keys were then shredded, making it nearly impossible for an enemy to uncover its meaning.

From 1959 to 1991, the Gong Station in East Germany broadcasted coded number groups that corresponded to specific times and locations where active spies would be dropped. Air Force printer Joachim Preuß (Preuss) used those recorded messages to transcribe over sixteen thousand documents for his superiors.

As recently as 1991, Russian stations made several unscheduled broadcasts with new numbers during an attempted coup in the USSR against President Mikhail Gorbachev.

Several years later, Cuban spies were caught decoding fourteen hundred pages worth of secret messages being transmitted by a local station. Some of those messages said things like "Prioritize and continue to strengthen friendship with Joe Dennis" and "Congratulate all female comrades for International Day of Woman."

Since the end of the Cold War, listeners have theorized as to why these stations still exist. Some believe drug cartels are using them to coordinate shipments across the US border. Others think they're still being utilized by the counterintelligence community for their original purpose.

In fact, many of the prevailing theories about the use of numbers stations were confirmed in the late nineties by a government official from the United Kingdom, who stated that the transmissions were not meant for regular listeners, including ham radio operators.

Despite the proliferation of technology, such as cell phones, email, and Twitter, numbers stations are still in use today and new ones have been known to crop up from time to time. They transmit all over the globe in different languages, including Russian, Chinese, Spanish, and English. Few people know they exist, and among those that do, there's a lot of confusion over these stations' true purpose.

All they know is someone, somewhere, is listening . . . and waiting.

ROYAL TREATMENT

History is a record. It tells future generations where we came from, and how we got to where we are today. History is chock full of failures, successes, and everything in between. It is a journey of cultures, yet many cultures have been lost—to time, to invaders, to fires and floods—and we have no way of learning about them aside from the few clues that remain.

The ancient Egyptians left behind pyramids, temples, and tombs, with the story of their people illustrated on their walls. We have statues and writings from the ancient Greeks to shed light on their way of life and how they contributed to the world at large. And then there's ancient Sumer, the basis for modern civilization as we know it today.

The Sumerians originally settled in Mesopotamia, a region in southern Iraq, around 4000 BC. They made great advances in agriculture, technology, and, most important, language.

Sumerian was the primary tongue in Mesopotamia for over a thousand years before other languages started to take hold.

Cuneiform, their written language, lasted two thousand years longer. It was comprised of triangular-shaped markings etched into clay tablets, and was used for all sorts of communications. A message from King Xerxes was uncovered in Turkey etched into the side of a mountain. It described the great deeds accomplished by his family in the region.

Cuneiform tablets have been found all across the Middle East, but one has perplexed historians for decades. It was a German-American man named Hermann Hilprecht who first discovered it at the beginning of the twentieth century. Known as the Sumerian King List, it details the names of ancient rulers across the region, and the lengths of their reigns.

There are a few things surprising about it. First, there are several versions known to exist—at least eighteen stone tablets have been found. However, the most comprehensive version is known as the Weld-Blundell Prism, a long, eight-inch column with four sides, each side jam-packed with the names of ancient Sumerian kings.

This list is more than a chronology, though. It opens up the door to endless questions about our past and what we think we know. According to the list, many of the ancient kings ruled for hundreds of years, such as the mythological Gilgamesh. Sumerian kingship was meant for the divinely chosen. According to one translation, one king ruled for 28,800 years, immediately followed by another king who reigned for 36,000 years. Two kings who ruled for a combined 65,000 years.

In fact, over the course of more than

241,000 years, only eight kings ruled Sumer. A staggering number, even when those reigns are broken down to more realistic ranges using a variety of formulas and mathematical computations.

Those realistic ranges number in the tens of hundreds of years, which are still well outside our modern expectations. People just don't live that long, and so historians have been left with a puzzle to solve. Did the ancient Sumerian kings actually reign for thousands of years, or are we missing a piece that unlocks the true meaning of these numbers?

Perhaps more information could be gleaned from other lists we haven't found yet—that is, if they exist. Until then, we'll have to keep looking. Although rare, new stone tablets show up from time to time, but it's hard to predict how helpful they are. Some help us connect one more dot, while others just make the mystery a little more foggy.

In the end, our best chance is to keep looking, keep thinking, and keep putting the pieces together.

Oh, and to make sure to never leave a stone unturned.

WORDSMITH

Easter Island, just off the coast of Chile, was settled by the Rapa Nui people sometime around AD 1200. It's perhaps most famous for its moai statues, the giant carved stone heads that populate the island. Its people have been through a lot over the last eight hundred years—deforestation, European imperialism, the slave trade, and the introduction of foreign diseases—and yet there are still things we don't know.

Every culture has its own myths and mysteries. The giant statues, of course, are the largest and best known examples. But there are also wood carvings, houses made of stone, and writings.

The writings are perhaps the most fascinating remnant of the ancient Rapa Nui. Petroglyphs, or rock carvings, have been catalogued all over the island as territory markers and headstones. Many ancient petroglyphs have been translated over the years, giving researchers a better understanding of Rapa Nui history, but there's one type of script that has perplexed them for years.

It's called Rongorongo, and word of its existence was first spread outside the island by a French missionary. His name was

Eugene Eyraud, and he'd been a mechanic and miner by trade. Later in life, he developed a passion for missionary work, which took him to China in the mid-1800s, then to Chile, Tahiti, and finally Easter Island in 1864.

It was during his first tour when he encountered Rongorongo. He would enter the homes of the native people and see wooden tablets on display featuring unfamiliar glyphs. No one, not even the locals, knew how to read them.

He didn't see anything of note in them. To him, everything about the island was strange and new. It wasn't until five years later when a colleague of his accidentally unveiled Rongorongo to the rest of the world. The colleague had presented one of the wooden tablets as a gift to a bishop who'd been working alongside him.

Its differences from the main language of the island were immediate. First of all, nearly every instance of it had been carved in wood, not stone. It's been said that wood was so valuable, only expert scribes ever used it for their writing. And secondly, the bishop could find no one on the island who could to read the tablet to him. One person knew its contents from memory, but not what any of the symbols meant.

The glyphs, which were comprised of shapes representing different plants, people, and animals, were arranged in a technique called reverse boustrophedon (boo-stroff-uh-don). To read the carving, the reader would start in the bottom left corner and read to the right, then rotate the tablet 180 degrees and continue to the next line.

However, despite the obvious pictorial style of the text, Rongorongo has remained nearly undecipherable for over a century. Part of one of the tablets has been translated into some kind of lunar calendar, though it can't be read or understood. There are over fifteen thousand known glyphs within the system and no contextual texts or artifacts to compare them against. This makes Rongorongo arguably an unknown language.

Some historians have claimed it really isn't a language at all, but rather a proto-language. A way to convey information to anyone who already knows what the symbols really mean. However, with so few texts remaining and no one with any knowledge of what any of them say, it's possible that a definitive Rongorongo translation may never come.

A picture may be worth a thousand words, as they say. But a glyph carved into a wooden tablet . . . could very well be priceless.

URAL HISTORY

Despite the collections we have of artifacts and fossils spanning millions of years, we still don't know a whole lot about early civilizations. We deduce and make inferences based on what we find, such as pottery and grave sites, but we still have much to learn about how ancient cultures truly lived. Especially when they leave behind things that aren't so easily explained.

Russian archaeologists found such an object in 1999 while working in the Ural Mountains. It was a slab of stone nearly five feet tall and three and a half feet wide. It also weighed a ton. Literally. It's called the Dashka Stone, or the Map of the Creator, and one scientist believes it could be over 120 million years old.

That in and of itself isn't so odd. We have fossils dating back billions of years. What sets the Dashka Stone apart from other artifacts are its structure and what it represents.

The slab is made up of three layers. The first is a seven-inch layer of a compound with a dolomite base. The middle layer is an inch thick and made up of diopside glass and silicon. And the top is only a few millimeters of calcium mixed with porcelain.

This kind of layering didn't happen in nature. Someone, they think, had to make it.

On its surface is a series of lines intersecting at various points. These lines were etched in with some kind of primitive tool. Cartographers from Russia and China looked more closely at the lines and noticed how similar they looked to a particular area of the Ural Mountains known as Bashkiria. The accuracy was uncanny.

What archaeologists had found wasn't just a slab with pictures on it, it was a topographical map, one drawn with a bird's-eye view of the mountains. There were also lines representing waterways and dams. Undecipherable inscriptions adorned the sides of the stone as well.

Now, naturally, they didn't have drones back then, or airplanes, so how could an ancient civilization depict such a precise image of the mountains without help? That's what has baffled scientists since the stone's discovery. However, the claim that it's 120 million years old doesn't sit well with everyone.

What some scientists get hung up on are the fossils that were found within the slab. One was dated to 120 million years ago, while the other is about 500 million years old. That makes dating the map more difficult. That's because Homo habilis, who lived roughly 2.8 million years ago, is one of the earliest species that has left us evidence they used stone tools. To declare that this map was created 117 million years earlier, well before we evolved enough to fashion rocks and sticks into makeshift hammers and chisels, does seem a bit far-fetched.

Still, what the map illustrates, aside from the Ural Mountains, is that the area was home to an advanced civilization that had figured out how to see the world from high above. Something almost no one else could do at the time. They didn't draw any roads on the map since none existed, but they did learn how to navigate the nearby rivers and streams to get to different places. There's also the possibility that there might be more than one map. According to some reports, there might be as many as two hundred similar stones in existence.

No other slabs have been found yet, though. For now, scientists, cartographers, and archaeologists have only the one stone to perform their research on, but there's a lot that single stone can teach us. It also opens up the possibility that what we think we know about ancient civilizations . . . could be all wrong.

We can only move forward based on the information—and artifacts—we already have. There's more out there waiting to be found. We just have to figure out how to use one map to find another.

And another.

And another.

Curious, isn't it?

DISC MEN

In Greek mythology, Minos was born to Zeus and Europa. He became the first king of Crete, the largest of the Greek islands, where he didn't exactly rule with kindness.

Every nine years, he would demand that another ruler send seven boys and seven girls into the labyrinth. The labyrinth was a kind of maze, created for Minos by the craftsman Daedalus, and within the its elusive center lived the king's son, the minotaur, a creature possessing the body of a man and the head of a bull.

King Minos, his labyrinth, and his minotaur were all just stories. Fables about gods and goddesses to help explain how Greece had come to be. However, to the ancient Greeks they were more than just stories. They were legendary tales of good and evil about deities that were worshipped by the masses.

And if you look at the ruins and remnants left behind by the early Greeks, you start to wonder if they were ever really stories at all. When English archaeologist Sir Arthur Evans found the palace at Knossos, he called upon his knowledge of the Greek myths to aid in his research.

He named the ancient people who once

lived there Minoans, after King Minos, and then worked for several years excavating a large palace at the site. By 1905, the work had been completed, and through it, Sir Arthur had learned much about the people who once lived in what he called the Palace of Minos.

But it wouldn't be until several years later, in 1908, when an Italian archaeologist by the name of Luigi Pernier would find a new piece of a very perplexing puzzle. Luigi had been digging around in the basement of one of the buildings set off from the main palace when he found a small disc. Only six inches in diameter, the circular object featured more than two hundred impressions of hieroglyphs arranged clockwise in a spiral pattern. He called it the Phaistos Disc.

As with many archaeological discoveries concerning ancient cultures, the first inclination was to write the Phaistos Disc off as a fake. Many historical objects had been revealed as forgeries or hoaxes, and there was no reason *not* to think the same about this one. But surprisingly, most scholars agreed it was legitimate. One reason for that was the later discovery of an axe nearby bearing similar glyphs as the disc.

The 242 impressions, or tokens, were comprised of forty-five numbered symbols, each one unique. These symbols stood for common things like "person" or "child" or "arrow." Yet, despite their clear pictorial intent, every actual decipherment of the disc had been unsuccessful. Amateur archaeologists had tried everything—turning the disc as they read it, proposing possible stories it might have told—but nothing seemed to work.

It was thought for decades that the disc might never be translated successfully at *all* if more symbols weren't found elsewhere, either in Crete or in the palace itself. Or perhaps from where the object originated. A scholar back in the 1920s claimed the clay that had been used to form the disc hadn't come from Crete, but from somewhere else in the Aegean Sea. There may be more out there, but we don't know where.

However, in 2014, two linguists claimed they'd broken the code. Dr. Gareth Owens, a researcher from Crete, and John Coleman, a professor of phonetics at Oxford University, worked together for six years analyzing what Owens referred to as the "first Minoan CD-ROM." Early theories about the disc posited it had been a story to entertain readers, a declaration of war, a game of some kind, or even a mathematical equation.

But Owens and Coleman figured out the trick to deciphering it. They read it in a spiral direction, working their way from the outside edge to the center, and compared with glyphs to Cretan hieroglyphics, as well as ancient Greek writings. What they came up with were three words, which translated to "pregnant mother," "shining mother," and "goddess."

According to Owens and Coleman, the Phaistos Disc wasn't a story or a call to arms, but a prayer to a Minoan goddess. It might not be as riveting a conclusion as some had hoped, but thanks to the work of these two language experts, we now have greater insight into an unknown religion of an ancient culture.

Just don't ask me to try to read the disc. Turns out . . . it's all Greek to me.

MESMERIZING

Some people are just born with innate talent. Mozart began composing when he was only five years old. Blaise Pascal, the French mathematician, wrote his first theorem when he was only eleven. And British philosopher John Stuart Mill had already learned how to speak several dead languages by the time he was eight.

Andrew Jackson Davis from Blooming Grove, New York, took a little longer to find his calling. Born in 1826, he had received only five months of formal classroom education by the age of seventeen. His father had been an alcoholic, and Andrew, along with his mother and sister, had to find work wherever they could to keep a roof over their heads. The young man was a cobbler's apprentice by trade and found other odd jobs around town so his family could stay afloat.

He'd been in Poughkeepsie, New York, in 1843 when he attended some lectures on hypnotism from mesmerist J. S. Grimes. At the time, it was called "animal magnetism," and the prevailing theory was that every living thing on earth was born with the ability to influence other creatures. Some could even use their powers to heal.

Davis believed he possessed special powers, specifically the ability to read minds. He explored these possibilities for the next three years, calling himself the Poughkeepsie Seer as he practiced his own form of medicine. He used his psychic sight to diagnose sick people, and to speak with spirits from the great beyond.

In 1844, he woke up in the Catskills, claiming he'd gone into a trance only hours before where he spoke to Galen, the Greek physician considered to be the father of modern medicine. Though relatively uneducated, that didn't stop Davis from writing books about magnetic healing, many of which he dictated while in a trance.

His first book, *Principles of Nature,* sold one thousand copies in the week after its release. One reason for its success—Davis wasn't a scholar. He was a below-average man born with above-average skills and that made him appealing to the masses. If he could become a kind of mental superhero, then so could anyone else.

Unfortunately, while his books were financially successful, they were a critical flop—especially among the intellectual crowd. Critics didn't take his work seriously, often citing factual errors as well as jargon-filled ramblings better suited toward fiction than credible textbooks. Things weren't looking good for Andrew Jackson Davis.

He even had a run-in with author Edgar Allan Poe, who didn't much care for his brand of shenanigans. Poe wrote a short story just before his death called "Mellonta Tauta" that featured a character named Martin Van Buren Mavis, the Tougkeepsie Seer. A nice little dig at the man whose trance sessions also influenced the story "The Facts in the Case of M. Valdemar." Poe had written that one in the same year he and Davis had first met.

But Davis and Poe would never patch things up. The Poughkeepsie Seer had grown too positive for the Baltimore native. You see, Davis had moved past séances and spiritual contact. He wasn't just a medium—he was a progressive thinker and the founder of a movement. One he coined in his magnum opus *The Great Harmonia*.

The concept was called the "law of attraction" and it was much different from the "law of attraction" we know today. To Davis, the spirits he contacted during a séance would be attracted to his attempts only if they shared the characters and intentions of the other living people present. Later on, as mesmerism fell out of fashion, the term evolved to be more about earthly prosperity for those with positive attitudes.

But Mr. Davis also gave us two more things before his death in 1910 in the form of predictions. In his book *The Penetralia,* published in 1856, Davis wrote: "Look out about these days for carriages and travelling saloons on country roads—without horses, without steam, without any visible motive power—moving with greater speed and far more safety than at present." He said these machines would move with the help of a mixture of gas and liquid that ignited safely within their shells.

He also mentioned in the same book a type of machine that could automatically transcribe words for him. He called it a soul-writer and said "It may be constructed something like a piano, one brace or scale of keys to represent the elementary sounds . . . so that a person, instead of playing a piece of music, may touch off a sermon or a poem."

In other words, the uneducated cobbler from upstate New York didn't just learn how to talk to the dead. He predicted the automobile and the typewriter decades before they were revealed to the rest of the world.

Quite the progressive thinker, indeed.

SHARK ATTACKED

A good card shark can build up a kind of reputation. They can be shifty. They know how to read people. And they know exactly how much trouble they can get themselves into before they're in too deep.

Joseph Elwell was quite the shark himself, and he was known for it all around New York City in the early 1900s. But it wasn't just his prowess with a deck of cards that earned him a reputation. It was his other obsession, one even more dangerous than any ticked off gangster waiting for his loan payment. You see, Joseph loved the ladies—particularly the newly married ones.

Aside from the obvious problems with his vice of choice, 1920s New York was nothing like current day New York. Women were still seen more as virtuous property of their husbands and fathers than as people in their own right, and if word ever got out of their misdeeds with Mr. Elwell, their reputations would be dragged down right along with his.

But Joseph couldn't help himself. He'd flash his bright white smile, say a few charming words, and they'd fall head over heels for the Bridge King of Manhattan.

You heard me right. Joseph Elwell's game of choice wasn't Texas Hold'em, or five-card stud—the kinds of games you might associate with a card shark. No, his game of choice was bridge, and Joseph was its Michael Jordan.

His skills both at and away from the table were legendary, as was the list of men who wanted him dead. Jilted lovers and overprotective fathers threatened him with all manner of violence. Even his own wife hated him, and as you might imagine, his infidelity eventually caused their separation.

However, none of the angry husbands ever seemed seriously threatening. They'd all been angry or jealous or hateful, but for all their posturing, Joseph just laughed them off and moved on to the next woman he saw. Which is what made what happened on June 11, 1920, so strange.

The night before, Joseph had spent the evening with Viola Kraus, who had recently divorced her husband and was looking for some fun. The two had dinner and drinks at the Ritz-Carlton Hotel, followed by some revelry at the Ziegfeld Midnight Frolic, a late-night performance put on by the women of the Ziegfeld Follies—just a less family-friendly version.

Around three in the morning, Joseph arrived back home, where he spent a few hours making phone calls. He placed the last call at just after 6:00 a.m., and then stepped outside to fetch his morning paper from his stoop.

Later that morning, Joseph's housekeeper arrived to begin her daily cleaning. As she started tidying, she noticed the door to his living room was locked. From the inside. She let herself in and saw a man sitting in a chair with the day's newspaper folded in his lap. He was nearly bald, had no teeth, and looked deathly ill.

For a moment she was taken aback by the presence of a stranger in her employer's house, but then she took a second look, and realized she recognized the man after all. It was Joseph Elwell.

The housekeeper said hello to him, but he didn't respond. So she went over to check on him. That's when she saw it—the red hole between his eyes. She screamed and fled the room to call the police. Surprisingly, Joseph's shot to the head hadn't killed him. He was still breathing when the authorities arrived to inspect the scene. He was too far gone to speak, though, and shortly after he was carted off, he passed away.

The NYPD noted that Joseph had been shot at point blank range with a .45, and yet they ruled out suicide. That's because the police found a single bullet on the table in front of him, and the cartridge on the floor beside him. The gun that fired it, though . . . was gone.

Nothing in the room had been disturbed. Joseph hadn't been robbed, and there were no signs of any kind of struggle. The blood spatter on the walls indicated the shooter had been crouched in front of the late bridge player, though, so they had probably known each other.

But despite the evidence left behind, there was one question still buzzing inside everyone's heads: how had the shooter gotten away? All the windows in the room were sealed and the door had been locked from the inside. No way in or out.

Joseph Elwell's murder remains unsolved to this day, and after all these years, it's unlikely anyone will end up cracking it. A mysterious end to a complicated character, if there ever was one. Now that's what I'd call . . . curious.

MAN vs. WILD

A picture is worth a thousand words, although some can be worth far more than that. The world-famous photo of the Loch Ness Monster, taken by Doctor Robert Kenneth Wilson in 1934, depicts the shadowy image of the creature's famous long neck sticking out of the water, the waves around it rippling outward.

It's an image that everyone knows. It's instantly recognizable, and it has inspired decades of speculation of what might be living beneath the waters of Loch Ness. But there is another photo, one that is also at the center of a decades-long debate over its authenticity and what it might signify about humanity . . . and where we really sit within the food chain.

It was taken by Eric Shipton in 1951. Shipton was a mountaineer who had climbed numerous Himalayan peaks, but had wanted to scale the venerable Mount Everest. Nowadays, Everest is a popular destination for thrill-seekers with money to burn, but during Eric Shipton's time, only a small handful of people had ever successfully reached the summit.

Those people had used known routes along the northern side. Shipton and his crew were set on exploring the southwestern side to see if there was a way up to the top no one had found yet. Along for the trip were three other British climbers—William Murray, Tom Bourdillon, and W. H. Ward—as well as local Sherpas to help guide them. One of those men, Sherpa Tenzing Norgay, became friends with Shipton, and would even accompany him on future expeditions.

The climb didn't pan out, though, and the climbers descended the mountain—but they never stopped trying. During another expedition several months later, Shipton, Norgay, and a Dr. Michael Ward were exploring a glacier west of Mount Everest when they stopped to look at something strange in the snow.

It was a footprint, thirteen inches long and twice as wide as a man's foot. It bore four small toes and one big toe, and was discovered at an altitude of nineteen thousand feet. Just ahead of that print was another, then another.

They were tracks. The men followed them for a mile to a chasm where it was clear that whatever creature had made the prints had jumped across. And from where they stood, they could see that the tracks continued on the other side.

Shipton, unable to follow them farther, returned to the trail and continued his work. He would later publish his findings in both a book and an article that each detailed what he'd found. Biologists and zoologists tried to discredit his claims, assuring people that the only creatures living at that elevation were bears and langur monkeys. London's Natural History Museum even commissioned a Himalayan bear to walk across a stretch of sand so they could compare its footprints with the photographs taken by Shipton.

But the test backfired, because they didn't match.

And the biggest langur monkey prints are only about eight inches long, much smaller than the imprint discovered near Mount Everest. Yet, despite the claims from experts all over the world that the prints were animal in nature, Shipton refused to believe it. So did the other Sherpas familiar with the region.

Because they'd all either seen the creature that made the prints firsthand, or personally knew someone who had.

It had been described as being about five feet six inches tall, and covered with reddish brown hair, except for its face. It stood upright, like a human being, and it lumbered through the snow with ease. It had only ever been seen in passing, and had never been captured on camera—which, of course, only added to the legend.

Tenzing Norgay went on to become the second man to summit Mount Everest, alongside Sir Edmund Hillary in 1953. He was clearly a brave and determined man.

But on that earlier trip in 1951—when he saw the enormous footprints in the snow with his own eyes—he had frozen in place with fear. And then he uttered a single word that would carry more weight than any photograph of a footprint ever could, at least to our modern ears.

He muttered the name of the creature he believed had left the footprint:

"Yeti."

BAFFLING ORIGINS

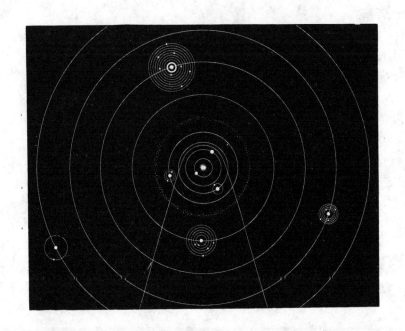

TUNNELS

They were surrounded, and had been for months. The Ottoman Empire had been spreading westward for decades, and by 1683 it had arrived on the doorstep of Vienna, capital of the Holy Roman Empire. If the city fell, the dam would burst, and the Ottomans would roll through like a wave.

They had sent for help, of course. King John III of Poland was most likely on his way with an army to free them, to push back that sea of red flags and golden crescents. But King John hadn't arrived, and they weren't sure how much longer they could hold on against an army of nearly a hundred thousand warriors.

The siege of the city had been going on for two months, and you have to wonder if the people of Vienna ever felt relief from that overwhelming sense of anxiety. They were in danger and at risk, and the thought that the Turks might breach the walls and kill them all was real and present. It hung over them like a dark cloud.

But the real danger wasn't above them, it was beneath the walls themselves. You see, the Turks had been using their time outside the city to dig tunnels. Rather than continue to launch themselves headlong into solid, sturdy walls, they had decided going under them would be more productive. So while the people of Vienna were waiting for help, their enemy was creeping up slowly beneath them.

During the day, the soldiers inside the city watched and waited. They were observant and careful and plentiful. But at night, there were fewer eyes on the enemy army, and that's when the Turkish diggers did most of their work. They could make a bit more noise, and had the cover of darkness to hide their movements in and out of the tunnels.

Another group of people who worked through the night were the bakers in the city. If the people were going to have fresh bread each morning, that meant long nights of grinding, kneading, and baking it. And it was during one of those quiet nights when the bakers thought they heard something odd. It was almost like the sounds of digging, but it seemed to be coming from nearby, which was impossible.

And then it clicked. The digging was coming from beneath the building they were in, beneath the very city itself. They rushed out and alerted the soldiers on duty, and the warning was sounded throughout Vienna. When they routed the Turkish diggers and examined the tunnels, they were shocked to discover at least ten large explosive devices, just waiting to be detonated.

Somehow, against all odds, they had discovered their enemy's plan before it was too late, and put a stop to the invasion. Soon after, King John arrived, and the city launched its counterattack against the Ottomans. And they won. They won the battle, and in the coming years, they put an end to the westward expansion of that red and yellow crescent flag.

Those bakers were heroes, but they were also relieved citizens, and they wanted to celebrate along with everyone else. So they got to work crafting a special treat, one that would mark their victory over the Turks.

What they created was something new and different; a pastry designed to mimic the central icon of their enemy's flag. They called it the *kipfel,* which meant "crescent" in German. It was a smash hit—so much so that it's still around today, although we know it by a different name *entirely.*

The *croissant.*

A WANTED MAN

Allan was born in Scotland in the early 1800s, and from the very beginning, life was rough. His neighborhood in Glasgow was known for its poverty and crime, making it very difficult to break outside of that pattern. But Allan tried.

His father passed away before he turned ten, causing him to enter the workforce to help support his family. As he grew and worked over the years, though, he encountered new ideas and movements, one of which was known as Chartism. It was a mid-nineteenth century reform movement in Britain that called for better rights for the working class.

It wasn't a bad thing. At its core, the Chartist movement was demanding better voting rights and representation in a government that had been a bit too inaccessible for a very long time. But as in all big movements, there were some who took things too far. Violent protests and demonstrations led to arrest warrants for a number of Chartists, and Allan's name was among them.

To avoid arrest, Allan hid out at the home of friends for months. In April of 1842, though, those friends managed to sneak him aboard a ship that was headed to the United

States. For a long while, he seemed to be safe—until, that is, the ship was wrecked off the coast of Nova Scotia. Thankfully, though, Allan survived.

He eventually made his way to the Chicago area, where he set up a new life in a Scottish community known as Dundee. Allan was safe there. He had left his troubled past behind and evaded the authorities. He might have had a price on his head back home, but in America he was a free man. All he needed to do was keep a low profile, and everything would be all right.

Five years after arriving in Dundee, though, something happened to change that. Allan had rowed out to a small island in the middle of the Fox River to cut some timber, and encountered evidence of a large campsite. It was unusual enough that Allan returned to town and told the sheriff about it, and together they set up watch to see who might be using the island, and for what.

When they discovered who it was, the sheriff was astounded. A well-known counterfeiting operation had been using the island for gatherings between crimes, and thanks to Allan, all of them were captured and taken to jail. The sheriff was more than grateful for Allan's help, and made the young man a deputy as a reward.

Within two years Allan had moved to Chicago, where he joined the police force there. He was good at his job, and had an eye for details that no one else seemed to have. Before long, he became Chicago's first official detective.

His career would become something of a legend. Hated by criminals, he was plagued by assassination attempts for years. A decade after arriving in Chicago, though, it was another man's assassination that Allan managed to stop. A group of people had planned to kill newly elected President Abraham Lincoln as he traveled to Washington, DC, for his inauguration. Allan managed to stop it, though.

He went on to build a business around his skills. He left the official police force and became a freelancer, offering his private investigation services to anyone who needed them. His reputation became so great that when the Department of Justice needed to supplement their team of investigators in 1871, they hired Allan's company.

It's all a bit ironic, isn't it? A man who fled his homeland to avoid arrest for criminal activities ended up becoming the *premier* detective of the nineteenth century. His team helped track down the notorious serial killer H. H. Holmes, toppled the largest New York City crime syndicate of the day, and did battle with the outlaw Jesse James.

Most people today would recognize Allan's company if they heard the name, because it's so unusual. That's not Allan's fault, though, because as far as he was concerned, he did the logical thing and named the business after himself. As a result, his surname has become synonymous with the concept of a detective agency.

The Pinkertons.

THE RUMOR MILL

Cities are proof that the sky is the limit. Soaring towers, crowded streets, people shuffling from one thing to the next, and those miraculous feats of engineering and artistry. Cities are organic and constantly changing, and yet they're anchored in our minds and hearts by their landmarks. Imagine New York without the Empire State Building, or Paris without the Eiffel Tower. They wouldn't just look different, it would be like they didn't exist at all.

Now imagine a city rich in history and culture, home to authors, politicians, and titans of industry. This one in particular is located in northwest Germany, a little over a hundred miles from Dusseldorf. It was founded in the early 1200s, and for a very long time was known as "the city of linen." In fact, it once produced so much of the fabric that in the 1920s, it started issuing linen currency, as well as notes made of velvet and silk. This, my friends, is Bielefeld.

It's a city much like any other. It boasts a university and serves as headquarters for a number of companies, including food, plas-

tics, textiles, and home appliance manufacturers. Bethel Institution, a hospital for the mentally ill, was built in 1867 and protected patients from Nazi forces during World War II, a time when Hitler had ordered the executions of all mentally ill people across Europe.

There's a local theater, several Gothic churches, an art museum, a concert hall, a botanical garden, and even a football team: the DSC Arminia Bielefeld. And if you've made it this far, you'll notice something interesting about Bielefeld: nothing. Even though its citizens might think differently, there is nothing particularly *special* about Bielefeld. At least when compared with other cities just like it around the world.

Which is what makes one particular claim so bizarre. You see, in the dial-up days of the internet—the mid-nineties—online forums were where people gathered to gossip, joke, and talk politics before social media took over our lives. In one such forum, a German computer science student named Achim Held, posited that "Bielefeld gibt es nicht."

As with many languages, such a sentiment has multiple meanings. It could mean "Bielefeld is empty," as in, there's nothing there to do or see. But it's the other meaning that went viral long before the idea of "going viral" was even a thing:

Bielefeld, they say, doesn't exist.

According to Achim Held, the city's existence was a hoax carried out by a clandestine organization known as THEM, and anyone who said otherwise was part of the conspiracy. Of course, he knew his claim wasn't real. It was an experiment. But as we've learned from stories of undead monsters and multiple personalities, experiments can take on a life of their own. From there, the joke spiraled into a full-blown conspiracy theory, including references to the Illuminati.

One good example would be the focus on the number 23. Bielefeld's city hall sits at 23 Niederwall and its area code, 05711000, adds up to the number 23. As the concepts of memes and online folktales took off in the mid-2000s, so too did this bizarre theory.

In 2014, Bielefeld mayor Pit Clausen used the conspiracy as a way to increase tourism for the city's eight hundredth anniversary. German chancellor Angela Merkel once attended a town hall meeting there, later adding as a joke, "if it even exists."

Bielefeld certainly *does* exist, but some people still resist the idea. If you claim to have been there, or know someone who has, you might get labeled as "one of THEM." And while some may see this tale as a harmless prank, it's also slightly disturbing. One offhand comment can wipe a city off the map—in our minds, at least.

It's crazy to think that a joke like this could ever be taken seriously, but it raced around the Web for years. In 1999, finally fed up with all the lies and rumors, the city decided to issue an official press release. In it, they assured everyone that, *yes,* the city *does* in fact exist. There was just one small problem with their efforts to dispel the rumors: the date they chose to publish their announcement just happened to be the first of April.

Otherwise known as April Fools' Day.

CRASH LANDING

Eugene was born in Texas in the early 1920s. His father was a police officer who moved the family to Los Angeles shortly after Eugene's birth. After high school, Eugene, eager to follow in his father's footsteps, was accepted to Los Angeles City College where he planned on studying police science.

But plans have a habit of changing, especially when your window to the world is opened wider than you've ever seen before. Eugene quickly abandoned the idea of wearing a badge when he discovered the science of aeronautical engineering. Designing airplanes and *flying* them? It was a dream come true.

Eugene joined the United States Army Air Corps in order to obtain his pilot's license and enlisted in December of 1941, eleven days after the attack on Pearl Harbor. With the USAAC in need of reinforcements, he was sent to Oahu as part of the 394th Bomb Squadron—the same squadron responsible for piloting the B-17 Flying Fortress.

He'd been flying for a few years when his B-17, on its way out of Vanuatu, missed the runway and crashed into nearby trees. Two members of his team were killed, and Eugene, not wanting this to happen to anyone else ever again, stopped flying planes and started investigating why they crashed. He earned medals for his work, but after he left the Army he found the courage to start flying again, this time for Pan American Airways.

He thought his days of crashes were over now that he no longer faced the threat of being shot out of the sky, but some people just can't escape their fate. On June 18 of 1947, Pan Am Flight 121 was scheduled to depart from Karachi, Pakistan, and deliver twenty-six passengers and ten crew members—including third officer Eugene—all the way to Istanbul.

Everything seemed to be going fine for several hours until one of the engines failed. Thankfully, the other engines compensated to keep the bird in the air, but that caused them to overheat. Eventually one of them caught fire, and then fell off the aircraft.

With two engines down, the plane descended, eventually crash-landing in the Syrian desert. Fifteen people had died, while another eleven passengers were in dire need of medical attention. Eugene suffered a few broken ribs, but that didn't stop him from assuming control of the situation and dragging passengers out of the burning wreckage to safety.

And that was the final straw for Eugene. Between the tragedies of his time in the military and this new civilian crash, he was ready to walk away from flying ships forever. He resigned from Pan Am a short while later, and began to pursue that original dream of becoming a police officer.

That dream brought him back to LA, where his father's footsteps were waiting for him. He served for a time in the traffic division, but was eventually moved to the Public Information Division, where he developed a taste for writing—a taste that grew into an insatiable hunger. Suddenly, Eugene saw a way to put all his expertise to better use.

The 1950s had arrived, and with them came the dawn of a new age in entertainment. Motion pictures were expensive to make, and audiences didn't always want to go out to enjoy a few hours of distraction. But television was a different story, and thanks to his police knowledge, Eugene landed a job as an advisor on a new crime procedural.

The show ran for just one year before being canceled. He went on to pitch a number of other TV shows—all with lawyers and cops—but none of them lasted beyond a handful of episodes. To pay his bills, he wrote scripts for already-established shows.

Life seemed to be one fiery wreck after another—both literal and metaphorical—but he understood that out of failure came new opportunities for success. If the networks didn't want shows centered around police officers and lawyers, then Eugene would look somewhere else for inspiration. So, he looked up.

Eugene had explored the sky and crashed to Earth. He was a survivor who had saved numerous lives, and a decorated pilot with a brilliant mind. So rather than give Hollywood more of the same-old, he used his past to make something futuristic. And in 1966, it arrived: a diverse new crew on a bold mission.

And it's still with us today. Thanks to everything he experienced in his early years, Eugene Wesley Roddenberry gifted us with one of the most beloved and influential science fiction worlds ever created.

Star Trek.

UNBALANCED BREAKFAST

Before Atkins. Before South Beach. Before Jazzercise and SoulCycle and Tae Bo, there was Battle Creek Sanitarium. Founded in 1866 in Battle Creek, Michigan, the sanitarium wasn't a mental health facility like we're used to seeing today. Back then, the word "sanitarium" was a variation on the word "sanatorium," which came to define a health resort for injured soldiers.

It had been owned and operated by the Seventh-day Adventists, a denomination of Protestants who believed in healthy living straight from the Good Book. No meat, no shellfish, and definitely no alcohol or tobacco were allowed. It was strict, but some people believed it was also beneficial.

Strangely enough, not a whole lot of people went for that sort of thing. Battle Creek started small, with no more than a hundred patients in the beginning. But when Dr. John Harvey arrived at the turn of the century, he wanted to change all that. Under Dr. John's leadership, he quickly grew the sanitarium's meager attendance from a hundred to more than seven thousand patients with a staff of over eight hundred assisting at any given time. He turned Battle Creek into a well-oiled machine dedicated to making lives better . . . for a nominal fee, of course.

John was himself a Seventh-day Adventist and, as part of his theology, believed strongly in the church's push toward vegetarianism and away from sin. In order to achieve the latter, he developed what was referred to as a "bland diet" consisting mostly of yogurt, nuts, peanut butter, and starches. A bland diet was the key to abstinence in his mind, brought on by the lack of stimulation of the taste buds.

Patients at Battle Creek were also encouraged to take part in various activities to aid in their recoveries, including light therapy, afternoon marches around the premises to assist with digestion, and even regular enemas. John believed the root of all evil in the body was bacterial toxins, and his combination of a bland diet with rigorous exercise was meant to help clear that nastiness right out.

While he ran Battle Creek, John filed patents for several inventions that would help those who stayed there, including a radiant-heat bath, massage tools, and exercise equipment. He'd made numerous strides in medical devices under what he called "physiotherapy," but there was something missing. Something from the other side of the equation. He'd done all he could for the patients physically, but now needed to revolutionize their diets.

The idea had come to him in a dream one night. It was for a new kind of bread, one that would be easier to chew at breakfast when people had just woken up. The following day, John walked down to the kitchen and mixed a dough made of wheat, oats, and corn. What came out wasn't very appetizing and he left it there for a few days while attending to sanitarium business. When he came back, the mixture had hardened and John almost threw it out, but then he had another idea.

Rather than waste all that food, he rolled it out and baked it and what he ended up with were crispy little flakes. John had stumbled onto something big here. So big, it would go on to spawn an entirely new category of food: the breakfast cereal. It just so happened that John Harvey Kellogg had invented corn flakes.

But the story doesn't end there. Just when Kellogg's corn flakes had hit the sanitarium's breakfast tables, a down-on-his-luck businessman sought out Dr. Kellogg to help cure his chronic health problems. This businessman, inspired by the doctor's delicious new breakfast cereal, returned home with ambitions of his own. While his first product, a cereal beverage called Postum, didn't do so well, his sophomore endeavor was a huge hit.

It was called Grape-Nuts, named for the fruity aroma given off during the manufacturing process. And its creator, C. W. Post, had inadvertently kicked off what would be known for decades as the Cereal Wars.

GETTING AHEAD

As a child, Larry Walters had dreams of soaring high above the clouds. After all, he was from Los Angeles, a place where people from all over the world came to follow their great big dreams and find great big success.

Larry applied for the United States Air Force after high school in the hopes of becoming a fighter pilot. Gliding through the sky and zooming past the clouds were all he wanted to do. The Air Force couldn't help him, though. Not with his terrible eyesight. He was rejected and eventually found work as a trucker, as well as a part-time gig at a television studio. Two jobs about as far from the sky as you can get without working on a submarine.

But his boyhood dreams never really went away. He remembered a trip to a military surplus store in his teen years where he saw weather balloons hanging from the ceiling, the kind meteorologists sent into the atmosphere to take readings of air pressure, temperature, and humidity. They were strong, made of rubber and meant to carry heavy loads.

They would have to do. Larry and his girlfriend forged a requisition from the TV studio for forty-five weather balloons and several tanks of helium, telling the vendor they were for a local commercial shoot. Well, Larry wasn't entirely lying. He'd definitely be on TV by the end of all this. It was 1982, long before the phrase "going viral" was attached to anything but deadly pandemics. Still, what he was about to attempt would definitely get him a slot on the six o'clock news.

Call it a midlife crisis. Call it *inspiration.* That's what Larry did when he filled all forty-five of his weather balloons and tied them to a metal lawn chair. He dubbed the vessel the "Inspiration I," and launched it from his home in San Pedro, California, with himself as its sole passenger, along with a BB gun, a CB radio, and a camera by his side.

Each balloon measured four feet across when fully inflated and together, all forty-five of them carried him to an altitude of sixteen thousand feet in no time. Two commercial airliners noticed the makeshift craft and notified the FAA of the not-so-unidentified flying object. Only a few minutes into his trip, and he was already famous.

But Larry was in a bind. The chair had risen so quickly and to such a height, he worried shooting the balloons might cause the chair to become unbalanced and spit him out. He lifted the BB gun to his shoulder and, one by one, popped a few balloons. The chair slowly descended with Larry holding on for dear life.

Forty-five minutes had passed since the launch and he was coasting his way to an easy landing when the worst happened: Larry lost his grip. Not on the chair, but on the BB gun. His landing gear, for lack of a better phrase, had fallen off and now it was up to gravity and the California winds to carry him to safety.

Well, safety was the first choice. The winds had another idea. As the chair floated down, the cables from the popped balloons dangled below and got caught on power lines in Long Beach. They caused a blackout across the entire town, but Larry *survived,* and managed to climb down from his first predicament and into a brand new one.

The Long Beach police department knew all about his little excursion, and they'd been waiting. They took him into custody for violating the Federal Aviation Act. He paid a fine, but since no one got hurt, he didn't face any jail time. He did, however, enjoy his fifteen minutes of fame, appearing in a Timex ad, and doing some motivational speaking across the country.

Eventually, Larry's wild idea led others to follow in his . . . air steps? No fewer than five people have attempted similar trips using balloons and deck chairs. And while Larry might not have fulfilled his dream of flying a fighter plane for the Air Force, his story *did* become the basis for several episodes of hit TV shows, including *The A-Team* and *Hill Street Blues.*

Oh, and a major film from Disney and Pixar: *Up.*

Let's face it, if you're looking for fame, you can't get much higher than that.

ART IMITATES LIFE

His name was Pedro Gonzalez, and to some he was known as "the man of the woods." No, he didn't live among the trees or off the grid. It was the mid-1500s— there *was* no grid yet. He was born in Tenerife, one of the Spanish Canary Islands off the coast of Africa, and he was . . . well, he was a little strange. To those who knew him, he was a curiosity, unlike anyone they'd ever seen before.

Pedro had a condition now known as hypertrichosis, although at the time those who suffered from the condition were simply called "wild men" or "animals." See, Pedro had hair. A *lot* of hair. I don't mean long locks like Rapunzel. Rather, his entire face and body, from his forehead to his toes, were covered in thick, dark hairs.

Given the lack of human rights laws at the time, it wasn't long before young Pedro's condition made him a target for opportunistic kidnappers. He was taken from his home and thrown in a metal cage, where he was fed raw meat and kept like property. A pet. In fact, he was eventually sent to

France as a gift for King Henry II's coronation in 1547.

Once in France, things didn't go as expected. I mean, they couldn't have gotten much worse, but King Henry didn't react the way another king might have. Rather than accept the gift and throw Pedro in a dungeon or parade him around the kingdom on a leash, he took mercy on the boy. He saw his humanity where others saw only an animal, and so the King decided to try something.

He plucked the young man from his cage and had him educated by the best teachers in the land. In a not-so-benevolent gesture, he forced Pedro to use the Latin form of his name, Petrus Gonsalvus. He wore clothes of fine silk, ate delicious, warm meals, and learned to speak, read, and write in three different languages. He had reached noble status without having to be born or marry into it. Quite a feat for someone who, only years earlier, had been forced to eat raw meat in a cage where he slept.

Unfortunately, no one else saw him as a nobleman. He still bore the symptoms of a man with hypertrichosis. Shaving didn't work—the hair just grew back. What's worse, Gonsalvus's adoptive father, King Henry, was killed in a jousting match twelve years after he'd taken the boy under his wing. Since he was still technically a gift for the king, he now became the property of the king's widow, Catherine de' Medici.

Catherine did not prove as generous as her late husband. She, too, had an experiment planned for Petrus, one that changed the lives of two innocent people in the name of morbid curiosity. Catherine wanted to know if Petrus and his wife could conceive children and pass on his condition.

There was only one problem: Petrus didn't have a wife. Not to worry, though. Catherine was resourceful. She ordered the young daughter of one of her servants to marry him, and it didn't take long for the newlyweds to start a family. All in all, they had seven children, four of whom were also born with hypertrichosis. The queen was thrilled her experiment had paid off.

Yeah, the whole story sounds awful and cringeworthy. These were not civilized times, but in a way, some good did come of Petrus's change in status.

His story was told for generations, and like with any story, it took on a life of its own. Soon, Petrus wasn't a medical anomaly, but a cursed prince. And his wife had turned into a villager held captive in a hidden castle. Eventually, someone wrote it all down, someone named Gabrielle-Suzanne Barbot de Villeneuve. And that story she wrote became the origin of a tale we all know and love today.

A tale as old as time, you might say.

That's right. Before the talking teapots and dancing candelabras, there was Petrus Gonsalvus and his wife, Catherine: the real-life inspirations for *Beauty and the Beast*.

SPACE CASE

We all have days where we don't quite feel like ourselves. We wake up on the wrong side of the bed, we miss that early morning latte to get ourselves going, or we notice something is just . . . off. It doesn't take much for one little thing to throw our whole world off balance. However, in one man's case, something had been wrong for some time; he didn't quite feel right on *two* worlds.

Kirk Allen first showed up on Dr. Lindner's Baltimore doorstep in the mid-1940s. A physician in a governmental research facility across the country had asked Dr. Lindner to provide a second opinion on his patient. Mr. Allen didn't have a deadly disease or anything, but his symptoms were unique. The physician just wanted to make sure the man did not pose a threat to himself or his colleagues.

Kirk Allen had had no outbursts or incidents while employed at the research station. He got along just fine with his coworkers and no one questioned the quality of his work. However, the people around him were worried. You see, Kirk Allen believed he had two homes. I don't mean two houses in different cities; he believed he spent half of his time on Earth and the other half on another planet.

He spoke matter-of-factly about it, as though it were perfectly normal for him. In a way, the other planet was a means of escape for him. He'd been born in Hawaii to a wealthy diplomat father. His mother, a native Hawaiian, spent most of her days working and was almost never with her son. With both parents absent, Kirk spent his formative years in the care of nurses and governesses.

The governesses were tasked with educating him, which proved difficult, as Kirk had an unquenchable curiosity and a passion for learning. He loved to read and his teachers had trouble keeping up. And one governess was so obsessed with cleanliness, she instilled in the young Kirk a debilitating fear of germs from the very environment and people he'd grown up around.

When *she* left, another governess, named Ms. Lilian, entered his life. By then, he'd already been living within two worlds: that of a child with everything he needed, and that of a child who lacked parents in a real and practical way. Because of that, crossing the line into adulthood wasn't easy.

But he still had books. When the world was weighing down on him and he felt like he needed to get away, he retreated into the pages of fantasy and science fiction stories. The Wizard of Oz books had been his favorite until one day when a crate of books was delivered to his house. There were religious texts, essay collections, and biographies, but Kirk found himself drawn to a novel by an English author he recognized.

The main character immediately caught

his attention, as he and Kirk shared the same name. He finished the book in a single day, then read it again. He reread it three times before moving on to another book with a character who also bore the name Kirk Allen. The third time he discovered a main character with the same name as his, he felt nothing, almost like it had been fated to happen.

It had been these latest stories, a series of American science fiction novels about an Earth-born man taken to another planet, that captivated him in a way no other books had. He didn't just become engrossed in the tales. The fourteen-year-old Allen truly believed they were about him. An older, wiser him. Biographies of a life he'd lived among the stars. Every detail, every character the fictional Kirk encountered was instantly recognizable to the real person.

To Kirk, while his physical body went to work, ate in diners, and slept in the same bed every night, another piece of him was off having fantastic adventures battling strange creatures and wooing galactic princesses. It was as though the author had found out about the real Kirk Allen and transcribed his life story. And once he'd read through all the volumes of his "biography," Kirk began writing his own.

Kirk did his best to stay grounded in reality. He earned a degree and tried to build a normal life for himself on Earth. But he never forgot about his obsession. He started filling in the gaps in the stories and building them out with what he thought were his own memories—memories that eventually turned into hallucinations. Kirk was told to seek help, or find employment elsewhere.

Which brings us to Dr. Lindner's office. The good doctor saw only one way of curing Kirk Allen of his delusions: by entertaining them. He went along with his patient, establishing that his memories of intergalactic space travel were real. From there, the two men worked back through his real biography, including all the neglect and abuse that had brought him to this point. It was only when Kirk understood *why* he'd believed the stories were about him that he was able to shake the delusion.

There was just one problem: Dr. Lindner had now become obsessed with Kirk's stories. He found himself daydreaming and fantasizing not just about new adventures on distant planets, but the very idea of allowing one's brain to exist on another plane of existence while the body languished on Earth.

It seemed a bit of Dr. Lindner's patient had rubbed off on him, though not to the same degree. He understood that none of it was real. But he wondered if it could be real. Could we be in two places at once? Could we bear memories of lives unlived? We may never know, just like we may never know the real Kirk Allen.

Kirk Allen was a pseudonym used to protect his identity. The fictional character's name was also not Kirk Allen. Some have theorized the books that kicked off the man's obsession was the Barsoom series by Edgar Rice Burroughs. To this day, though, we still don't know his real identity, which only adds to the mystery behind the man.

What isn't so mysterious is how what happened to Kirk Allen could have happened to *anyone*. The books we read have a tendency to affect us in ways we aren't even aware of at the time. Perhaps the author George R. R. Martin said it best:

"A reader lives a thousand lives before he dies. The man who never reads lives only one."

LOVE NOTES

It doesn't take a lot to change the world. Just one small act can set off a chain of events that could shape the future for generations to come. And oftentimes, those acts occur under duress, when there is much to lose and little to gain in the short term.

During Prohibition, the government took away alcohol across the US under the belief they were curing the nation of abhorrent behavior. Working-class folks turned to bootlegging and hoarding to get by, and their combined efforts eventually led to the repeal of the draconian law.

However, 1,600 years earlier, it was a Roman priest who broke the law of the land, and his rebellion against the Empire did more than change that law—it changed the *world*.

Around AD 269, at the height of the rule of Emperor Claudius II, Rome was on a bloody path of war and destruction. Claudius needed his armies to be bigger and stronger. There was only one problem: nobody wanted to join up.

Roman men at the time had no interest in traveling across Europe to fight on behalf of a cruel and despotic leader. Legend has it that Claudius was so strong that he could knock out a horse's tooth with a single punch. He had no patience for formalities, and positioned himself as the opposite of the aristocratic emperors who had come before. He was a soldier through and through—and he expected his men to follow suit.

Because he was a soldier with deep affinity for the military, he had no time for silly things like marriage or family life. In fact, Claudius believed it was the concept of family that was keeping men from joining his ranks. They were soft and weak, he said.

By getting married and raising children, they were not living up to their full potential as soldiers of Rome. However, rather than incentivize new recruits with promises of fame and glory—you know, positive reinforcement—Claudius took the opposite turn: he simply banned marriage.

It was a harsh move, for sure, and one that did not go unnoticed by the church. A local priest did not agree with the declaration. He believed people should be able to pursue their love despite what the emperor thought. Government had no right to deny what God had already blessed.

Though he knew it was illegal, the priest found a way to rebel against Claudius. He began performing clandestine marriage ceremonies for Roman couples looking to build better lives for themselves. Unfortunately, just as had happened with speakeasies during Prohibition, the authorities found out about the secret ceremonies taking place right under the emperor's nose.

They arrested the priest and paraded him in front of the prefect of Rome for a trial. Neither his testimony on true love, nor his duties as a man of the cloth made any difference to the Roman courts. He had defied Emperor Claudius, and made a mockery of his position.

The priest's fate had been sealed long before his trial. He was sentenced to death, which sentence was to be carried out over a series of beatings and stonings before his eventual decapitation. Claudius was going to make an example out of this traitor for anyone else looking to challenge him so defiantly.

The priest was held in prison for a short time before his death, and during his stay, something unexpected happened. He found love, not unlike the young couple he had married in secret. And despite the obvious barriers keeping the two apart, their relationship flourished.

You see, he had fallen in love with someone outside his prison cell: the daughter of one of his jailers. During the brief time they had, they exchanged notes and letters professing their love for each other, all the way up to the day of the priest's execution.

He was beheaded for his crimes as ordered, and went down in history as a martyr for his cause on behalf of lovers everywhere. And it was because of his efforts to stand up to an unjust and immoral law that he was later named a saint.

And because he died on February 14, we remember him on that same day each year, signing letters and cards to our loved ones with *his* name, not ours.

"From . . . your *Valentine*."

AND THE
WINNER IS . . .

Good help can be hard to find. When it comes to fixing things around the house, or repairing our cars, we want to know the people we're depending on are skilled and reliable.

Sometimes, we might ask a friend for a recommendation. Or we'll search online and read reviews. Well, Louis B. Mayer didn't have the internet to help him back in 1926.

The West Coast head of a major film studio had a very big job and an army of workers on his payroll. He just didn't realize how much it would cost him in the long run.

Mayer had come to the United States from Russia with his family in 1887. He then relocated with them to Canada where he started attending school. He grew up poor in what his nephew would later call "a crappy childhood."

But Mayer eventually found his way back to the United States. He worked his way up from Massachusetts theater owner, to film distributor, all the way to the head of his own studio by the 1920s.

Louis B. Mayer Pictures did well at first, but really started to make waves once the it merged with two other studios: Metro Pictures and Goldwyn Pictures, forming the colossal Hollywood Voltron known as Metro-Goldwyn-Mayer, or MGM Studios.

Mayer was made head of West Coast operations and saw great success, especially as the studio made the move from silent film to talkies. And with that success . . . came a lot of money. So Mayer did what any millionaire would do in his situation: he invested in real estate.

He decided to build a house near the Santa Monica beach, a ritzy area where the wealthy liked to play. There was just one problem: building a house was a massive undertaking. It required architects, construction workers, electricians, and an army of others to bring his dream to fruition.

All those laborers would cost a lot of money, and waiting for an architect to draft plans would mean more time not being spent in a brand-new mansion on the beach. Rather than go through all of that, he turned to the set designers at MGM to build his new home in time for the summer.

They would accomplish in weeks what would take carpenters months to complete.

Head of design at the studio, Cedric Gibbons, sketched out a plan for the home, while Joe Cohn, his production manager, put together a build schedule with his team. The whole project would take six weeks and require three shifts of builders working 24/7.

Unfortunately for Mayer, there was yet another wrench waiting to be thrown into his well-oiled machine: the studio's labor union. They were about to sign a new contract guaranteeing them overtime pay and higher rates.

This meant the cost of Mayer's summer home was about to skyrocket. Cohn managed to work out a deal where a few workers from the studio would work on the house while the rest of the labor was outsourced somewhere cheaper. The plan worked and Mayer's summer home was finished in the spring of 1926.

But the whole ordeal made him nervous. Carpenters and painters were one thing, but what would happen if the actors got the idea to unionize? Or the directors? A union meant more than just better pay. It also meant health insurance and a pension . . . and less money for MGM.

Mayer wasn't about to lose the studio's profits to the people who kept it afloat. So he got an idea. He reached out to other Hollywood bigwigs and got them involved in creating a new organization—the Academy of Motion Picture Arts and Sciences, or AMPAS.

It would unite all five branches of the film industry under one banner—actors, writers, directors, producers, and technicians—and give Mayer the opportunity to decorate them in gold.

He believed that filmmakers were simple folk. All they really wanted was recognition for their craft. That recognition took

the form of an awards ceremony, the first of which was held at the Hollywood Roosevelt Hotel on May 16 of 1929.

It was hosted by actor and AMPAS president Douglas Fairbanks and honored the members of the industry responsible for making some of the best pictures released between August of 1927 and July of 1928.

Those who won took home a bronze statue plated in gold. It was designed by the person who had helped Mayer craft his summer house, Cedric Gibbons. He'd designed it to look like a man standing on a film reel and holding a sword with its tip pointed down.

According to one Hollywood legend, Academy librarian Margaret Herrick took one look at the statue and remarked that it looked just like her uncle Oscar. Well, the name stuck, and today, the Academy Awards—or "Oscars"—are held every year to pay respect to the men, women, and children of the film industry who continue to entertain us, all year round.

But more important, now *you* know that the Academy Awards were nothing more than a star-studded union-busting tactic meant to keep laborers from organizing.

Of course, it failed to work, and the unions came anyway. Despite that, they kept the award ceremony around—because who doesn't love getting dressed up to take home a trophy?

UNCANNY

PEOPLE

ALWAYS PRESENT

He was a philosopher by trade, which gave him the tools he needed to be an extraordinary social reformer. Jeremy Bentham was born in London in 1748, and graduated with his masters from The Queen's College, Oxford at the young age of just eighteen. And he seems like a progressive personality born well ahead of his time.

Bentham was an advocate for the separation of church and state, for equal rights for women, and for the abolition of slavery. He fought to put an end to corporal punishment and the death penalty, and called for the fair treatment of animals. And on top of all of that, he's considered one of the spiritual founders of University College London, and is still remembered fondly there today.

He also lived in an age when it was difficult to find enough corpses for medical study. Back then, only executed criminals were acceptable subjects for dissection by medical students. Unless, of course, a generous individual chose to donate their own body willingly. Which, at the age of twenty-one, is exactly what Bentham promised to do.

He lived a long and fruitful life after that, don't worry. He made contributions to the fields of economics, legal reform, and gender studies, and he also published extensively. But I think you get it. Bentham was a smart guy who did a lot of great things. A lot of people still look back with respect and admiration for what he accomplished. Got it? Good.

Because then he died. People saw it coming, of course; he was eighty-four when it happened, which was impressive for the 1830s. But in the month prior to his death, he set about putting two connected projects into action. The first was the donation of his body to science that he had promised more than sixty years before, and sure enough, two days after his death a group of friends and students gathered to watch Dr. Thomas Southwood Smith conduct the procedure.

Afterward, Bentham's skeleton was preserved and set aside for the next step. Except his head. With flesh and hair and teeth all intact and untouched, Smith used a procedure to mummify Bentham's head and freeze the decay. But something went wrong, and the dead man's head was left a bit too dark and taut for most people's taste. In the end, they were forced to make a wax replica.

When they were ready, they brought all of Bentham's parts over to his second project: his cabinet. It had been built prior to his death and set aside for this very moment. It's a large wooden display case that sort of resembles a really nice phone booth, complete with doors that open and lovely dark paneling inside. And it's big enough for a grown man to sit inside comfortably.

One of Bentham's favorite chairs was

placed inside the cabinet, and then his skeleton was dressed in his own clothing. They stuffed hay inside the outfit to flesh it out, so to speak, and then sat the whole thing down in the chair, with that wax head on top. They even added his walking cane for good measure.

His real head caused a lot more trouble than people expected, if you'd care to know. Other than the fact that it's just a bit too gruesome to look at, it's also been stolen a few times by University students. These days, it's locked away and safely out of sight—and out of reach, as well.

All these years later, you can still visit Jeremy Bentham. His wooden cabinet is typically on display in the main building of the University College London. Although on rare occasions his body has been removed from its cabinet so that he can sit in on important gatherings of the College Council. They even record his presence in the meeting minutes.

His status? "Present, but not voting."

COPIED

When the King arrived in the small town just a few miles from Milan, Italy, he was exhausted and hungry from his long day of travel. He had come to oversee a sporting competition the following day, and to present all of the awards to the winners. But first order of business was to find a meal and then get rest.

King Umberto I was born in 1844, and had been king of Italy for over twelve years when he arrived in town that day in July of 1900. Historians consider him to be a fairly unimpressive king, even after taking his prior military career into consideration. That's all right, though; not every ruler can be extraordinary.

Umberto and a friend located a small restaurant nearby, and found a seat in the back. Honored to have the king in his restaurant, the owner himself came out to take their orders, which was when the conversation stopped. There was something familiar about the owner that caused the king to stare in astonishment.

The two men were nearly identical in appearance, and both of them mentioned as much. Same face, same height, same weight. They two of them could easily have passed as twins. So the king asked for more details. It turned out they both even shared the same birthdate—right down to the year—and each of them had married a woman with the same name on the same date.

The coincidences continued to pile up. Similar military careers, although with different ranks, and two separate occasions when both men were in the same promotional ceremony at the same time. The king was astounded, and said as much.

After the restaurant owner left to have the food prepared, the king told his friend that he would give this amazing stranger the gift of a royal position the following day, and asked that the man be invited to the award ceremony, which he dutifully did.

But the man never showed up. With the events of the day playing out around him, the king had taken a seat and asked his friend where the restaurant owner had gone. The friend was sad to inform him of the terrible news that the man had gone hunting that morning and been killed by a stray bullet. The king's double—the man who had mirrored every significant moment of his own life, and even looked like him—was gone, less than a day after meeting him.

The king didn't have time to grieve, though. A moment after learning of the man's death, a number of gunshots rang out in the crowd around him, and the king toppled over, the red blossoms of gunshot wounds appearing on his clothing.

They had shared everything, it seems. Even death.

BROTHERHOOD

Jimmy ran away to join the circus.

I know, it's a bit stereotypical, but I promise you it's the truth. He jumped on a train in Brooklyn, and let it take him all the way to Nebraska. Somewhere between those two locations, though, he tossed the circus idea out the window and decided to see what else life might have in store for him.

When he arrived in Nebraska, he stepped off the train and began a new life with a clean slate. He even changed his name. From that moment on, he would be Richard Hart. He worked to get rid of his thick Brooklyn accent, made friends, and built a career. Life was good.

He spent time in the army, and served as an officer in France during World War I, but eventually returned home. Because that's what Homer, Nebraska, had become for him. It was home.

In 1919, a flash flood swept through town. Hart managed to save the local grocery store owner, and as a result the grocer thought so highly of Hart that he allowed the man to date his daughter. The pair eventually married, too.

During Prohibition, Hart served as an investigator, seeking out bootleggers and bringing them to justice. When he began wearing a pair of guns—one pistol on each hip—the locals started calling him "Two-Gun" Hart. He was effective, too, making numerous arrests and shutting down dozens of operations, and all that success earned him a new job as the town marshal there in Homer.

But that's when the cracks started to show. Richard Hart, they said, was a wolf in sheep's clothing. He had a track record for being more than a little too violent with the Native Americans he encountered, and he had been accused a number of times of petty theft while performing his duty as marshal.

His true nature was catching up with him, it seemed. When he was removed from his post as marshal, he found himself unemployed and running out of money. So he reached out to the family he had abandoned years before, sending a letter to one of his brothers for help. In response, that brother sent a check. The following month, he sent another. And on and on it went, with the generosity of his family helping him stay afloat and pay the bills.

That's the thing about family. When times are tough, they always seem to be there. They rally around us, lift us up, and give us what we need. Richard Hart's own family seemed completely normal in that respect.

Expect they weren't. They were so *far* from normal that it's no wonder little Jimmy had left town decades before and then changed his name. Because even though they were blood, they were dangerous.

Don't believe me? Then I'd recommend doing a bit of light reading about Jimmy's brother Alphonse, because I guarantee it'll open your eyes. After all, there's a reason Jimmy's brother had a lot of money. He was a mobster—perhaps *the* mobster—who'd built a career and fortune in the illegal bootlegging industry.

Jimmy's brother Alphonse, you see, was none other than the legendary crime boss himself: Al Capone.

GET ME OUT

William was what you might call an explorer. He grew up at the end of the nineteenth century at a time in America when war was raging across the state of Kentucky. No, not that kind of war. This was the Kentucky Cave Wars, which was a sort of competition between the people lucky enough to own land over large cave systems who wanted to sell tickets to tourists.

Honestly, it was like a lot of things in life: if there's money to be made, people have a tendency to get competitive about it. But of course, this was a pretty odd business opportunity. If you owned land with access to a cave that people could walk into and look around, you could sell tickets for admission and make a living. Except in Kentucky there are a *lot* of caves.

William was thirty-seven years old, and lived on his father's land in central Kentucky. About a decade before, he had discovered a cave on the family property there, and had begun selling tickets to visitors—but there was a problem. The more popular Mammoth Cave was easier to get to, so it had the majority of the business in the area.

Not one to be deterred, William formed a plan. If he could find another entrance to his family's own cave system—perhaps even one that was closer to the foot traffic near Mammoth Cave—they might be able to increase their business. So William went exploring, and in 1925 he found something promising.

He called it Sand Cave, and set about exploring it properly, to make sure it would work for his goals. On January 30, though, he was crawling through a narrow part of the cave when his lantern went out, leaving him in the dark. Normally a very careful man, William accidentally kicked a large boulder, which somehow rolled onto one of his legs, crushing it and trapping him in the dark.

His brothers and friends tried to get him out but failed. Rescue workers failed as well. A local college offered to send their entire basketball team, but the offer was politely declined. They did their best to keep William's spirits up, and brought him food and water, but at the end of the day he was trapped in a small cave, and that horror wasn't about to just go away.

On February 4—six days after becoming trapped—a group of men took him a meal, and on their way out the entrance to the cave collapsed. William was still pinned beneath the boulder, but now he was also cut off from the rest of the world. His rescuers began to dig down from a different location, but it took them ten days. When they finally broke through and reached him on February 16, he was already dead.

It took William's family another two months to retrieve his body, which they buried on their farm on April 24 of 1925. And then, oddly, the entire family sold the farm two years later, moving away and leaving the family cemetery behind.

The new owner, being very aware of the story of William's death, saw a business opportunity. He dug up the explorer's body and moved it to the cave there on his own land. He even had a glass box made for it so that everyone who visited would have a good view, like the curiosity it was.

It sat in its glass case for nearly two years, but in March of 1929 someone broke in and stole William's body. When it was recovered a week later, the damaged leg was missing. They had the corpse put inside a metal coffin, secured it with chains, and then placed it deeper inside the cave. It stayed there until 1989.

There might be a silver lining to all of this, though. When William became trapped in the cave back in 1925, the media went wild. Historians believe that roughly fifty thousand tourists came to the cave during those two weeks of agony for William. They bought food and drink from the local vendors, and then visited other nearby caves. Over fifty reporters traveled there as well, each one hoping to write *the* great account of the ordeal. William Floyd Collins was a star—for a while.

The result was an explosion in public awareness of the Kentucky cave systems. In 1941, the US government declared the entire Mammoth Cave area to be a national park, protecting it for future generations to enjoy. Each year, over half a million people step inside and do a little exploring of their own.

Safely, I hope.

THE KNOCKOUT

John L. Sullivan was known as the "Boston Strong Boy." Born in 1858 to Irish immigrants, John grew up in the South End of Boston. His parents wanted him to become a priest, but during his first year of college he discovered two things: he loved to play baseball, and he was really good at it.

Sullivan dropped out of college around 1875 and entered the world of professional baseball, a journey that lasted about eight years. According to him, that was about the time that he switched over to a new sport: boxing.

He started out as part of a boxing tour. He and five other men traveled the country by train, stopping almost every day in a new place to fight each other and sometimes even a local volunteer. The tour lasted 238 days, during which time they participated in 195 matches in 136 different places. Sullivan knocked out eleven opponents during the tour.

Now keep in mind, this was the late 1880s. Sullivan sometimes fought bareknuckled, meaning his opponents weren't always given the benefit of a padded glove to the face. Then again, neither was Sullivan. That's okay, though, he loved the sport and was considered the best in the world during his time. And over the course of his decade-long career, he was only ever knocked out once, which was how he lost his final match in 1892, in fact.

Which is sort of true, but not really. Yes, Sullivan was officially knocked out only once, but someone else had laid the Boston Strong Boy out cold shortly before he retired. That fighter was named Donahue. Donahue helped run a boxing school out of the city of Worcester, Massachusetts, but in 1892, Sullivan had been participating in a small theater tour where he boxed with others onstage in front of large crowds, and a friend introduced him to Donahue.

The thing is, Donahue wasn't actually a boxer, but working in a boxing school was a great way to pick up all the tricks of the trade. Sort of like how kids learn things from their parents just by watching and practicing what they see. Donahue, it turned out, was a quick study.

One night during this touring boxing exhibition, Sullivan called out from the stage that he would beat any man who came onstage. If he failed, he would pay them a reward, but of course, Sullivan never failed. He was the Boston Strong Boy, after all. Most of the time, Sullivan would hit them once and they would fall over and not get back up.

But Donahue changed all of that. They actually managed to last two full rounds before things got interesting in the third when Sullivan caught Donahue with a powerful blow to the face. But Donahue, unlike all the other contenders that night, refused to go down. Instead, all of that pain and rage became a sort of rocket fuel, ready to explode.

With a savage scream, Donahue lashed out and connected with the champion's jaw. For a brief instant, it looked as if nothing would happen. Then, like a tall pine hit with a lumberjack's ax, the Boston Strong Boy silently toppled over, hitting the canvas with a sick thud. He was out cold.

Boxers get knocked out, we all know that. And while it's unusual for Sullivan to have gone a decade without that happening to him during an official match, we might be able to accept that there were other moments when it could have taken place. This theater match in 1892 was just that rare moment. Few would ever be able to claim they had seem the champion felled by another fighter. The folks in this audience became members of an elite crowd.

Because of the knockout, sure, but also because of something else. Like I mentioned before, Donahue wasn't a boxer. Amateurs weren't supposed to be able to level a professional like that.

Could it have been a lucky punch? Sure. But that still wouldn't change the most surprising detail of all: John L. Sullivan, the Boston Strong Boy, had been knocked out by a woman.

Mrs. *Hessie* Donahue.

FROZEN DINNER

Francis had found himself in possession of an abundance of free time. It's a long story that I honestly don't want to get into here, but let's just say that he had been working in one field for most of his life, but a mistake at the age of sixty-five earned him some prison time, a hefty fine, and permanent expulsion from the industry he loved.

So there he was, in March of 1626, with not much else to occupy his time. As the story goes, he was riding in his carriage through the snow-covered streets of the village of Highgate, now a suburb located to the north of London, when he called for his driver to stop near Pond Square. An *idea* had fallen out of the air and struck him—metaphorically, of course.

He had been watching other carriages pass by, and noticed how their wheels pulled up the snow to reveal the grass beneath. What struck him as odd, though, was that the grass was always perfectly green, rather than dead and yellow. And it occurred to him that maybe the snow had something to do with that.

Francis climbed out of the carriage into the damp, cold air, and looked around. Calling his driver over, he instructed the man to go to a nearby farm and purchase a chicken. When the coachman returned, he was told to kill the bird, pluck it clean, and clean its insides out, as if he were preparing it for a meal.

When the pale white remnant of the chicken was ready, Francis took it and laid it in the snow alongside the park there. A crowd began to gather as this strange man started doing even stranger things. First, he scooped up handful after handful of snow and packed it into the chicken's abdominal cavity. Then, after retrieving a cloth sack from the carriage, he put the chicken inside and packed it in with even more snow.

Remember, this was 1626, so even though the sight of a frozen chicken at the grocery store might strike us as normal, there were no freezers back then. What Francis was testing was a theory that we all know would pay off—snow, because of its cold temperature, could preserve raw meat for later. It was genius.

Sadly, Francis wouldn't live to see if his hypothesis worked. That hour out in the wet and cold must have weakened his body, and by that evening he was in bed with pneumonia. A few days later he was dead. The frozen chicken, as far as I can tell, disappeared after that.

There are stories, of course. There always are in situations like this. Many people over the years have claimed to see the pale shape of a naked chicken running around the area of Pond Square. The most common version of these sightings is that the bird appears from nowhere, runs in a circle two or three times, and then vanishes.

While the tales of the ghostly chicken

might fall within the realm of fantasy, Francis is embedded firmly in the pages of history. He's been referred to as the "father of empiricism" who used inductive reasoning to build scientific knowledge, much as he did that cold day in Pond Square with his frozen chicken. But he did much more.

He served Queen Elizabeth I as her legal advisor, and was knighted by King James I. You and I might know him as that crazy old guy with a bag full of snow and a dead chicken, but thankfully history will remember him with a bit more respect.

Our Francis was none other than the Lord High Chancellor of England.

Sir Francis Bacon.

MOURNING

Few rulers stick out from the pages of history like Queen Victoria. She was almost larger than life. So much so that the time period she lived in took on her own name: the Victorian Era. And what a time it *was*.

During her sixty-two-year reign, the world changed dramatically. The British Empire expanded around the globe, and the modern constitutional monarchy as we know it today took shape and matured. The world saw the first powered flight and the invention of the telephone, and went from paintings and horse-drawn carriages to photography and automobiles.

Queen Victoria impacted Europe in a very particular way, too. She and Prince Albert had nine children, and between them there were forty-two grandchildren. And that family tree spread wide. Today, five European countries have monarchs who are descended from Victoria, including King Charles III. Clearly, she left her mark on the world.

Victoria and Albert were a beloved couple, and it was hard to blame the public for that. Prince Albert was a man that leaned toward the progressive side of the political scale. He helped influence reforms in the areas of welfare, slavery, and education, along with the ever-expanding world of manufacturing.

And of course, what royal family would be complete without multiple palatial homes to live in? There was Kensington, of course, and everyone knows Buckingham Palace. But in 1851 the Queen added one more house to that list, down on the northern tip of the Isle of Wight. They called it Osborne House, and it served as a summer home.

But summer turned to winter. In 1862, at the age of just forty-two, Prince Albert died, leaving Victoria all alone. What happened over the next four decades has sometimes been described as the birth of a culture of death. She wore the black of mourning for the rest of her life, and made sure that the servants never stopped taking care of Albert's daily needs, even though he was no longer alive.

When her children eventually married, each of them posed for wedding photographs that included a bust of Albert. She never slept in a bed that didn't have a photo of him beside it, and kept a plaster cast of his hand so she could hold it. In fact, when she passed away in 1901, that hand was placed inside her coffin. It's fair to say that Albert's death altered hers completely, and not in a healthy way.

The most interesting obsession of her later years, though, was not discovered until after her death. When Osborne House fell into the hands of her son and heir, King Edward VII, he explored the areas of the house that had been off limits to anyone other than his mother. And there, behind locked doors, he found an unusual display.

Hundreds of photographs that covered generations of people Victoria had known. Portraits of people who had been important to her, right there in the house where she could visit whenever she wanted. Despite the fact that these photographs spanned decades, and each one showed the face of different friend or family member, there was one common feature tying them all together.

None of the subjects were alive.

Queen Victoria's secret gallery was a tour of what most of us would consider to be a hauntingly personal moment.

Her funeral.

PRECIOUS CARGO

Henry Brown knew nothing but slavery for most of his life. Despite his upbringing on the Hermitage plantation in Virginia, Henry had a surprisingly positive outlook on life. He appreciated nature and enjoyed showing the children on the plantation the flowers that grew there. He was a religious man with a whole lot of faith in a world that had done him so much wrong.

Henry's faith brought him to Nancy, another slave, and the two of them got married and had three children of their own. He'd been making regular payments to his wife's master as a way to keep him from selling her and the children off, but the master had other ideas. There was more money in selling Nancy and the kids to the highest bidder than there was in taking Henry's meager payments, so the master separated the family, leaving Henry despondent and alone.

You might think something like that would break Henry's faith in people, but it didn't. In fact, he was about to take the biggest leap of faith in his life with the help of two men who had a plan. After the loss of his family, Henry knew he had to get out. He refused to go through something as heartbreaking as that again if he could help it, so he contacted a friend, a free Black man named James Smith, who helped orchestrate his escape.

James and a white shoemaker named Sam Smith came up with an ingenious way to get Henry out of Virginia and into the North where he could be free. Except, Henry didn't use the abolitionist safe houses along the Underground Railroad to escape. He chose a very *different* route. Actually, several different routes, including a trip by wagon, then by railroad, transferring to a steamboat, another wagon, a second journey by train, a ferry, and another railroad, until he finally reached Philadelphia.

After twenty-seven grueling hours, Henry was free, and he used that freedom to advocate on behalf of other enslaved people. He spoke out as an abolitionist against the South and its barbaric practices. To avoid the Fugitive Slave Law of 1850, he moved to England and became a magician to entertain crowds and earn a living. He eventually remarried and began a new family, taking them back to the US with him after the end of the Civil War.

Now, you might be asking yourself, what is it about Henry's story that still resonates today? Many enslaved people escaped their fates, but we never got to hear their stories. Well, Henry's tale is a special one. Like other enslaved people, he was so desperate to leave a life of pain and suffering, he embarked on a journey where—at any moment—he could either die or be discovered.

But of course, his efforts were a success, and literature about how he'd earned his freedom found its way back south, boosting the morale among other enslaved people. He became a sort of celebrity, for better or worse.

You see, Henry Brown was the first enslaved person to mail himself to freedom. He spent a little over one day in a three-foot-by-two-foot crate that was hauled from his home in Virginia to the Philadelphia Vigilant Association in Pennsylvania. He survived with the help of a single air hole cut in the side of the box, and a small portion of biscuits and water by his side.

Any person might be dehydrated, exhausted, or even unconscious after such a long, difficult journey. He even spent part of that journey *upside down*. But Henry "Box" Brown never lost his positive attitude, either. Upon opening the crate in Philadelphia, one of the men remembered hearing Henry's very first words as a free man.

True to his positive attitude, they were anything but frustrated, tired, angry, or afraid. He simply smiled from inside the dark wooden crate, waved his hand, and cheerfully said, "How do you do, gentlemen?"

Henry Brown, it seems, knew how to deliver a powerful message.

BIRD BRAIN

Livestock never fares well in a tornado. I think many of us remember that iconic scene in the movie *Twister* when a cow moos across the screen as it's carried away in a funnel of wind and debris. But tornadoes—and the creatures caught up within them—can teach us a few things about the wind and the way it moves.

That was the thought mathematician Elias Loomis had in 1842 after hearing reports about naked chickens. Yes, you heard that right: *naked* chickens. Farmers in Ohio had noticed their poultry walking around without their feathers following a tornado that tore through their town. And it happened enough that folks didn't really think anything of it.

Loomis saw the featherless fowl as an opportunity to measure a tornado's wind speeds, a feat previously thought impossible. Keep in mind, this was the 1840s, well before animal rights organizations monitored how scientists used living creatures in their studies. Elias Loomis had a hypothesis and almost *no* oversight. I'm sure you can see where this is going.

Loomis killed a chicken, and launched its body out of a small cannon, clocking in a top speed of over 340 miles per hour. The bird flew high and far, leaving in its wake a cloud of feathers . . . and enough meat to make a few chicken nuggets. Tornadoes must spin at a slower rate, he thought, and continued with his research.

Unfortunately, his tests proved unsuccessful. The technology being what it was at the time, he was unable to gather enough data on just how quickly tornadoes turned, nor their effects on the local livestock. It wasn't until over a century later when Bernard, an atmospheric scientist at SUNY Albany, took a closer look.

Bernard had spent his early career at General Electric, researching the atmosphere. He'd discovered the effects of what happened when silver iodide was injected into clouds. It formed ice crystals, and Bernard thought he might be able to use this to control precipitation. In fact, his work is still used today by cloud seeding companies that can produce rain on demand in drought-stricken areas.

After he left GE, Bernard went to work at Arthur D. Little, the company that helped create the word processor and the NASDAQ stock exchange, which eventually led him to the University at Albany. It was there where he learned about Elias Loomis's research on wind speed and naked chickens.

Bernard wasn't sure Loomis had been on the right track, but technology had advanced to the point where new research wouldn't need to harm animals in the process, so he took a crack at it himself. He dropped some chickens in a wind tunnel—the kind they use to test aircraft—and then turned it on. And it worked . . . well, sort of.

The chickens lost plenty of feathers, but inconsistently and not enough to classify them as "naked." They were honestly just sort of patchy, and ran around clucking angrily. It didn't take long for Bernard to realize that chickens made terrible gauges of wind speed.

But that didn't stop him from earning an Ig Nobel Prize in 1997. No, not a *Nobel* Prize, an *Ig* Nobel Prize. Ignoble, get it? It's a satirical award given to ten bizarre or benign achievements in scientific research. Bernard won it for his paper, "Chicken Plucking as Measure of Tornado Wind Speed."

Bernard's work also found its way into popular culture. His research of ice crystal formations in clouds became the basis for the substance ice-nine in Kurt Vonnegut's 1963 novel *Cat's Cradle*. It turns out, Vonnegut had worked as a publicist for General Electric in the late 1940s, so he knew all about Bernard's work. Even though he didn't have a college degree himself, GE hired Kurt to help advertise the company's scientific breakthroughs.

To be honest, any other applicant as unqualified as Kurt would have been turned away at the door, but he had two things working in his favor. First, he lied. He'd told GE that he held a master's degree in anthropology from the University of Chicago, which he most certainly didn't.

His other advantage was that he had a little help from the inside. It turns out that his brother already worked for GE, where he worked as an atmospheric scientist.

His brother . . . *Bernard* Vonnegut.

THAT GIRL IS POISON

Her name was Locusta and she was born in Gaul, an area known today as France, during the first-century Roman empire. Her origins are a mystery. It was suspected she was a peasant, but one who had developed a green thumb of sorts. Not for crops, though. And she didn't care much for growing roses, either. She went for something with a little more . . . kick.

Locusta discovered that if she mixed fungi, deadly nightshade, other types of plants, and even blood, she could create something toxic. Something . . . poisonous. She started out by testing her various potions on animals she found, then adjusted the ratios for maximum potency.

Her only problem was her location. There just wasn't a call for a professional poisoner out in the countryside, where people were more concerned with getting by than casting vengeance upon their enemies. So she took her services where she knew there'd be in demand: the city. Namely, Rome, chock full of intrigue and political backstabbing.

Locusta fancied herself an entrepreneur, and saw an opportunity to help the wealthiest Roman influencers take each other out without anyone knowing. Oftentimes, her assassinations looked like run-of-the-mill heart attacks. Enemies of Emperor Claudius fell to the ground clutching their chests or their throats as they foamed at the mouth, the muscles in their bodies tensing up to the point of snapping until all went black.

Her talents went viral in a way, with her name being passed along through the underground networks of ill repute. If you needed someone killed without it looking like a murder, you called "Locusta the Poisoner." Of course, once the bad guys knew about her, so did the authorities, and Locusta found herself arrested on murder charges more than once. It didn't matter, though, because the throne saw her as an asset. One royal decree from Claudius and minutes later, she was back to toiling and troubling.

Claudius's fourth wife, Juila Agrippina, took a liking to Locusta and employed her as her own personal poison consultant. Agrippina had a history of poisoning her husbands and inheriting their wealth, all with one eye on the throne. Not for herself, however, but for her son, Lucius. She couldn't rule, but she could control a ruler from behind the scenes. Lucius's father had already died, but Agrippina's third husband, Claudius, needed an heir after his son from his previous wife had been deemed unfit to lead. What better way to secure a new heir than adopting the one living under his roof?

And he did, having the boy change his name to Nero. But it didn't take long for Agrippina to grow restless. She didn't want to wait for her husband to die and her son to take over as emperor, so she paid a little visit to an old friend. Locusta mixed a poison to get rid of the emperor's bodyguard, then paid the royal food taster to take the day off so she could enact her plan.

A few death cap mushrooms in his stew were all it took for Claudius to go down. The emperor's doctor was summoned immediately. He performed the standard procedure to help a choking victim: sticking a feather down Claudius's throat to trigger vomiting. Locusta had seen to that, too, though. Moments before, she had doused the feather in strychnine.

Claudius died, and Nero took his place, with his mother in his ear at all times. Agrippina had finally made it to the top—well, as close as she was going to get. Her personal poisoner, however, did not fare so well. There was still one loose end to tie up, so Agrippina accused Locusta of poisoning her husband, and had her sentenced to death.

It's okay, though, because Nero knew a good thing when he saw it, and had the young woman released. He had fallen out with his mother, who had become too great a burden, and the two had parted ways.

Locusta didn't do too badly, either. She moved into a palace, and started a school to teach other women in the art of poisoning. She also developed new formulas and tested them out on thieves, enslaved people, and others she thought deserving of death.

But as we've learned, political turmoil exacts a heavy toll on everyone involved, and nobody gets out unscathed. Locusta's past eventually caught up with her after Nero's tragic suicide. His successor, Galba, had grown sick of all the poisoning and the woman behind it. He sentenced Locusta to death, and had her dragged through the streets in chains before being publicly executed.

A gruesome end for a gruesome person. Experts have called Locusta "history's first serial killer," but that title isn't quite right. She didn't kill out of compulsion or passion or some sociopathic tendency. No, Locusta the Poisoner was something more.

She was history's first hit woman.

RAVENOUS

Some talents have universal appeal. A good musical performance. A beautiful painting. A functional and inspiring architectural design. These are things that almost everyone can appreciate.

Other talents are a bit less mainstream. They sit at the edges, and while a few people might find them interesting, the vast majority of the world is either uninterested, unprepared, or *both*. In the case of one man, it might be fair to say that his skill was simply not their cup of tea.

The world had never seen someone quite like Tarrare, and they certainly weren't ready. He was born in France in the 1700s, and from the very beginning, everyone could tell he was different. It wasn't in his looks, or the way he spoke. It was how his stomach was kind of a bottomless pit.

By the time he was a teenager, he could easily eat his weight in beef each day, and somehow never gain a pound. His mouth could stretch wider than average, and people who knew him at the time described his figure as, of all things, skinny. However, his appetite was so grand, his family couldn't afford to feed him. That meant they couldn't afford to keep him, either. And just like that, Tarrare was on his own.

He didn't starve, though. To be honest, it wasn't a challenge for someone with a talent for stuffing his face to find work as a sideshow act. He fell in with a group of street performers who kept him fed, and quickly exploited his outrageous metabolism.

Audiences didn't just want to see him eat hundreds of pounds of steak and chicken. The man with the iron stomach began varying his diet with less edible additions, including rocks, corks, and live animals. If he could fit it in his mouth, he ate it, and got paid pretty well for it, too. Unfortunately, he also paid for it.

Tarrare was a notoriously foul-smelling individual who ran into serious intestinal troubles because of his sideshow work. After one particularly long hospital stay, he realized he needed to do better for himself—and his stomach. He joined the French military, but although his newfound sense of purpose should have been enough to sustain him, he became just as sick not eating as he did when he was.

It was while he was wandering around the base's medical ward when military scientists decided to perform some tests on Tarrare's incredible appetite. They realized that when his enormous stomach was empty, it became a perfect way of transporting messages to imprisoned soldiers across enemy lines.

If only they'd trained him a little better before sending him into the field. It didn't take long for Tarrare to be spotted and captured. Soon, he was being questioned about his reasons for being there. Tarrare, naïve and afraid, told them all about the box in his stomach containing the note. So they chained him to a toilet and waited patiently for his, um, deposit.

If only it had been worth the wait. The message said nothing. Well, nothing that meant a great deal to the enemy, nor the imprisoned soldier. The entire ordeal had been an experiment as to whether his gut would be a viable way of smuggling information long-term.

Tarrare was eventually released to France where he resumed his civilian life, searching for food wherever he could find it. And he was sick of it. He'd been studied and exploited, and all it had gotten him was the torture of an upset stomach.

Soon after, he checked himself into a local hospital in hopes of a cure. He couldn't live with this affliction any longer. Unfortunately, medicine at the time just wasn't very advanced, and treatments consisted of filling his insides with an assortment of powerful drugs to see how they performed. But nothing worked.

Tarrare spent his nights wandering the halls looking for something to eat. He branched out from his usual fare of everyday objects and started eating off-menu. He drank patients' blood and ate limbs in the morgue.

Sometimes he escaped and feasted on the entrails discarded behind butcher shops, or stray dogs and cats in the neighborhood. One day, a fourteen-month old child went missing and though Tarrare was never accused of anything outright, it was enough to have him evicted from the hospital.

Years later, Tarrare would find himself back there one last time—as a corpse. Doctors tried performing an autopsy on him, but they didn't get too far. The odor coming off his body simply made a full examination all but impossible.

Any number of things could've killed the man who ate literally everything in his path. After all, his gigantic stomach was riddled with countless infections caused by his strange dining habits. But no. Tarrare hadn't been undone by rocks, or corks, or even human limbs. It wasn't cats or dogs, or all those rotten butcher castoffs.

No, the man who seemed to be able to eat anything without consequence died of something entirely unrelated, taking his reputation for an iron stomach with him to the grave . . . completely intact. So what *did* kill the man who seemingly could consume anything?

Tuberculosis. Otherwise known as "consumption."

MUMMY DEAREST

Her name was Xin Zhui, but she's now known to many as Lady Dai. Born around 213 BC, Lady Dai was an important figure during the Han Dynasty. She had an eye for the finer things in life, and was considered one of the societal elite. She wore mostly silk clothing, and cosmetics, such as blush and powders, to show off her wealth. Her lavish parties were catered with foods and wines only ever tasted by the royal family and ruling class.

She also entertained her guests with performances by musicians who played only for her. When she wasn't hosting elaborate gatherings, Lady Dai could be found playing the *guqin*, a string instrument typically studied by the upper crust of Chinese society.

Unfortunately, for all the wining and dining she did, Lady Dai didn't get around much. It was her sedentary lifestyle that most likely contributed to her premature death. It is believed that at the age of fifty, she suffered from a heart attack brought on by high cholesterol.

Her body was interred alongside her late husband, and eventually her son, in tombs deep underground. Buried with her were clothing, boxes of makeup, musical instruments, eating utensils, and other personal items. However, it wasn't Lady Dai's life that proved to be that interesting. Based on what we know today, she lived like many of her peers and died young, her lifestyle proving a little too rich in more ways than one.

It wasn't until over two thousand years later, in 1971, that we learned about the one thing that set Lady Dai apart from everyone else. As Mao Zedong spread fear across China of vague threats from a capitalist nation—meaning the United States—citizens all over the country started digging bomb shelters beneath their homes. Which is why workers at a hospital in the capital of the Hunan Province had been digging into the side of a nearby hill.

They had only dug about a hundred feet down before stopping for a smoke break. What they didn't know was that just on the other side of the dirt was an open shaft leaking a flammable gas right beside them. They lit their cigarettes, which in turn ignited the air in dazzling bursts of blue fire. A team of archaeologists were called in to examine the scene, but the level of funding needed for a full investigation could not be procured, so they reached out for help to an unlikely source: local high school students.

Fifteen hundred teens volunteered to dig and sift as they worked their way down fifty feet of clay into a series of cavernous tombs. Each of the three noble corpses occupied their own tomb, but it was Lady Dai's that proved to be the most extraordinary.

In the tomb's center stood a coffin painted black—a color signifying death. Within that coffin were three others, nested one inside the other, painted in different color schemes to depict the journey to the afterlife. They had been adorned with images of clouds, animals, and important places designed to tell a story of life, death, and rebirth.

It was inside the fourth and smallest coffin where archaeologists made their most important discovery. Up until then, the mummies discovered in places, such as Egypt had experienced significant levels of decay. Even with no exposure to the sun or the elements, their bodies had desiccated into little more than dry skin on brittle bones.

Lady Dai, however, was a sight to behold. Her skin was soft and pale with a presence of moisture. Her arms and legs could still bend at the joints, and none of her organs had deteriorated. Even her hair and eyelashes had remained in place, and there were trace amounts of red blood within her veins.

An autopsy was performed, the results of which gave doctors deep insight into how she might have lived when she was still alive. They even found the vagus nerve, which is as thin as a hair and controls the expansion and constriction of the lungs. It often disintegrates with other tissue as a body decays, but it was still present in Lady Dai.

We know more about the Han Dynasty today than we ever had before . . . all thanks to Lady Dai. Her near-perfectly preserved corpse, as well as the array of items found inside her tomb, have shed light on an era of China's history long thought lost forever. And there may still be more to learn, either from her, or the other tombs still hidden beneath the streets.

It seems the ancient Chinese understood that the preservation of their dead was just as important as the preservation of their history. We just have to dig a little deeper to find it.

ROCK MUSIC

Listen. Pay attention. Tune your ear to the world around you and you'll hear music everywhere. In the rhythm of a footstep on a tile floor, or in the chime of the elevator in the lobby. A baby's cry, a squeaky brake—anything can become a song with a keen ear and a little imagination.

A stonemason from Keswick, England, possessed such an ear and it took him quite far. In 1840, Joseph Richardson had been wandering around near a mountain about five miles from his home, when he struck one of the rocks along the mountainside. Surprisingly, it rang out with a clear, crisp tone . . . and it gave Joseph an idea.

He took the rock home and stored it away. It had been the first step in a journey that would take him thirteen years to complete. He returned to the mountain over the course of those thirteen years in search of more rocks, or hornfels, just like it. He hit each one just like the first to hear its tone and he did this until he'd amassed over sixty of them.

His goal was to compile them into a musical instrument known as a lithophone. Now, the lithophone wasn't too different from a xylophone. It consisted of carefully assembled tiers of rocks arranged like piano keys. When struck, each rock elicited a specific tone on the musical scale.

His first lithophone had too small a range to play most songs of the time, but his second version was so large it could reach eight octaves. And Joseph was obsessed with building the instrument, spending most of his time and money on its construction. The effort nearly bankrupted his family, but don't worry . . . he had a plan to earn it all back.

With a special set of mallets and his children by his side, Joseph took his lithophone on a European tour. He and his sons toured Germany, France, Italy and other European countries playing for all kinds of crowds. Audiences were in awe of the unique sound of his lithophone. The concerts proved so successful, in fact, that the Richardsons didn't return home for three years. He even performed for the queen at Buckingham Palace.

The papers reported that his stones sounded like the "warble of a lark" at its upper register, and like the bellowing toll of a "funeral bell" at the lower register. Others described the music as haunting. It sounded like a relic from an ancient era, not a modern musical instrument.

As Joseph traveled and put wear and tear on his creation, he modified it with steel bars for reinforcement. He also added bells and other pieces to produce additional sounds during performances. However, all that travel had exacted a heavy toll on his children.

They'd grown tired, and his youngest son had caught pneumonia. On the night before a planned trip to America, the boy passed away. The grief was too much for Joseph and his other two children, and so they ended the tour. And that was the end of the Richardson family band.

It's not known whether Joseph ever performed with the stones again after that, but we do know that they stayed in the family. In 1917, more than sixty years after Joseph's death, his great-grandson donated the lithophone to the Keswick Museum and Art Gallery in his hometown, where it still resides today. Its sound has been recorded and converted digitally, too, so today's musicians can incorporate its ethereal notes into their modern compositions.

Joseph Richardson contributed to the world of music in a powerful way: he built his influence one stone at a time for thirteen years with blood, sweat, and a lot of tears. And even though the record books might not agree, one might say he also has a pretty big claim to fame.

After all, he did create the world's first *rock* band.

FOOD FOR THOUGHT

William Buckland wanted to do it all. One look at his life and it's clear he had a dream to be the most interesting person in the world. Born in England in 1784, William found a home in education, but he wasn't content with merely being a teacher.

He also named the first non-avian dinosaur, the *Megalosaurus*. Then in 1823, while exploring a cave in south Wales, he came across a skeleton that he dubbed the Red Lady of Paviland, known today as the oldest modern human found in the United Kingdom. William was also unique in his teaching style, as he was prone to shouting questions at his students while shoving a hyena skull in front of them to throw them off.

Obviously William had a knack for standing out, but he felt there was more for him out there. He sought another way to be the first, to rise above his peers in a meaningful and lasting way. So he turned to one of his greatest passions: food.

It's probably safe to say William was the only man around known for eating mice on toast. He often threw parties where he served panther and dolphin, among other unconventional meats, to his guests. And his friends didn't seem to mind. In fact, they supported him in his ultimate goal: to eat one of every animal on earth.

He sampled sea slugs, crunched on kangaroo, and munched on mole—the last of which he claimed was one of the worst things he'd ever tasted. Well, that and the bluebottle fly. No animal was off-limits, though, including hedgehog, ostrich, and even crocodile.

But William didn't just *eat* animals—he kept many of them as pets, too. Sure, there were guinea pigs and frogs and ferrets, the usual fare you might find in a child's bedroom or kindergarten class. But he also kept hawks, owls, and a pet hyena in his house. It seemed his eccentricities were not limited to the dinner table *or* his classroom.

But eventually, William's palate grew tired of even the most exotic creatures he could get his teeth on. On a trip to Italy in the early 1800s, he was touring a local cathedral and asked about the wet floor. It was slippery, but not from water. The priest told him about the blood spilled by saints that sloshed beneath their feet. William, skeptical of the priest's story, dropped to the floor and lapped up some of the fluid, only to realize that it hadn't been blood at all. It was bat urine.

However, perhaps the most egregious act William Buckland ever performed came during a trip to visit British politician Lord Harcourt. Harcourt was in possession of a locket that held within it a small parcel of brown pumice. A stone by the looks of it.

One evening, the Harcourts held a dinner for many important guests and put the piece on display for all to admire. And eventually—perhaps while they served dessert and brandy—the locket was passed around the table for everyone to admire. Each dinner guest took turns opening it to gaze upon the hardened, walnut-sized remnant . . . of King Louis XIV's mummified heart.

But William, not one to let the attention drift away from himself, didn't merely want to look at the piece of heart. Ever the showman, he announced to the group, "I have eaten many strange things, but I have never eaten the heart of a king before," and then popped the little nugget into his mouth.

Believe it or not, the eccentric gourmand wasn't immediately ostracized from high society. No one knows how the Harcourts handled their prized king's heart being devoured like a common peanut, but William Buckland eventually went on to great success and acclaim as a scientist and educator.

Upon his death in 1856, he was buried in Westminster Abbey, and his son, Francis, continued his father's legacy by also eating as many different animals as possible. He also tried becoming a full-fledged scientist, just like his father, but decided a life spent traveling the world and writing about the animals he ate was more fulfilling.

William had been an academic, a man of letters who enjoyed teaching and discussing his field of study with his peers.

His son, though?

It turns out . . . he just didn't have the stomach for it.

BOOKSMART

Everyone has their vices. Some enjoy playing the lottery. Others love a good chocolate bar. For Antonio Magliabechi, though, his vice was knowledge.

Born in Florence, Italy, in 1633, Antonio apprenticed for a local goldsmith until he was forty years old. It was then when he met Michele Ermini, a librarian for Cardinal de' Medici. Michele saw something in Antonio: a passion for learning, and a desire to rise above his status as an apprentice and do more with the mind he was given. With Michele's help, Antonio learned several languages, including Greek, Latin, and Hebrew.

Years later, after decades of study, Antonio found himself in the same position as his onetime tutor, becoming the librarian to the Grand Duke of Tuscany. From there, his reputation stretched far beyond the confines of his bookshelves. He became an academic celebrity of sorts, engaging with scholars from all over the world who wanted to learn more about the self-taught genius from Florence.

However, genius often breeds other problems. For all his intelligence, Antonio was quite negligent about his state of dress. He tended to wear his clothes until they were literally falling off of him in tatters. He typically ate only three hardboiled eggs for dinner with a glass of water, and if someone came to his door who he didn't care to entertain, he wouldn't let them in.

He was an incredibly private man devoid of pride or extravagance. He once worked for an entire year without taking a salary. In fact, the concept of money or bills just didn't occur to him, allowing him to amass quite a fortune. But he didn't really spend it on anything. Well, almost. Antonio enjoyed spending what money he had on his greatest obsession: books.

He was known as a literary glutton, filling his work library with over forty thousand titles and more than ten thousand manuscripts. His home also held thousands of volumes, many of which lined stairways and extended outside the house to his porch.

Even more impressive was the fact that he had read every single one of them. As someone whose side table practically groans under the weight of all the new books I want to read, I can't help but be a little jealous. Clearly, Antonio dedicated his life to expanding his mind with the written word.

Perhaps all that reading had a profound effect on him, or maybe his brain had always been wired a certain way, but aside from his extensive library, Antonio was also known for his extensive memory. Today, he might be called a human search engine, capable of citing the exact book, author, and even page number asked of him.

According to the stories, he was once asked by his employer the duke where he might find a specific title. Without hesitation, Antonio told him there was only *one* copy of it in *existence*. It rested in the Grand Seignior's library in Constantinople, on the second bookcase from the right, eleven volumes in.

It's said that a priest asking for a eulogy on a certain saint would often get a list of more than a hundred authors who had ever written about them, and where their books could be found among the many thousands in his possession.

All that book knowledge came at a price, though. Antonio almost never traveled outside of Florence to see the world. He slept in his clothes, rarely ate anything other than those hardboiled eggs, and spent hours each day reading in the palace library. And yet he lived to be eighty-one years old, and was revered for his sharp mind and endless memory. For him, a work-life balance didn't exist . . . because his work *was* his life.

When he died, Antonio left his entire fortune to the poor. His library, though—tens of thousands of books—all went to the Grand Duke, but with one condition: that they be used to found a public library. It was called the *Magliabechiana,* and through various mergers with other private libraries around Italy, it went on to become the National Central Library of Florence, the largest public library in all of Italy.

Antonio didn't just believe in learning—he believed that knowledge was meant to be shared with everyone. If he were alive today, he'd be amazed at how easily the internet has made that dream come true.

Either that, or he'd spend his entire life online, reading everything he could get his hands on. I'd expect nothing less . . . from the world's most ravenous bookworm.

O BROTHER

It's a widely held belief that a person cannot give themselves a nickname. Nicknames are often terms of endearment, a way for others to show someone they care about is recognized for what makes them special.

Of course, on the playground, a nickname might also be a way for a bully to punch down at someone different from them. They might call someone with glasses "four-eyes," or they'll chant "cry-baby" at someone weeping after being hit.

Nicknames may disappear after some time, or they might stick with a person all their life—just as they did for five brothers from New York. In fact, had it not been for their nicknames, these siblings might not have become celebrities at all.

They were born to Jewish immigrants named Minnie and Samuel. The eldest son, Leonard, arrived first in 1887, followed by his brother Adolph in 1888 and Julius in 1890. Milton was born in 1892 and the youngest of the brood, Herbert, arrived in 1901.

There was another son, named Manny, who had sadly passed away several months after his birth in 1886, most likely from influenza.

Their mother, Minnie, grew up in a German household of entertainers—her mother a harpist who yodeled, while her father performed ventriloquism. She knew show business like the back of her hand, so when her brother, Abraham, expressed a desire to enter the vaudeville circuit, she became his manager.

As her boys got older, she saw vaudeville as pathway to success—not just for them, but for the family as a whole. Minnie took them under her wing and adopted the last name of "Palmer," so booking agents wouldn't suspect her relation to the group.

Each of her sons had a special talent. Adolph could play as many as six instruments, including the harp—just like his grandmother. Julius knew his way around a guitar. Leonard could play the piano better than most, and Herbert had a beautiful singing voice.

Milton often accompanied his uncle, Abraham—now known as Al Shean—onstage. He'd wear a papier-mâché head and pretend to be a dummy while Uncle Al played the ventriloquist operating him.

Meanwhile, Julius bounced from act to act. He toured the country performing with various vaudeville entertainers to minor success. Eventually, he and three of his brothers formed their own group, creating characters and writing skits, which they performed for raucous audiences everywhere.

But there was still something missing. Something catchy—a hook, a way to differentiate themselves from the other acts on the road. It finally landed in their laps during a poker game in 1915.

The boys were in Galesburg, Illinois, sitting around a card table with a monologist named Art Fisher. As he dealt each brother a card, he referred to them by a nickname based on their different personality traits.

It was a common fad at the time to append an "O" to the end of a nickname, so that's what Fisher did. Adolph was first. Since he played the harp, his was easiest to come up with: Harpo.

Leonard was something of a womanizer and women at the time were often called "chickens," so he was considered a "chicken chaser," hence his new nickname: Chicko. The moniker later lost the "K" when a typesetter printing up advertisements for one of the brothers' performances accidentally left it out. The variation stuck and he was known as "Chico" from then on.

Third was Julius. Fisher placed a card in front of him and said, "Here's a card for Groucho." It's been debated for decades as to the origins of the name. One story claims that Julius was just a moody person—a grouch—and that's why Fisher called him that.

The other legend is that Groucho often kept his earnings in a small pouch around his neck known as a "grouch bag."

Fourth was Milton, who often wore rubber-soled shoes known as "gumshoes." Fisher dubbed him "Gummo."

The fifth brother, Herbert, didn't get his name until later, once he'd replaced Gummo as the fourth brother in the act. According to Harpo, the nickname "Zeppo" was given in honor of a trained chimp named "Mr. Zippo," who performed acrobatic feats onstage. Apparently, Herbert was also prone to showing off by doing chin-ups and other acts of strength, but hated the name "Zippo," so he changed it to "Zeppo."

Groucho had a different take. He claimed Zeppo got his name due to the popularity of a new invention that had appeared just before his birth: the zeppelin airship.

But the origins of Zeppo's nickname aren't as important as the man himself, who helped his brothers build one of the most influential and important comedy acts in history.

There you have it, the story of how Groucho, Harpo, Chico, and Zeppo Marx—otherwise known as "the Marx Brothers"—would not be nearly as beloved today if it hadn't been for one fateful poker game.

PECULIAR PLACES

THE WAITING GAME

D r. Thornwell Jacobs was a key figure in the life of Atlanta's Oglethorpe University. The school actually predates him—dating all the way back to 1835—but the Civil War managed to close the place down for a number of years. It reopened in 1870, but went bankrupt just two years later.

For a very long while after that, it seemed the old college would never come back. But that's where Dr. Jacobs entered the picture. In 1913 he managed to get a new charter for the school, and two years after that, it opened its doors to the public again. It was a fitting accomplishment for Jacobs, too, since his own grandfather had served on the faculty there years before. Poetic, even.

Jacobs was an *interesting* man. For example, shortly after the school reopened, he dreamed up the unusual plan to travel to England and bring back the body of the man who founded Georgia, and who the University was named after—British general James Oglethorpe. It turns out that after establishing the colony in what is now Savannah, the general returned to England, where he passed away in 1785.

Jacobs had this dream of burying Oglethorpe beneath the university, so he traveled to England to locate the general's tomb, which had been lost to time. Like a real-life Indiana Jones, Jacobs found it—and, after digging down into it, had himself lowered in just to verify his discovery. After that, he put his request in to have the body moved back across the Atlantic. And it was declined.

Jacobs certainly had a fascination with buried objects. When Ringling Brothers donated several dead elephants to the university, they first dissected them, and then had them buried under the Weltner Library. But that wasn't the weirdest thing Jacobs oversaw. No, his crowning achievement came a few years earlier, in the late thirties, when he started plans for something that had never been done before.

Troubled by the lack of well-preserved artifacts from human history, he set about making sure future generations wouldn't feel the same about our modern world. In the basement of Phoebe Hearst Hall, where an old swimming pool once sat, he began construction of a large chamber.

His design called for a space measuring twenty feet long by ten feet wide, which would sit on a foundation of solid granite bedrock. The floor and walls would be covered in plates of enameled porcelain, and then waterproofed with pitch. It was a massive project with exacting specifications, but that's because Jacobs had a very particular vision.

When it was completed three years later, the room was filled with a huge assortment of objects that represented the world of 1940s America. There were microfilm records of more than eight hundred books on "every subject known to mankind" and voice recordings of prominent individuals—including Stalin, Hitler, and a champion hog caller.

I'll let you make your own assumptions about that one.

They put hundreds of other objects in there as well. A television, various pieces of furniture, sewing machines, artwork, and even seeds. But nothing precious or theftworthy. In fact, jewelry wasn't allowed, or precious metals of any kind. It was a collection of easily attainable, everyday objects.

And then it was sealed. They had a massive stainless steel door set into the wall of the chamber, closed it tight, and then welded it shut. Jacobs called it the Crypt of Civilization, but although it might seem to us like nothing more than an elaborate time capsule, it was so much more than that.

Did it work? Well, nearly eighty years later, no one knows. Everything could have rusted into piles of scrap by now, or it all might be as pristine as the day they sealed it. We'll never know, though. Because this time capsule isn't one of those hundred-year projects, or something designed to be opened on a significant national or local anniversary. No, Jacobs had a much bigger target in mind when he had it built.

The Crypt of Civilization won't be opened for another 6,095 years.

I hope you're patient; it seems we've got a lot of waiting to do.

POTPOURRI

The cow had disappeared right before his eye.

It was March of 1924, and young Emile Fradin was standing in the field that he worked with his father in the small village of Glozel in central France. It was just by chance that he'd been looking in the right direction at all. The cow had been standing there one moment, and the next . . . well, it was gone.

Emile ran over to the spot where the cow had vanished from and discovered the reason why. There was a large hole in the ground. It had chosen that very moment to open wide and had dropped out beneath the cow like a trapdoor in a Scooby-Doo cartoon.

Of course, their first priority was to get the cow back out, and that took a bit of time. Cows are heavy, after all, and they have a tendency to kick and fight. But they eventually managed to free the fallen beast from the pit, and that's when they got a good look at what was down there—and it baffled them.

They could see bricks. Neat, tidy rows of uniform bricks were visible in the soil and roots below the surface of the field. So Emile grabbed a shovel and began to dig around them. Soon enough he and his father were standing in a small chamber with walls of brick and a tiled floor. And there were objects inside.

Word quickly spread. A local teacher visited the farm and alerted the government to the discovery. Local scholars began to flock to the farm for their chance in helping with the excavation. Over the next five years, the dig site was extended, eventually revealing a number of chambers, each with their own collection of artifacts.

That's where things got strange. First, you have to remember that no one knew these chambers were there in the field until the cow had fallen through the ceiling of one of the rooms. But they were an odd collection of items that made that difficult to believe. Yes, while some of the items in the chambers dated back to the first century BC, others were much newer, possibly as recent as the fifteenth century.

There has been a lot of controversy about the discovery over the years. Emile was accused of forging the entire site, but that claim was finally dismissed in court. More modern tools in the last couple of decades have also allowed scientists to determine the true age of some of the oldest pottery there—dating back roughly two thousand years.

There are bone fragments from the thirteenth century, and ceramic tablets with Phoenician writing on them. It's like a potpourri of archeological clues, making it very difficult to nail down exactly when the chambers were built. And none of that even comes close to the biggest question of them all: why?

Why was this set of chambers constructed? Why did someone want to gather up so many of these seemingly disparate items and store them all in one place. And why were they hidden away, buried beneath the surface of a field in the middle of France?

Nearly a century later, the answer is the same as it's always been: we just don't know.

RESTLESS

Thomas was a plantation owner in colonial Barbados, an island in the Caribbean. He lived there with his entire family, and preferred it to life back in England. But when you live someplace, there's always the risk of dying there as well. In 1807, Thomas purchased a large family vault in the local cemetery in anticipation of just that sort of eventuality.

That same year the family suffered through the loss of Thomas's aunt, and she became the first to occupy the tomb. The following year, Thomas and his wife lost a daughter—Mary Anna—and in July of 1812 another of their children passed away. It was a lot to work through, for sure. Losing a child is never an easy thing. But each of them had a home in the family tomb.

Later that same year, Thomas himself passed away. When they opened the vault, though, they were met with a surprise. All three of the coffins inside were no longer where they had left them, neatly arranged in a row on the stone floor. Instead, they seemed to have been tossed against the walls, and some of them had even opened.

The family suspected grave robbers, but there didn't appear to be anything missing.

In the end, they simply replaced all the coffins and added Thomas's to the room, and then made sure to lock up and seal the vault. And then life moved on.

In 1816, another of the children passed away, and after a somber funeral, the family took the small casket to the family tomb and unlocked the door. Inside, though, chaos had visited the original coffins once again. They were beginning to think that something darker was going on, that an unseen force might be at work. Oh, how right they were.

Just two months later, the family lost another of their own, and they returned to the all-to-familiar vault. Again, the door was still locked, but again, the coffins inside had been tossed against the walls and into general disarray. They straightened up things just like before, but word began to spread throughout the island about what was going on in their tomb.

When another of the family passed away in 1819, news spread fast enough that the governor of Barbados himself, Field Marshal Stapleton Cotton, traveled to the cemetery on the southwest corner of the island to watch the burial with his own eyes. Inside they found the same scene of disarray, and the governor personally inspected it, before helping with sealing the tomb.

This time, at his request, they covered the floor of the tomb with a layer of sand, hoping it would reveal footprints if it were ever to happen again. Then they locked the door, sealed it, and even placed "secret marks" on the doorframe to help them know if the vault had been tampered with.

It was less than a year before the authorities were made aware of reports of noises from inside the tomb. Governor Cotton made the journey back to the tomb, and the community and family gathered around to watch him inspect it. He reportedly found the seal intact, but when he unlocked the door and pushed it inward, it resisted suspiciously. With help, he was able to open it wide enough to look in, which is when he discovered two very different clues.

First, the coffins had all been tossed against the walls, which explained why the door was difficult to move. Some had tipped over, and others were standing on end. But to make matters more confusing, the sand on the floor was as smooth as it had been in 1819. Not a single footprint could be seen, which of course reinforced the local belief that the tomb was home to more than just wooden coffins. There was a spirit in there as well, and it wasn't happy.

This was apparently the final straw. In April of that year, the family pulled all of the coffins back out and transported them to new, underground graves, and left the old family vault empty and unused. The spirit never gave them trouble again.

Over the years, people have offered up their own theories about why the coffins kept moving. Some blame earthquakes, while others think the cemetery has been plagued by flooding from underground sources. To be honest, no one really knows for sure, leaving this story in the realm of the myth, rather than fact.

When it's all said and done, I suppose, there really is only one truth we can glean from this tale: let's all hope our own final resting place is exactly *that*.

Restful.

MEDIUM-SIZED TOWN

Everyone needs a home. Sometimes we plant roots where we're born, choosing to stay among what's safe and familiar. Other times, we have to leave one home in order to find another where we can be accepted and thrive. George P. Colby was in search of such a place in 1875 when he left his home in Pike, New York.

George was a trance medium, someone who would speak as though the dead were communicating through them during a séance. He traveled all over the country conducting sessions and giving readings to the public. But it was during a stay in Iowa when his travels took him on a journey he never expected.

He'd been contacted during one of his seances by a Native American spirit called Seneca. Seneca told George to go to Florida. It was *there* where he was meant to establish a community for others like him. Mediums, psychics, and other spiritual men and women would flock to this place to practice their craft, making a home for themselves apart from a world that called them hacks and frauds.

As he made his way south, George contracted a bad case of tuberculosis. By the time he'd reached his destination, he was in bad shape and close to death. Seneca, now deemed his spirit guide by the intrepid medium, led him to a spring deep in the wilds of Florida. George drank from the spring, and according to his tale, its waters cured him of his ailment.

This was the beginning of a town he would call the Cassadaga Spiritualist Camp Meeting Association, more commonly known as simply Cassadaga, named after a spiritual community near his hometown back in New York. Perhaps Seneca had been right, or maybe George just happened to tap into something needed at the time, but Cassadaga became an overnight sensation.

Psychics and mediums quickly found their way to the town and built houses for themselves across its fifty-seven acres. Many of the homes became makeshift business establishments, as their occupants were known to host séances for tourists who had come to learn of their loved ones' fate in the afterlife.

Growth kind of stalled in the 1930s, but the mediums never left and their descendants eventually took over both the homes and the family businesses, conducting séances and readings for curious tourists passing through.

Of course, a town populated by spiritualists was bound to attract *other* entities as well. The Hotel Cassadaga, which still looks just like it did in 1927, continues to rent rooms to folks looking to indulge their otherworldly side for more than a day. It's been said guests have even run into a friendly ghost or two during their time there.

It's not surprising to learn that the hotel isn't the only part of the town that's remained the same since its inception. Cassadaga itself hasn't really changed much since the 1930s when it was a major destination for spiritualists from all over the country. Today, while the world around Cassadaga marches forward, those who live there and maintain it make sure the camp remains true to its roots.

Resident psychics there claim to have spoken with the spirits of famous people like Abraham Lincoln, and have witnessed all sorts of paranormal phenomena around town. Computers and photocopiers have been known to malfunction out of nowhere. Ghosts wander around homes, peering from windows to pedestrians outside.

In the cemetery on the edge of town, there's something called the Devil's Chair, a place for mourners to rest and reflect on the passing of loved ones. However, as time has passed, a more sinister narrative has come to surround the chair. Allegedly, anyone brave enough to sit in it is said to come face-to-face with the Devil himself.

There's a curfew within the camp that lasts from dusk until dawn, discouraging anyone who might be looking to cause trouble after dark. Psychic readings, handwriting analysis, and séances are still conducted today, and the town continues to be a beacon for those in touch with the other side.

I assume George Colby would be proud to know his little community is still around, but he died decades ago, long before it reached its peak.

But if we really wanted to know, maybe someone there . . . could just ask him.

IMPULSE BUY

No one knows how it got there or its true purpose. Its builders left no written records. It has existed for thousands of years in the middle of a field in Wiltshire, England, where it draws nearly one million visitors each year. Its thirteen-foot-tall stones stand straight up, each weighing about twenty-five tons, and the method of its construction continues to baffle historians to this day.

Stonehenge may not be one of the seven wonders of the world, but it is no less awe inspiring when examined up close. The sheer enormity of the stones does make people wonder how they were moved and arranged in the first place. According to twelfth-century writer Geoffrey of Monmouth, King Arthur's faithful wizard, Merlin, constructed it himself.

But although it sits in a wide open meadow surrounded by grass, visiting Stonehenge today requires the purchase of a ticket. It takes a whole team of guards, groundskeepers, and restoration experts to keep the Neolithic structure intact, and that costs money. I've been there myself, and paid the price of admission. In fact, money is what begins our story in the first place.

During the early 1500s, King Henry VIII owned Stonehenge after seizing the land upon which it sat. It eventually passed down to the Earl of Hertford, followed by countless other owners until 1824. At that time, the site was purchased by a wealthy family from Cheshire who maintained ownership for almost a century. Then in 1915, after the last heir to the land was killed fighting in France during World War I, the family put the land up for auction.

The auction was held at the Palace Theatre in Salisbury. Of all the people present, one stood out: Cecil Chubb. He was born in Shrewton, about four miles from Stonehenge, and, being a successful lawyer, had become quite wealthy. When the lot was announced, Cecil hadn't expected to bid, but the more he thought about it, the better the idea sounded to him.

Lot 15 contained a little over thirty acres of land, including Stonehenge itself. When the final bid was collected it was Cecil Chubb who came out on top, having spent 6,600 pounds. By today's standards, that puts the total at almost $700,000. He didn't hold on to the property for long, though.

He believed such an iconic and wondrous sight should not belong to just one man, but to the nation as a whole. In 1918, three years after purchasing it, he formally rescinded his ownership, and gave Stonehenge to England, though he also included a number of conditions. First, all local residents should have free access to see it at any time. Second, outside visitors should be charged no more than a shilling for entry.

Since then, Stonehenge's value has only gone up. Locals are still allowed in at no cost, but visitors must pay five pounds to gaze upon the stones. If it were being sold at auction today, it's estimated that the ancient site could fetch as high as 65 million American dollars.

Quite a smart investment with hindsight, but at the time there really wasn't any reason to own the land other than to build upon it. Chubb had no interest in using the area for new construction, so why purchase it at all?

Well, he did it for the best reason of all: love, of course. Love for his hometown, and love for his wife.

He believed that if anyone was going to own that ring of stones, it should be a local man, not some company or investor from overseas. And more important, he wanted to give his wife a special gift. Something she could look at and remember just how much he loved her.

As it turned out, she wasn't thrilled with his last-minute purchase, which may have fueled his desire to give it back to England. However, his philanthropic gesture was recognized in 1919, when he was made a baronet by Prime Minister Lloyd George, so perhaps the investment paid off after all.

If there's a lesson to be learned here, I think it's this: while it's a good idea to buy your true love a ring, buying them Stonehenge might be a bit too much.

AMUSE IT OR LOSE IT

Speak the name Transylvania and you might feel a chill. It evokes a certain image, one of a man clad in black, with sharp fangs dripping with blood. Its people have often been portrayed as hapless peasants, fearful of the creature living in the scary castle at the top of the hill.

In fact, Transylvania is almost nothing like the way Bram Stoker portrayed it in his novel. Even Dracula's castle, which many have claimed is based on Transylvania's real Bran Castle, is in no way associated with the historical roots of the famous character. Almost everything we know about the region is thanks to one famous book and its countless film adaptations—and it's wrong.

The historic area located in central Romania is actually lush and green. It is populated by people of all different backgrounds who live and work in any one of the region's vibrant cities. There is a rich history within Transylvania, which can be seen in things like its well-preserved gothic architecture.

And for potential tourists looking to explore the hometown of one of the greatest characters in all of literature, there's a lot more to see than just castles. There are glorious churches, the Apuseni Mountains, and countless little hamlets and villages to give you a taste of the local culture.

There's also an amusement park.

It's not as well-known as it should be, considering the engineering it must have taken to build it. The park features numerous attractions, such as a Ferris wheel and a playground. There's also a bowling alley, a mini-golf course, and a natural lake for visitors to paddle around in.

You might be wondering why this place required such advanced engineering to build since none of its attractions are any different from those you might find at an amusement park in the America. Its Ferris wheel isn't that tall. The playground is mostly comprised of jungle gym equipment.

What makes the park so special is its location—and how one gets to it. In order to visit the site known as Salina Turda, you have to board an elevator that will take you down almost four hundred feet below the earth. That's right—the whole park was constructed underground . . . inside an old abandoned salt mine.

The mine had been in use right up till 1932, before it was turned into a bomb shelter during the Second World War. After that, it was used to store copious amounts of cheese. Then, in 1992, millions of dollars were spent converting the space into a full-fledged tourist trap, complete with a museum, eighty-seat amphitheater, and spa.

That spa boasts some of the purest air in the world thanks to the salt, which acts as a natural defense against allergens. Temperatures remain at a steady 54 degrees Fahrenheit and the humidity never breaks 80 percent. It seems the weather is always perfect when there's no weather to worry about.

And Salina Turda isn't just home to an amusement park. It's also a big destination for folks looking to practice halotherapy in the former salt mine. Breathing in the salty air helps treat their asthma and other respiratory conditions, and has been in practice for hundreds of years.

It's a pretty unique idea—taking a place that used to be nothing but a big hole in the ground and turning it into a tourist destination. So if you ever have the chance to visit the beautiful Transylvanian countryside, be sure to budget some time for a little fun *underneath* all that scenic beauty.

And breathe easy knowing that you're in the happiest place *under* the earth.

WINDY CITY

You can't change the weather. Whatever it wants to do, it will do, and all *we* can do is grin and bear it. Florida will always face hurricanes in the summer while Minnesota can plan on sub-zero winters every January and February.

In Iran, where temperatures can reach up to 128 degrees Fahrenheit, high winds are a given. These winds, which can gust as high as seventy miles an hour or more, kick up sand and dust, resulting in some pretty devastating sandstorms.

When that happens, day turns to night as sand sweeps through towns, knocking over trees, taking out power lines, and swallowing cars—or even people. They're a deadly nuisance, but also a fact of life, and it's been that way for thousands of years. However, if you look at the top of an old wall in the small village of Nashtifan, you'll see how the Iranian people have learned to live with these dustups—and how they've used them to drive innovation.

The town's name is appropriate, too. Nashtifan translates roughly as "storm's sting." The winds that blow there can be powerful and damaging, but Nashtifan has found a way to harness them into something more constructive. The people there built sixty-five-foot tall vertical windmills that look more like revolving doors than an alternative energy source, but there's a reason for their unique design.

These windmills weren't constructed like the ones we are used to seeing in America today. Instead of the planks being mounted in a circular formation and then attached to the top of the central column, these windmills had their planks connected to the columns themselves. When the wind blows, the paddles catch the air and turn the central post.

This does two things. First, the array of windmills slows the wind down, throttling its speed through a bottleneck. The village on the other side is spared from the worst of any storms passing through, saving them from the usual devastation.

And second, grindstones beneath the columns turn as well, grinding grain into flour. The strength of these structures using power derived only from the wind is impressive. They possess no extra motors or turbines, functioning only on what nature provides.

But it doesn't look like Iran's deep dive into alternative energy will last much longer. No, they won't be switching to natural gas or fossil fuels. It's just that there's only one man maintaining the windmills, and no one has offered to follow in his footsteps when he's gone.

Because of that, out of the hundreds that used to stand there, only a handful are still around today. It's hard for just one man to keep them operating, after all—especially since they're made of wood, clay, and straw.

Oh, and they're also about fifteen hundred years old.

Yes, these vertical axis windmills, a design used in state-of-the-art wind turbines coming out of research companies today, got their start in ancient Persia around AD 500. They still work just as well as they did back then, too. It's just a shame that they'll probably disappear in a few years, unless someone volunteers to take over their maintenance.

It's not clear what will happen to the village when they eventually fall apart. Perhaps they'll build new versions in their place, ones made of metal and plastic that can withstand higher wind speeds and generate power for the village. But it won't be the same. That any of these artifacts still exists is a testament to their construction and the ingenuity of the people who built them.

After all, the old cliché has never been more true:

"They sure don't make them like they used to."

FIRESTARTER

It doesn't take much for a fire to spread. It starts with a spark, then a small flame. Give it some air, and a little kindling, and it isn't long before that flame has grown into an uncontrollable blaze.

Some fires are necessary. They're deliberately set to clear old brush to make way for new growth. And sometimes nature steps in and starts the fire itself. In the Everglades, for example, fires triggered by lightning strikes engulf the grass along the river basin, improving water flow and habitats for local wildlife.

But not all fires help the environment. During the mid-1800s, fires were set to clear land for farms and railroad tracks. Such a fire had been set in the Wisconsin town of Peshtigo in October of 1871. It had been one of many controlled blazes started in order to pave the way for new development.

However, an unexpected weather pattern brought in a cold front that day, and with it came high winds. These winds spread the fire out, causing it to grow into what experts called a "firestorm." Firestorms possess specific traits that set them apart from other kinds of fires. Flames in firestorms burn at

2,000 degrees Fahrenheit or higher, with winds that blow at over one hundred miles per hour.

Firestorms are bad enough in open areas like plains or prairies, but if one were to occur in the middle of a dense forest, it could erupt like a nuclear blast.

As the fire spread, it grew so large and powerful that it actually made it across the Peshtigo River, burning the town on both sides. A flaming tornado, also called a "fire whirl," incinerated homes and train cars as it picked up and tossed their smoldering hulls in the air.

Townsfolk fled as quickly as they could, their first thought being to jump into the river. Its waters were ice-cold despite the flames burning on both sides. Many drowned, while others fell victim to hypothermia. And those who couldn't make it out of town in time? They succumbed to the fire itself as it blazed across 1.2 million acres of land.

Before the fire started, Peshtigo, Wisconsin, had a population of roughly seventeen hundred residents. A report filed two years later listed the number of deceased as high as twelve hundred, although the final number is thought to be much higher. We may never know just how bad it was, though, because town records were destroyed in the blaze.

Coincidentally, at the same time the Peshtigo fire was raging, another fire had begun on the Door Peninsula in northeastern Wisconsin. It had originally been thought that the fire in Peshtigo had gotten so big and powerful that it had migrated across the Green Bay and onto the peninsula.

When that fire had reached the small town of Robinsonville, a group of nuns and families from the town hid inside the local church and prayed for protection. But the fire quickly consumed the town and lingered outside the chapel, surrounding it on all sides. The nuns and the people they'd helped stood inside, helpless. Ultimately, though, their prayers seemed to have worked. The church and those inside it somehow survived the fire.

About ten years after the Peshtigo and Door Peninsula fires had been extinguished, theories surrounding their origins began coming out of the woodwork. Perhaps they hadn't been started by reckless railroad hands or overzealous farmers, after all. In fact, some people believe that fragments of a comet had landed in Wisconsin and ignited the areas where they made impact.

Scientists dispute this idea, as meteorites are cold when they hit Earth's surface, but there is something odd about two such large fires burning at the same time in roughly the same area of Wisconsin. Both events are relatively unheard of. And you might think two thousand people dying over a million acres would be more well-known.

But it's not surprising that nobody covered what had happened in Peshtigo. They probably had their hands full with another blaze burning at the exact same time. One that killed three hundred people, and destroyed over seventeen thousand buildings in the process.

And everyone has heard of this one.

The Great Chicago Fire.

MORE THAN
HUMAN

FIGURE 9.

THE GROUPIE

Harry was *really* good at chess. I don't mean that in a casual way, either. Harry was tried and tested in dozens of large tournaments, and proven to be incredibly good at it.

He started playing at the age of fifteen, and over the years that followed became a master of the game. In 1895 he managed to become the United States representative in a British competition known as the Hastings Tournament.

Most of the other chess players there were a lot older than him, and there's a rumor that they were a bit rude to him. It might have something to do with his age, sure, but it was more than likely to be connected to the cigars he smoked while he played. Whether or not they liked him didn't matter, though; Harry beat them all.

I'm not going to sugarcoat this story; Harry didn't live long. He passed away in 1906 at the age of thirty-three, but he left behind a legacy that still makes people scratch their heads today. Not for his typical victories in normal chess competitions, though. No, Harry built a reputation for something entirely different: group matches.

He would sit down with a number of other chess players—each with their own game board and pieces set up—and then play against all of them simultaneously. It would often take place during an official tournament, when many of the players had the day off, so these weren't just random players off the street. He was playing groups of the best chess players in the world, all at the same time.

And he would *win*. Once, he sat down with a group of sixteen players and beat thirteen of them. Another time he played against twenty contestants at a German tournament and managed to record eleven draws, three wins, and six losses. It was incredible to see, as many people recorded. One player managing to think through and compete with a dozen or more high-level opponents at the same time . . . well, it was amazing.

His best match was in Moscow in 1902. There he sat down with twenty-two tournament players and beat all but one of them. If he hadn't died four years later, there's no telling what else he would have been capable of accomplishing. Harry Nelson Pillsbury was a phenomenon. And not just because he beat so many players at the same time.

No, as if that weren't enough of a handicap, Henry managed to secure all of these records with one additional limitation. You see, he played each and every one of those group matches seated in a chair . . . facing *away* from his opponents' boards . . . while others called out the moves to him.

Harry Nelson Pillsbury wasn't blind, but he played each of these games as if he was.

FANCY FOOTWORK

Not everyone has it easy growing up. Many of us are forced to make our own way due to any number of hardships. Carl knew that better than most.

He grew up in Germany and his father had a certain kind of idea about how men should behave. He told Carl's mother not to coddle him. His boy had to make his own way, forge his own path, like he had done.

So Carl learned early on that he had to be self-sufficient in order to get want he wanted or needed. By the age of two, he had learned to feed himself. By ten, his interest in music had led him to take up the violin—and with no one around to teach him, Carl taught himself instead. He got pretty good, too. So good, in fact, that when he turned sixteen, his parents sent him off to a music conservatory to continue his education.

Carl studied with some of the finest teachers in Germany for several years. After he graduated, he used his talents to take him far beyond what even he believed possible. Before he was old enough to drink, he was playing with international orchestras in sold-out concert halls. His skills were so renowned, he was invited to perform before the famous composer Johann Strauss in Vienna.

He also developed a little trick previously unseen during your average concert. Whenever he'd break a string, Carl would change it in the middle of the show while the rest of the band played on. Then, he'd rejoin the group and continue the performance.

But he didn't do it backstage or off to the side. He made it part of the act. It got so popular that he started using a weakened string in his shows just so he would be forced to demonstrate his ability each time he played.

And his talents weren't limited to just music or impromptu violin repairs. It's hard to imagine how someone might learn to shoot at a music conservatory, but Carl had also managed to become an ace marksman. He was so good it was said that he could shoot the spots off a playing card.

Of course, word about it spread, and the public wanted to see this new skill with their own eyes, so Carl added it to his repertoire. Anything to keep people in their seats, right?

Throughout his career, he shared his gifts with audiences all over the world. Carl even took his unique brand of music and marksmanship to America, where he eventually settled with his wife and gained citizenship.

Carl had lived the kind of life most men only dreamed of, becoming a celebrity both at home and abroad. But when his later years were upended by the First World War, he saw a bigger calling for himself. He wanted to help the veterans returning from battle, specifically those who had lost their limbs.

To do this, he wrote and illustrated a guidebook for them. It took him less than a month to finish and it taught recent amputees how to use their feet for things they used to do with their hands.

I know, it sounds strange for a master violinist—a man who could change a broken string in the middle of a performance or shoot a playing card—to write a book about using one's feet to perform everyday tasks.

Well, as the old saying goes, you have to write what you know, and Carl knew all about *doing* things with his feet. From shuffling cards, to smoking cigarettes, to writing his autobiography, Carl was a phenom with his feet.

That's because he had no choice. Carl Unthan had been born without hands.

NICK OF TIME

Since the beginning of time, civilizations all over the world have found new and innovative ways of telling the time. The sundial, which calculated the time of day for ancient Egyptians using the sun's position in the sky, is one of the oldest techniques we know of. The Saxons cut up candles into sections instead, with each segment meant to burn for just one hour.

As time advanced, so too did the methods by which people measured it. It was in the late 1300s when the first mechanical clock chimed for the world. Though the device has been lost to history, we can get a good idea about how it might have functioned thanks to the Salisbury Cathedral in England, which boasts the oldest working clock in the world.

As with most new inventions, early clocks tended to have flaws. They were notoriously inaccurate and complicated due to their use of weights, which also made them too large for the average house. Churches were the primary locations for most mechanical clocks until the coiled spring was invented in the mid-fifteenth century, allowing clockmakers to shrink them down to a more manageable—and accurate—size.

Later on, new materials and techniques were added. Pendulums, hairsprings, quartz, and magnets all found their way into these machines, bringing their costs down and allowing them to live in our homes and even on our wrists. Over the centuries, they're transformed from enormous structures to mass-produced commodities.

And that's the funny thing about the common clock. We don't really think about it. We expect it to be there, on the wall or on our wrist, or now, on our cell phones. We've never had a reason to ask the biggest question of all: why can't we tell time? Our bodies are capable of incredible things, like creating life and healing our own wounds, but counting the seconds to the same degree as a ten-dollar watch is impossible.

Some extraordinary people are capable of hearing a tone and telling you exactly what musical note it is. Others have photographic memories so vast, they're able to recall ten-year-old conversations word-for-word as though they were reciting lines from a play. But an accurate internal clock has eluded our evolution for millennia.

At least until 1825, when J. D. Chevalley demonstrated his unique talent for telling time. He'd developed it as a child when he began counting the intervals between bell chimes and pendulum vibrations of the clocks around him. He once gathered a crowd on a steamboat on Lake Geneva and told them he could calculate any number of minutes or seconds they called out without fail. When the time had passed, he would announce it with startling accuracy while a spectator with a watch verified his claim.

He was never wrong.

What's more amazing is that he did this while carrying on conversations with the members of the crowd. His internal clock was wound so tightly, nothing could throw it off. He once said of his gift, "I have acquired by imitation, labour, and patience, a movement, which neither thoughts nor labour nor anything can stop."

Not much else is known about Chevalley. He'd had his fifteen minutes of fame, which I'm sure he counted down to the second, and wasn't heard from again. Telling time better than a wristwatch is a fun party trick, but not something to earn a living on. Though, I do wonder why no one else has come forward with a similar ability.

Perhaps our reliance on technology has made such a talent unnecessary. Maybe our memories will be next to go as we rely on the internet to do our remembering for us.

Or maybe J. D. Chevalley was just born at the right time in the right place, like he'd been destined to become the perfect human clock.

After all, he was *Swiss*.

CLIMB EVERY MOUNTAIN

G oran Kropp loved mountains. Some might say he was even built like one. The man topped out at six foot three and 240 pounds. He was born in Sweden in 1966, and his father introduced him to climbing at a very young age. When Goran was six, he and his father climbed the highest mountain in Norway together, cementing Goran's obsession then and there.

Mountains change over time, but never go away. They're solid. Permanent. If only Mr. and Mrs. Kropp's marriage had been as strong. Several years after Goran's life-changing adventure, his parents divorced.

Goran didn't take it well, but after a few years of endless partying and excessive drinking, he knew something had to change. He couldn't keep going on this way, so Goran made a complete 180-degree turn and joined the Swedish paratroopers. It was there he built up his strength and stamina, marching for miles with 150 pounds of gear strapped to his back, and gaining the admiration of his fellow soldiers.

But he never forgot his love of climbing, the feel of rocks under his fingers, and the thrill of reaching the top of a place man was not meant to see. Goran lived a simple life outside of being a paratrooper. He saved his meager military earnings by living in a tent, and climbed mountains in his free time. By the late 1980s, he'd climbed five peaks, each of them nearly four miles tall . . . and all by himself.

After that, it was all about climbing higher and farther. He was the first Swede to climb to the top of K2 in the Himalayas, and by the mid-nineties, he'd reached the summit of five of the fourteen tallest mountains in the world, most of them by himself. There was a reason he was known as "the Crazy Swede."

But one peak stood out above all the rest—literally. Survivors have written books about it and countless men and women have died trying to reach the top. That's right, Mount Everest. He still had yet to summit the granddaddy of them all.

He was Goran Kropp, the Crazy Swede, and climbing to the top of Mount Everest like everyone else was out of the question. He couldn't just fly from his home in Stockholm all the way to Nepal. No, he wanted to make an entrance—one that would take him six months to make.

He loaded up a specially designed bicycle with 250 pounds of food and gear, and left his home on October 16 of 1995. He rode six thousand miles on that bicycle—all the way to the Everest base camp—arriving in April of 1996.

Once there, he convinced the other on-going expeditions at the time to let him summit first . . . alone. No Sherpa, no partner;

just Goran and his gear. This was it. Everything he'd been training for—all those other mountains he'd conquered—had been nothing more than appetizers. And *this* was the main course.

He began his ascent on May 3, trudging all day through snow as deep as his thighs, until he found himself three hundred feet from the summit. Unfortunately, the day had gotten away from him, and darkness was closing in. Goran wasn't worried about reaching the top, but about being stranded alone on the mountain until morning. Up to his waist in snow and ice, he would surely die of exposure.

Instead, he climbed back down and bided his time in base camp. Then the unthinkable happened. A blizzard had struck another group of climbers descending Everest a few days later. They'd left too late in the day, and had been caught in the storm after dark.

Goran helped carry medical supplies up the mountain over the next several weeks.

When the weather finally cleared up three weeks later, he saw his chance. He was going to try again. On his second attempt, the Crazy Swede did it. He climbed to the top of Mount Everest all by himself, accomplishing something very few others had done before him. Then, with nothing left to prove, Goran descended the mountain.

Waiting for him back at base camp was his only companion, the one who had come with him all the way from Stockholm, Sweden—his trusty bicycle. Goran Kropp packed up his gear, mounted his mighty steed, and said goodbye to everyone at base camp before beginning his ride home.

It seems that even after climbing the tallest and most dangerous mountain in the world, he just couldn't help going the extra mile.

THE LITTLE GIANT

People change over the course of their lives. As they grow up, they grow in other ways. Their tastes change, their styles change, even the kinds of friends they keep change. But most people tend not to change in . . . other ways.

Oh, sure, they might get a drastic haircut or have a little work done. And some people might hit the gym five times a week so they can look like a superhero by beach season. But nobody changes the way Adam did. That's because he was one of a kind.

Adam was born in Austria at the turn of the century. Ever the patriotic fellow, he attempted to enlist in the German army during World War I, but he was turned away. And for very good reason: there was no way they'd allow a four foot six man on the front lines. They didn't even make uniforms in his size.

But he kept trying. He felt he had a duty to serve his country, and he wouldn't let his diminutive stature hold him back. Adam managed to add another two inches to his frame the following year, but the army

wouldn't have it. He still came in at under five feet tall and to the powers that be, he proved more a liability than an asset.

Oddly enough, though, were the parts of Adam that had developed beyond his undersized build. Namely, his hands and feet. He was like a mastiff puppy in that respect, with a shoe size that had doubled within two years even though his height remained mostly the same. When he reached the age of twenty-one, it was like a switch had been flipped.

Adam shot up like a redwood—almost three feet in ten years. Doctors examined him thoroughly, discovering he was born with a condition known as acromegaly, in which the pituitary gland produces too much growth hormone. Even if you haven't heard of it, there's no doubt you've seen it. The condition affects fewer than twenty thousand cases per year, but some notable individuals include celebrities like Andre the Giant and Richard Kiel, who played the metal-mouthed henchman Jaws in several James Bond movies.

Adam's condition worsened later in life due to a tumor on his pituitary gland. If you were to look at pictures of him from when he was barely twenty all the way to the end of his life, you'd see how stark the transition was. One moment, he's the picture of perfect health, all of his facial features within a standard proportion. The next, his forehead has enlarged, as has his chin, and his cheeks are puffed out like a chipmunk's. Within ten years, Adam had gone through a sort of Jekyll-and-Hyde physical transformation into someone completely different.

The doctors tried to operate and remove

the tumor, but given how long it had been growing, chances of curing his condition were slim. They managed to slow down the growth rate, but unfortunately, it wasn't enough. He kept getting taller, his body contorting and modulating to accommodate the rapid growth. He went blind in one eye and deaf in his left ear. His spine curved so severely he was bedridden by his late forties.

Most people stop growing by the time they reach adulthood, and might even begin shrinking as they approach old age, perhaps hunched over by years spent at a desk or performing manual labor. Not Adam, though. By the time he died at the age of fifty-one, he'd grown from the meager four feet six inches of his youth to a staggering seven feet eight inches tall.

He had lived two lives as part of two different worlds, making Adam Rainer the only man on earth who ever lived as both a dwarf . . . and a giant.

TALL ORDER

Some guys just feel like they have something to prove. How else would you explain someone like Jeffrey Hudson? Born in England in 1619, Jeffrey's family worked under British royalty as keepers of their livestock. The Duchess of Buckingham took particular interest in Jeffrey when he was very young and invited him become a part of the family.

They were so infatuated with him, in fact, they thought it would be selfish to keep him to themselves. Months after Jeffrey joined the Duchess's household, he was presented to King Charles I and his wife, Queen Henrietta Maria, at a grand feast in their honor.

As the dinner came to a close and dessert was being served, the young Jeffrey popped out of a pie before the queen, clad in a suit of armor. The sight was terribly amusing and the duke and duchess gifted Jeffrey to the king and queen.

Jeffrey moved in with his new royal "parents," so to speak, and got along quite well with the rest of the household. His cuteness, however, began to fade as he grew up, and so to maintain favor with the royal family, he started wearing elaborate costumes and telling jokes to entertain them. He became known as quite the wit among the nobles who visited the king and queen.

His talents once took him all the way to the French court, but upon his return to England, his ship was besieged by a band of pirates. He escaped unharmed and resumed his life among his royal family. Though they saw him as nothing more than a clown, they nevertheless educated him in all the various customs of the court, including horseback riding and shooting. He was also raised in the Roman Catholic church. He was never a royal himself, but he was cared for as though he'd been born one.

In the 1640s, as tensions between King Charles and Parliament rose over a coming Irish insurrection, Queen Henrietta fled to the Netherlands with several members of her house, including Jeffrey. He tried to use his unique skills to help drum up support and funds for the king's crusade, but proved unsuccessful with the Protestant Dutch government. With no other way out of the coming war, the queen returned to her husband, who had already begun to fight.

The war grew more violent in the subsequent months, and the queen knew she had to get out if she hoped to survive. Just as she had done before, she gathered her courtiers and Jeffrey, and this time escaped to France, where he eventually grew tired of being her court jester. He stopped performing and started standing up for himself.

It is unknown exactly what transpired between Jeffrey and the brother of English baron William Crofts while he was there in France, but it had been offensive enough for the young Mr. Hudson to challenge the man to a duel.

The Crofts brother, thinking the whole affair nothing but a joke, arrived with a kind of seventeenth-century squirt gun. An insult to Jeffrey. When the time came for them to draw their weapons, Jeffrey aimed his pistol and fired at the arrogant Mr. Crofts. The bullet hit him square between the eyes, killing him.

Unbeknownst to Jeffrey, dueling was considered illegal, and seeing as how he had murdered a man from a very powerful family, he was quickly sentenced to death. Thankfully, at the last minute, Queen Henrietta managed to step in and get his sentence commuted. Rather than hang for his crime, her surrogate son was exiled back to England.

Jeffrey led a fairly charmed life, especially compared with others in the royal court. The queen often looked after him, as though he were her own child, and in a way he was. At least, that's how she saw *him*. Jeffrey, however, didn't see it that way. To him, he was more of a pet. A novelty. Something to amuse rich elites.

You see, Sir Jeffrey Hudson was only eighteen inches tall.

What happened to him in the months following his exile is largely unknown. However, it's been noted that he was captured by Barbary pirates and shipped to North Africa where he was enslaved for twenty-five years. During his time there, he was said to have grown to forty-five inches tall, putting him at a final height of three feet nine inches.

Eventually, Jeffrey returned to England, but not to the queen's court. He soon found himself imprisoned once again during a time when Catholics were under persecution by the English crown. He died in 1682, penni-less, and buried in an unmarked grave.

It seems that in both life *and* death, Sir Jeffrey Hudson came up short.

YOU MUST REMEMBER THIS

O ur memories—not the memories them-selves, but the act of remembering—are fragile. As we get older, it gets harder for us to hold on to our past. It starts simply, sometimes without us even noticing what's going on.

We forget to pick up an item at the store. It wasn't on the list. We'll add it for next time, but we never do. Or we walk into a room and forget why we're there in the first place. We look around for clues as to what brought us there, only to leave empty-handed until we can remember again.

The brain is a fickle thing. However, that fickleness can go both ways. Just ask Dan-iel McCartney. In the mid-1880s, Daniel's brain was a bit of a celebrity. He began his life in Muscatine, Iowa, but moved to Mor-row County, Ohio, where he spent most of his life.

And if you were to ask him about that life, he could tell you anything you wanted to know. The weather conditions of a partic-ular day, or what he had for every meal, or how he occupied his time from the moment he woke up until he fell asleep. You see, Daniel McCartney had a special skill.

What used to be called hyperthymesia is now known today as HSAM—Highly Superior Autobiographical Memory—and from the age of nine years old, it gave Daniel the ability to recall every detail from every day of his life. He could even tell you the day of the week certain events fell on. Ask him what he was doing on March 6, 1880, and Daniel could recount his breakfast, lunch, and dinner, as well as who he spoke to, what they talked about, whether it was raining, and more. Within Daniel's head resided a complete encyclopedia of his own life, available to him within seconds.

He was also known as a human calculator. Mildly challenging equations could be solved in seconds without need for pencil and paper, although the truly difficult ones would take minutes. In 1870, mathematicians in Salem, Ohio, asked Daniel to calculate eighty-nine to the sixth power. It took him ten minutes to work out the correct answer. On another occasion, he was asked to find the cube root of 4,741,632. Three minutes later, he rattled off the solution.

If it sounds like Daniel was a kind of mental superhero, that's because he was. Only twelve people in the world currently possess HSAM, including actress Marilu Henner and author Jill Price. When a newspaper asked Jill in 2017 what she was doing on August 29, 1980, she had no problem remembering it was a Friday, and that she was with her friends and their family on a Labor Day trip to Palm Springs.

Nor had she forgotten about the spa she and her girlfriends had gone to before they arrived at Palm Springs. She'd been just over fourteen at the time. The third time she drove a car? She remembered that one, too: January 10, 1981. It was a Saturday and she'd just turned fifteen two weeks earlier.

Surprisingly, all of the men who have been diagnosed with the condition have turned out to be left-handed. And while all people with HSAM can recall personal memories and minute details, that doesn't mean they have photographic memories for the purposes of retaining information. For example, Daniel McCartney couldn't cram for an exam the night before and simply *expect* to remember everything he'd read.

Ask anyone with the condition, and they might tell you how hard their lives can be. Every conversation, every cringe, every misspoken sentiment that has ruined a relationship can never be forgotten. What some might look at as a blessing can sometimes be a curse to the person living with it.

But in the late 1800s, Daniel McCartney made the best of it. He entertained crowds of people who had never seen someone with such insight into their own brain, who could perform mental calculations faster than most mathematicians. Daniel was a force of nature and the epitome of that age-old phrase:

"Knowledge is power."

BIG MISTAKE

Charles had always been a little different. His family looked up to him. Everyone he met did, too. They couldn't help it. He was over seven feet tall.

His parents claimed his towering height was due to his conception atop a haystack, though the real reason for his stature didn't matter to him. All he knew was that in Ireland in 1761, he was an anomaly. A freak, as they used to call him, and it wasn't long before he had outgrown the tiny village where he lived. Literally.

Charles set out for Scotland as a teenager, and began performing fun tricks for people he met. He liked to see the reactions on their faces as he lit his pipe using a nearby streetlamp. His charm and personality made him a sensation. So much so that a stage show was written and performed about the larger-than-life Irish transplant.

Charles's fame had earned him quite a bit of money, too, which he carried on him at all times. He didn't use banks, nor did he keep anything in a secret hiding place at home. Unfortunately, many locals knew about his wealth, which made him a target. After a night of heavy drinking, a pickpocket man-aged to lift every last bill off of the seven-foot giant, leaving him penniless.

To make matters worse, it started to come to light that Charles's height had come at a cost. While the story about the haystack was a fun way to play off their son's situation, the truth had actually been much darker. Charles Byrne had been born with a tumor on his pituitary gland, which had accelerated his growth. His health eventually took a bad turn and, compounded with his sudden extreme poverty, left him without any kind of a fighting chance at survival. He died at twenty-two years old, broke and homeless.

But the story of the Irish Giant doesn't end there. In fact, it gets a little stranger. See, Charles had died at a time when the medical field was entering an era of intense research, when patients—alive or dead—were being experimented on in new, sometimes inhumane ways. The dead rarely got a chance to rest as undertakers sold bodies on the black market to desperate medical researchers.

Charles Byrne had known all about these kinds of doctors and how they'd want to study his body after he was gone. One in particular had been on his radar for some time. He was a surgeon and collector of biological specimens named John Hunter—an apt name for someone who spent his life in pursuit of rare cadavers.

Prior to his death, Charles had asked a group of friends to make sure his body would be buried at sea, far from the hands of Dr. Hunter. They agreed to his wishes and after he died, had his body placed in a lead-lined coffin before casting it to the bottom of the ocean.

It's a wonder it sank at all, given that it had been empty.

There would have been no way for Dr. Hunter to retrieve Charles's body once it had slipped beneath the waves, so he turned to his trusty assistant: cold, hard cash. He paid Charles Byrne's embalmer to steal the corpse before it went into the coffin. Charles's friends had had no idea, at least not for a year. During that time, Dr. Hunter performed all sorts of experiments on the late Irish Giant's corpse, leaving behind nothing more than his oversized bones.

His skeleton remains the centerpiece of the Hunterian Museum at the Royal College of Surgeons in London. John Hunter's contributions to medicine cannot be understated. Thanks to his research, we have a greater understanding of how our bones develop over time, and how gunshot wounds and venereal diseases affect the body.

His legacy, however, will always have a large blemish upon it for not letting a poor young man rest in peace.

Just how large? I'd say about seven and a half feet.

PUZZLING

CRIMES

MATCHING SET

John Osborne lived a charmed life. Born in 1858 to immigrant parents, he worked hard and built a reputation as a smart young man. He graduated in 1880 from the University of Vermont with a degree in medicine, and was quickly hired by the Union Pacific Railroad as a company surgeon, which ultimately led him from the East Coast to the western town of Rawlins, Wyoming.

He dabbled in other occupations, and seemed to find success in all of them. He was a farmer, a banker, a chemist, and a rancher, and together with his day job as a physician, these careers all seemed to fill his coffers and bolster his reputation. By the age of twenty-five he was an elected official in Wyoming, kicking off a career that led him to the US House of Representatives and even a two-year term as governor of Wyoming.

It's said that Osborne could often be seem around town, smiling and waving to people he knew, all dressed up in his fine suit with his two-tone leather shoes and matching leather medicine bag. He was normal, successful, and the sort of man you'd want on your side if you were feeling ill or needed the advice of a kind doctor.

That's John Osborne. But I want to tell you about another man, as well. Because if John Osborne had an exact opposite, George "Big Nose" Warden was it. Born around the same time, George hadn't managed to find the same path to success that John had. In fact, by 1878, Big Nose George was an outlaw, running his own gang of criminals.

That was the same year that George and his associates tried to rob a train outside Rawlins, Wyoming—home to good old Dr. John Osborne—but it turns out there were a couple of undercover sheriffs working alongside him. George ran, and then when he had the lawmen in sight, he killed them.

He managed to live on the run for two years before making the mistake of telling someone about the murders. He was turned in, arrested, and then transported back to Rawlins for his trial. On March 22 of 1881, before his trial could actually begin, George was pulled out of jail by an angry mob and dragged kicking and screaming to a nearby telegraph pole where a noose had been arranged.

George was the opposite of John Osborne. John was popular, but the entire mob hated poor George. So when he managed to get his hands free from the rope that bound him, and then wrap his arms around the pole to keep himself from hanging, the crowd just watched and waited.

No one helped him. No one took him up on his request to shoot him and prevent the slow death by strangulation. They just mocked him and watched the clock. Before long, Big Nose George's arms gave out, and he dropped. He was dead a few minutes later, slowly choked by the noose around his neck.

He was buried in a plain pine box. Legend

says that George's nose was so big that the undertaker had to get help to hold the lid down so he could nail it shut. I've seen pictures of the guy, and honestly, I can believe it. Big Nose George earned that nickname.

A short while after he was buried, though, someone dug him up. A local physician wanted to do an autopsy and study the remains of the murderer, to see what physical reasons there might be for George's deviant behavior. But he didn't find anything.

He did, however, keep some souvenirs. This doctor took the skin from George's chest and legs and had it tanned. He made leather from the flesh of a dead human. Then he took that leather to a cobbler and had a pair of shoes made.

Oh, and a medicine bag. Naturally.

So there you go; the story of two very different men: a convicted killer, and the well-respected local doctor who wanted to better understand him. Which reminds me of an old saying: sometimes, in order to understand a person, you need to walk a mile in their shoes.

If that's true, the one thing is certain: no one understood Big Nose George Warden better than Dr. John Osborne.

COLLECTOR'S ITEM

New York's Metropolitan Museum of Art paid a handsome sum for the statue. In 1921, the $40,000 price tag was the equivalent of over $600,000 today. But to the Met, it was worth it.

The statue—known as "the Big Warrior"—stood nearly seven feet tall, and showed the likeness of a soldier from the Etruscan civilization. They were a culture that lived in central Italy but were absorbed into the Roman Empire as it grew and took over the region. It's an older and lesser-known culture, and relics from that period are incredibly difficult to find. So, yeah, the Met knew a good deal when it saw one.

The statue was part of a collection that the Met purchased over the span of six years from a team of restoration experts in Italy. The Big Warrior had been pieced back together by this team—two brothers and their sons, all with the last name Riccardi—but other items were in a less complete state. One example was the four-foot-tall sculpture of a warrior's head, the body lost to time. Experts at the Met concluded that when it was new, the head had sat atop a statue nearly twenty-five feet tall.

The last item purchased was another warrior of similar height to the Big Warrior. This one was put on display as "the Old Warrior," but it was in much worse shape. The entire right arm had been lost, as had the thumb from the left hand. But it was still beautiful, and made for a great addition to their growing Etruscan collection.

The exhibit featuring them opened in 1933, but right from the start there were scholars who had doubts. There were debates and papers published from both sides of the argument, but by the 1960s most archaeologists were in agreement: the Etruscan statues were fakes.

There were a number of pieces of evidence that helped seal the case. Part of it came down to a chemical analysis of the glaze used on the terra-cotta, but there were also some discrepancies regarding the way these statues were crafted and fired. Etruscans made everything in one piece, while these were clearly built in segments and later assembled.

Finally, in 1961, an elderly man named Alfredo Fioravanti slowly walked into the American consulate in Rome, where he sat down and wrote out a formal confession. He had been a sculptor employed by the Riccardis back in the early 1900s, helping them craft elaborate forgeries that were later sold to museums like the Met in New York. He even had photographs of the statutes to show them.

Fioravanti told them how they did it, too. They would work for months to craft a statue and get it just right. And then, when it was finished, they would push it over and watch it shatter into hundreds of pieces. Then, painstakingly, they would reassemble it, as any restoration expert might do with a broken archaeological find. If parts were ever missing, that was entirely by design—as in the case of the Old Warrior.

The authorities were skeptical, though. One man, decades later, claiming to have the answers to a long-forgotten mystery . . . well, that's the stuff of movie plots and paperback thrillers, not real life. But the old man insisted he was telling the truth.

To prove it, he pulled a small object out of his pocket and placed it on the table. The authorities there gave him a puzzled look before picking the item up and turning it over in their hands. When they recognized what it was, they knew the mystery had been solved.

It was a piece of the Old Warrior that no one had ever seen before, but everyone had assumed once existed.

The missing left thumb.

FOOLED

Henri had made fools of them all.

As he stood there in the middle of the crowd of people who had come for the museum's new gallery opening, he couldn't help but smile. My, how far he had come.

Decades earlier, he'd been a brilliant young artist. His paintings were spectacular and eye-catching, and he had a promising career ahead of him. And yet . . . well, he was just too honest. When an art critic offered to print a favorable review of his work for a hefty price, Henri refused. The resulting review destroyed his career before it had even begun.

But standing here, in the middle of the exhibit crowd, while hundreds of people filed past his work, all of the suffering seemed worth it. Along the way, of course, he had picked up new skills, and transformed himself into an entirely new artist. That's how you learn and grow, after all. But Henri took it one step further.

The exhibit, you see, was of a newly discovered Vermeer painting. There weren't many of the seventeenth century Dutch master's paintings in existence, so finding a new one was guaranteed to draw a crowd. What none of them knew, though, is that Henri—and not Vermeer—had been the man to paint it.

It was his sweet moment of revenge. All of those critics and peers who had doubted him and pushed him down were now nothing more than fools, tricked into believing that a painting Henri had created was actually the work of a Dutch Master. It was validating.

That was 1937. Over the next few years, Henri tried his hand at more forgeries. He managed to sell another fake Vermeer to the infamous Nazi Hermann Goering, one of the most powerful figures in Hitler's Germany. Goering had been gathering stolen artwork all across Europe, but occasionally purchased pieces he loved. A newly discovered Vermeer was just too tempting to pass up, and Henri walked away with half a million dollars.

When the war ended and Goering's hoard of treasure was recovered, experts began to look through the collection and attempt to determine where each piece came from. The new Vermeer, though, proved tricky. After months of chasing leads, though, it the authorities managed to arrive on Henri's doorstep.

At first they arrested him for collaborating with the Nazi forces, believing he had stolen the painting and given it to Goering personally. Henri insisted, though, that the painting was fake, and that he had actually fooled Goering into buying it. For a long time, though, no one would believe him. After all, how could this man—this unknown, washed-up artist—ever manage to create paintings that might be confused with the work of the legendary Vermeer?

So Henri proved it. Under the supervision of the authorities, Henri gathered the tools, chemicals, and paints necessary to complete another of his knockoff masterpieces, and then got to work. As the story goes, he wasn't even finished with the painting before the experts caved in and accepted defeat. Henri really *was* that good.

In the end, the court convicted him of forging signatures, and delivered a short, one-year jail sentence. Henri, however, had a heart attack a few days after the trial, and passed away before he could serve his time.

Oh, and one last thing. After going through everything recovered from Henri's home, the authorities found the bag of cash that Goering has used to purchase the fake Vermeer. Henri had barely touched it, already wealthy from the sale of other fakes to a handful of European museums. That's when they discovered something absolutely amazing: the cash was fake.

The unlikely fraud, it seems, had become the victim of his own game.

A CHILLING MYSTERY

Everyone needs a hero.

I think it's fair to say that many of us have been inspired by the amazing lives of other people. Heroes give us a target, a destination that we might try to reach for ourselves. They drive us forward and call us to action.

So it's no wonder that Charlie fell in love with the story of Sir John Franklin. He was a British naval officer in the first half of the nineteenth century who had a taste for adventure. This was a time when people were still trying to find an easier way to get from the Atlantic Ocean to the Pacific than sailing all the way around the tip of South America.

They called this elusive route the Northwest Passage, and assumed that it was somewhere north of Canada, through the icy waters of the Arctic. Franklin had the experience to get the job done, too. He was a rear admiral, had served as governor of Tasmania, and over the years had already helped explore the Hudson Bay in North America. He wasn't a slouch, that's for sure.

And he was a fighter, too. On one expedition that ended in 1822, he and his crew got into such dire straits that at one point they were forced to try to eat their own leather shoes. But it was his last journey that he's best known for: his own expedition to find that undiscovered Northwest Passage.

He was given a large crew, food for three years, and two sturdy ships that you might have heard of: the *Terror* and the *Erebus*—named after the Greek god of darkness. If you know your history, then you also know that the voyage was a failure. In fact, Franklin and his crew were never heard from again.

And that's the inspirational story that caught Charlie's attention. He read about it in his local Vermont newspaper when it happened in 1847, and it stuck with him every day after that. He wanted to be an explorer like Franklin. In fact, he wanted to be the explorer who *found* Franklin. So he set out aboard a ship in 1860 to do just that.

He and the others made it about as far as Baffin Island's Frobisher Bay, and then winter caused them to stop and wait. He heard about Franklin from the local Inuit people, and got the impression that the legendary explorer and his crew might actually still be alive. So after returning from that first voyage in 1862, he immediately began planning a return trip. He was *this* close to learning the truth, and possibly even making his own great contribution to the world of exploration. Charlie could feel it in his bones.

His second expedition began in July of 1864, and lasted five whole years. On King William Island, Charlie was able to find the remains of Franklin's expedition, but it was

nothing more than artifacts. No one had survived the tragedy of the *Terror* and the *Erebus*, and that was a realization that must have crushed Charlie's spirit.

He didn't give up, though. In some ways, he'd succeeded. He gave the world a definitive answer about the Franklin expedition, and closure was a good thing. But it also left Charlie believing that he was somehow fated to follow in Franklin's footsteps—to leave his own mark on history through brave, daring exploration—so he planned yet another trip.

With funding from the US Congress and a ship of his own, Charlie headed out in July of 1871 to try to reach the North Pole. He had a crew of twenty-five with him, including a German physician named Dr. Bessels who was there to serve as his science officer, but even with all of those resources, things were rocky.

His sailing master was a drunk who kept sneaking alcohol from the cargo area, Dr. Bessels was constantly arguing with him, and the weather wasn't cooperating with their plans. In fact, even though they'd gone farther north than any previous expedition, the sea ice was becoming too thick to move forward, so they guided their ship into a nearby bay for a rest.

Side note: Charlie was so grateful for that bay that he named it Thank God Harbor. Because why not, right?

Anyway, things didn't improve. In fact, as the winter got colder, the ice got thicker, and so their wait got longer. Days became weeks, weeks became months, and patient people became unbearable. At one point, Charlie left the ship on a short solo expedition to look around and see if there might be another way through the ice. But after reading about all the personal issues on the trapped ship, I think he also just needed some space to think.

When he returned, he was exhausted and cold. The first thing he apparently did was ask for a cup of hot coffee, which was quickly rounded up for him and delivered to his cabin. A short while later, though, he began to complain about not feeling well. Within days he could barely talk or sit up in bed, and a short while after that he was dead. Later, the crew took his body to shore and managed to dig a shallow grave for his coffin. They held a little funeral there in the frigid cold, and then waited for their chance to go home.

It's interesting to note that *Franklin* was killed by the *elements,* but *Charlie*—Charles Francis Hall, as history will remember him—was killed by something *else*. At least, that's what two historians believed back in 1968. So they traveled north to Greenland, following in Charlie's footsteps to the very shore of Thank God Harbor, where they searched for his frozen grave.

And they found it. They found it and they dug it up. Inside, Charlie's corpse was little more than a skeleton with a bit of skin and tissue still attached, his head resting on a pillow as if sleeping. An American flag was draped over his body, but the entire coffin had flooded and was frozen. Perfect conditions for preserving a body for certain kinds of testing.

The two scholars, Doctors Loomis and Paddock, took samples of Charlie's hair and fingernails, and then brought them to Toronto for examination. What they discovered was that Charlie hadn't gotten sick and died at all. He'd been murdered. The trouble is, on a ship as big as his, with twenty-five other tired, trapped, and angry shipmates, anyone could have been the suspect.

Charles Francis Hall left Vermont to solve the mystery of what really happened to Franklin's expedition—and he managed to do that. But in the process, he left us with a mystery of his own. We may never know for sure who killed Charlie, but maybe that's okay. Maybe this *new* mystery will inspire someone else to do great things as well.

Everyone needs a hero, after all. Even a dead one.

NUTSHELL

A lifeless body beside a bloody knife. A woman in her living room, dangling by her neck from a clothesline. A man slumped over the door of his convertible in his garage. At first glance, some of these deaths might seem like suicides or accidents. Not so. They are three of twenty unsolved murders, each with a different motive, but connected by one common thread: a woman named Fanny.

Born in Chicago in 1878, Fanny led a traditional, sheltered, nineteenth century life. Her father was a successful farm equipment manufacturer who expected his family to adhere to the strict gender norms of the time. Men, he said, should go to college and then get jobs to support their wives, who were meant to stay at home with the children.

Fanny and her brother were homeschooled, and both dreamed of attending Harvard. However, only her brother was allowed to go, which was disappointing, because Fanny had dreams of her own. The kinds of dreams she couldn't share with anyone else, and no way of fulfilling them while she still lived in her father's home. Respecting his wishes, she instead got married at the age of nineteen.

The marriage was perfectly fine for a while. They had three children and Fanny seemed satisfied. But deep down, she never forgot about her dreams. Eventually, they proved too powerful to hold back, driving her to divorce her husband in order to make them all come true, something that was unheard of at the time. Fanny, now in her forties, used the inheritance from her late father and her recently deceased brother to pursue a passion that she'd repressed for far too long: murder.

Specifically, the homicide cases described to her by one of her brother's college classmates. With his help and her newfound wealth, she created a new department at Harvard: the department of legal medicine. She also helped set up a library named in his honor, as well as a curriculum known today as the Harvard Seminars in Homicide Investigation.

Of course, Fanny did all of this in the 1940s, so it should come as no surprise that she was often discouraged from visiting crime scenes. Instead, she decided to create her own. It was the perfect cover, really—inserting herself into the growing world of murder investigation to better understand how to study and teach it.

Throughout the second half of her life, Fanny went from housewife to homicidal architect. She carried out elaborate murders, mostly of women, who had strayed from the safety of their domestic lives. She then used her crimes to educate others on best practices in analyzing crime scenes.

Her technique required the students to employ a geometric search pattern, such as a clockwise spiral, when examining the crime scene. Scanning from one side of the room to the next in a 360-degree fashion, students would get an idea of how her murders had been committed.

Despite her grisly actions, Fanny's work earned her numerous accolades, and she was even made an honorary captain in the New Hampshire State Police, making her the first female police captain in the United States.

As I said at the beginning, her crimes remain unsolved. You might be asking yourself, if we know who Fanny *was* and what she *did*, why would her murders still be unsolved today? The answer is a lot more simple than you'd imagine: they never happened.

You see, while her crimes were based on real cases, they were actually completed as highly detailed *dioramas*. Today they're known as "The Nutshell Studies of Unexplained Death." Each scene is like a room from a grotesque dollhouse, meticulously researched and recreated in order to teach detectives how to look for clues.

And Fanny—known throughout law enforcement as Frances Glessner Lee—is the pioneer who made it all possible. In fact, eighteen of the twenty dioramas that she created are still used today by Maryland's Medical Examiner's office, who also keep their solutions hidden from the public.

The old cliché reminds us that the best way to learn is to *do*.

Let's all be grateful that Fanny didn't take that piece of advice too far.

LAST DANCE

We're taught from a very young age that lightning never strikes the same place twice, but lightning is unpredictable and uncontrollable, and it lacks an agenda. You might say that lightning is definitely not a serial killer.

Serial killers do have an agenda. They can and do hunt the same areas for new victims. They often have a particular victim type or a compulsion for what they do and who they do it to. That was the case in Birmingham, England.

Her name was Mary Ashford and she had plans to go dancing with her friend Hannah Cox one Monday evening. She walked from her home in Langley Heath to Hannah's house and dropped off her party dress for that night. After work, she came by to change, and then the two of them headed out to the party together.

Mary and Hannah had danced with several men throughout the night, but two had entirely captured their attentions: Benjamin Carter and Abraham Thornton. The two couples departed the dance around midnight, but after walking Hannah to her door, Benjamin headed back to the dance.

Mr. Thornton and Mary, however, had

other plans. They walked the route to Mary's grandfather's house, talking until about four in the morning, when Mary went back to Hannah's to pick up her work clothes from the night before.

That was the last time anyone saw her alive.

Early the next morning, a man walking through Pype Hayes Park came across a pile of women's clothing next to large pit filled with water. He told the locals what he'd found and, filled with a growing sense of dread, knew what had to be done.

They dredged the pit and came up with a body. A woman who, according to the police, had been drowned. She had bruises up and down her arms, clear signs of a struggle just before her murder.

Beside the pit, authorities also found two sets of footprints in the mud. One was Mary Ashford's. The other set belonged to Abraham Thornton.

He admitted to spending the evening with the late Miss Ashford, but swore up and down that he didn't kill her. The police didn't see it that way, and, despite having no evidence beyond his muddy footprints, Thornton went on trial for her murder. He was their only suspect, and his odds of beating the rap were slim. Everyone, especially the public, thought he was guilty, but public opinion was not enough to build a case upon.

The police just didn't have the evidence to convict him, and Thornton was acquitted of the charges. Even after numerous petitions for retrials by Mary's family, it could never be proven that he killed her.

When one of Mary's brothers attempted to ask the judge for a retrial, Thornton defended himself by dredging up a piece of medieval law that allowed him to challenge Mary's brother to a trial by battle. If he won, he would be acquitted. If he lost, then he would be hanged. Mary's brother refused the challenge, and Abraham Thornton was once again a free man.

Then . . . another body turned up.

She was found in the same place—Pype Hayes Park—under the same circumstances. Her name was Barbara Forrest and she worked as a nurse at a children's hospital. She, too, had been assaulted and strangled after a night of dancing, and guess where the police began their questioning? That's right. With a man named Thornton. As it turned out, he'd been her coworker at the children's home, and there was *blood* on his pants.

Unfortunately, DNA testing still had years to go before it would be used in police investigations. There just wasn't enough evidence to convict him, and Thornton walked away without ever seeing the inside of a cell.

People close to the victims remembered both women feeling uneasy about their lives just before they were taken. Mary had told Hannah's mother she had "bad feelings about the week to come."

Barbara Forrest had told a coworker a little over a week before her murder, "This is going to be my unlucky month. I just know it."

Both murders had been committed in the same place using the same method, under similar circumstances . . . all by a man named Thornton. But it wasn't the work of a serial killer, and we know that to be 100 percent true.

Why? Because Mary Ashford was murdered in 1817, while Barbara Forrest's death occurred much later.

One hundred fifty-seven years later, to be precise.

UNLUCKY HAND

The Old West. A time of change and growth. Of outlaws and renegades, gunfights in the streets, and swift justice without all the red tape. Disagreements were settled where they happened, and often the only form of mediation required was a bullet. If the movies, television shows, and video games are true, the Old West was a time when laws meant less than one's own personal code of honor. If someone thought you did them wrong, you made it right . . . or you died trying.

One man thought Robert Fallon had done them wrong during a poker game in 1858. It happened in San Francisco just eight years after California joined the country as a full-fledged state. The city was growing out from under the thumb of Mexico's rule, and planting the seeds of the San Francisco we know today. Originally nothing more than a trading post for the West, San Francisco's dirt roads had been paved over, and its hills leveled for new homes and businesses.

One of those new businesses happened to be a saloon. You'd recognize the scene immediately: a dusty wooden floor, men in heavy jackets and tall hats, all sitting around a table drinking whiskey, and in one dark corner, a game of cards with the stakes higher than they'd ever been. Lose a hand? Lose your shirt . . . or maybe more.

Robert Fallon had been playing for a while with a group of men who nursed their beers and downed shots between hands. Some won a little, some lost a little, but Robert had something about him. A kind of aura that had skipped over the other players. A kind of luck.

But they didn't see it that way, and they didn't take kindly to cheaters, either. Actually, they didn't take kindly to anyone winning who wasn't them. Robert had amassed a small fortune at his seat. About $600. And his companions thought something was amiss. Tired of losing every hand, one man stood up and called him out for cheating.

Robert, surprised by the allegation, tried to explain he'd done nothing wrong, but no one wanted to hear it. More excuses from a lying cheat, they figured, so they shot him before he'd had a chance to prove his innocence. His opponents, not wanting to stop the game for something as inconsequential as a dead cheater, looked for someone else to take his place at the table.

The new player hunkered down in the dead man's seat and the table gifted him with the $600 his predecessor had already won. Hand after hand, this new young man seemed to display a similar brand of luck as Robert. He turned that $600 into $2,200 in no time, and just like before, his opponents weren't happy.

But before anyone could pull a revolver from their holster, the police burst into the saloon. Word had traveled fast, and they were on the hunt for the late Fallon's killer. They surveyed the scene and asked a few questions before telling the players that the $600 Robert had won should go to his next of kin.

The players looked around, unsure of how to find Robert's family. They didn't know anything about him—where he'd come from, where he was headed—all of it a mystery. The new player, however—the young man who'd almost quadrupled Robert's winnings that night—wanted to see whose money it was he'd taken.

He got one good look at the body and knew . . . the money had been his all along. Robert Fallon had been killed that night, only to have his estranged son take his place. The two hadn't spoken in seven years.

And that right there is what some might call . . . the luck of the draw.

PROS AND CONS

You have to wonder if some people are born to be conned the way others are born to con them. We believed David Copperfield made the Statue of Liberty disappear because we wanted to. We want to believe the prince promising us untold millions in an email because of what it would mean, how it would change our lives. What we don't often think about is why people deceive us.

In the case of David Copperfield and other magicians, it's for entertainment. To get a rise out of us, to instill a sense of wonder and awe in the audience. The supposed prince is just looking for a quick buck from an unwitting victim.

Then there are people like Victor. Victor was born in Austria-Hungary at the turn of the century, and he had a gift: he was a reader. Of books . . . and of people. There was no real reason for him to turn to a life of crime. It's not like he fell into a deep pit of debt, or lived on the streets. As a teenager, he studied in Paris and gained fluency in multiple languages. Victor was on track to be a great student. He might have gone on to be a great man, but we'll never know.

At nineteen years old, Victor needed a break from his education. He went on holiday where he discovered gambling . . . and women. Those two didn't mix, however, and Victor found himself on the receiving end of a nasty scar on one side of his face. One of the women he'd met had had a boyfriend with a jealous streak.

But Victor recovered and took his talents to the open seas, where he pulled schemes on unsuspecting travelers sailing between France and New York. In one, he pretended to be a Broadway producer and solicited investor funds for a nonexistent production.

As the years passed, Victor's scams grew in size and boldness. By 1925, the time had come to do something big. Something that would establish his legacy all over the world. He returned to Paris and came upon a newspaper story about the Eiffel Tower. The monument had fallen into disrepair and the money to fix it had run dry.

The article mentioned how the time might come one day when the city would have to simply tear it down. But where Paris saw an eyesore, Victor saw a way to get rich in the most ludicrous way possible.

He hired a forger to draft fake credentials for him, then invited several scrap metal dealers to a large hotel. He introduced himself as a high-ranking official within the government, and claimed that Paris just couldn't afford to keep the Eiffel Tower up anymore. It had to go, and Victor had been selected to choose the scrap metal dealer who would haul the pieces away.

He read their faces as he spoke, paying attention to mannerisms and tics that might give away the perfect mark for his con. They weren't hard to spot, either. The man who would end up with the winning bid for Victor's sham business was relatively unknown in the Parisian business community. His name was André and he wanted to make a name for himself, so after all the bids were sent in, he put in a little extra just for Victor.

It worked. Victor accepted André's offer and collected both his bribe and the money necessary to secure the tower's supposed sale. And then he fled to Austria with his winnings.

Poor André didn't know what had hit him. He couldn't go to the police, nor could he tell his fellow businessmen without looking foolish. Victor made sure to read the French newspapers for any mention of his scheme, but when nothing surfaced, he knew he'd done it. He'd sold the Eiffel Tower.

If that had been me, I'd have stopped there. To pull off one of the greatest cons in history without anyone else knowing about it, including the police, would have been enough. But I'm not Victor Lustig. He wanted to press his luck, to see if he could hit the jackpot twice.

So one year later, he returned to Paris and tried the same scam again, this time with a new group of scrap metal dealers. Only this time they were prepared. The police had been tipped off about Victor's meeting and went after him, but his craftiness got the better of them once again. He went to the United States where he returned to a life of smaller, pettier crimes.

Well, almost.

You see, he'd found a new mark, a businessman from Chicago—a man no other conman would have thought to cross. Victor promised the man he would double his money if he just invested in an amazing new business opportunity he had planned. The mark agreed and gave him $5,000. Victor promised him he'd have twice that much in one month.

Well, the month came and Victor hadn't doubled the man's money. Except this time, the conman didn't flee the country. Honestly, there wasn't anywhere he could've gone, anyway. His mark would have found him and made him pay one way or the other, so Victor returned his fifty thousand to him without a cent missing.

The mark was so impressed with Victor's honesty, he refused it, telling him to keep it for his trouble. And the man he tried to swindle out of that fifty grand? None other than the king of crime himself.

Al Capone.

BANK ROLLED

Charles De Ville Wells was known for two things: gambling and fraud. Though, that wasn't always the case. In the mid-nineteenth century, Wells worked on the docks as an engineer and inventor. One of his inventions, a device for regulating the speed of ships' propellers, sold for five thousand francs. With his newfound fortune, Wells moved to Paris—and that's where the trouble started.

He left his old life behind in favor of a new one, and along the way he discovered gambling. He became addicted to the thrill, and having a few extra francs in his pocket made it easier to get hooked. But as much as Wells loved to play the tables, he wasn't very good at it.

Eventually, the onetime inventor went broke, so he turned to less-than-legal ways of feeding the monkey on his back. He convinced investors to finance a new railway he was building in Berck-sur-Mer, a commune in the north of France.

Well, the railway never materialized, and when the courts demanded he answer for his deception, neither did he. He fled Paris for England, where he found new casinos to lose his money in. When it was all gone, he started another con. This time, he had the public invest in original inventions of his own design, promising huge payouts over time once they hit the market.

You can probably guess what happened. That's right—the profits Wells had promised never came. He led the investors on for years, with one man losing about nineteen thousand pounds in the deal—that's almost $2.5 million today.

And the money? Also gone, flushed away at any number of casinos Wells had been known to frequent. But he wasn't through. There was always another mark, one with money to give. Money that he was only too happy to take off their hands and spend at the table.

Wells had been well-known among the casinos in France prior to his relocation. In 1891, his travels led him to Monaco, home of the world famous Monte Carlo Casino. This place held one hundred thousand francs in its daily cash reserve—also known as "the bank." Anyone who happened to hit a streak and win more than that amount triggered a shutdown of all table play. Casino officials would drape a black cloth over the winner's table, then withdraw money from the vault to cover the difference. This was known as "breaking the bank."

Wells pulled up to the roulette table and placed a bet. The dealer spun the wheel and the little white ball bounced from space to space until finally landing on a number. Wells's number. He'd won.

He placed another bet and that proved to be a winner as well. For eleven hours, Wells sat at that roulette table and placed bet after bet, eventually accumulating a whopping one million francs in winnings. When he was ready to cash out, the casino draped a black cloth over the table and pulled out 900,000 francs from its vault. Charles Wells had become only the sixth person in history to break the bank at Monte Carlo.

A song was written about him shortly thereafter, titled "The Man Who Broke the Bank at Monte Carlo," immortalizing the famous fraudster for all time. No one knows how he did it. Given his criminal past, everyone assumed Wells had found a way to cheat. Perhaps the dealer had been in on it, rigging the wheel to give him the correct slot each time so they'd split the winnings at the end. Or maybe Wells had finally found a system that worked.

The most likely explanation was that he just happened to get lucky for the second time in his life. It didn't last, though. Eventually, the authorities caught up with Wells and made him answer for his crimes back in England, where he served eight years in prison for fraud. When he got out, he went right back to his old conniving ways—and back to the casinos, hoping to recapture some of that glory he'd felt in Monte Carlo.

But it never came. Wells died at the age of fifty-one from kidney failure, without a single cent to his name.

His winning streak finally over.

KILLER ACT

Hypnosis is one of those things most people laugh about when it's discussed as entertainment. It's fake, they say. You can't control someone just by swinging a pocket watch in front of their face like a pendulum. The people in those Vegas shows must be plants, individuals hired to pretend that they have no control over their bodies. They hop on one foot, or bite into an onion like it's an apple, and the audience applauds because they don't know any better.

But hypnosis is one of those strange places where art and science intersect. As a therapy tool, hypnosis can be incredibly beneficial to those who need it, but it takes time. It can't be induced in the time it takes to put on a short stage show. Not unless you're Arthur Everton, whose powers of persuasion were second to none.

Arthur was a professional hypnotist way back in 1909, often inviting audience members to come up onstage and be a part of his act. At a performance in Somerville, New Jersey, one night, he polled the crowd for a volunteer. The man who raised his hand was a piano mover and streetcar conductor from Newark named Robert Simpson. A moment later, Simpson climbed onstage and then awaited Arthur's instructions.

The hypnotist placed him under a trance, one meant to induce a cataleptic state. In other words, Simpson's body went as stiff as a board. Arthur lowered him down, positioning him between two chairs like a kind of bridge, with his head on one chair and his feet on the other.

Everton then put his skills—and Simpson's body—to the test by climbing up and standing on the volunteer's chest for a few seconds. The audience went wild. Amazingly, Simpson didn't move. He showed no signs of pain or stress, even though Arthur had just used him as a makeshift platform.

After Arthur stepped down, he eased Simpson down off the chairs before standing him back up. It was time to bring him out of his trance and back to reality. Arthur called to him, demanding he wake up. But Simpson just stood there, rigid and unmoving. Arthur tried again, but Simpson still refused to pop out of his trace and return to normal.

This was surprising to the audience, for sure. But it was even more troublesome for Arthur. Why? Because he and Simpson had performed the trick dozens of times before. Yes, Robert Simpson was a plant. In fact, he was what they called a "leader," someone planted in the audience to lead the rest of the crowd into the fantasy.

Finally, after several moments with no movement, Simpson's body began to relax, and then he collapsed to the floor. Arthur quickly dragged his friend offstage, where he attempted to revive him, but shockingly, it was too late. A doctor in the audience pronounced Robert Simpson dead at the scene, much to Arthur's consternation.

Arthur believed the man wasn't dead, but merely still stuck in his trance. Given time, he'd be able to wake him up just as he had before. The doctor let him accompany Simpson to the hospital where the hypnotist spent all night trying to pull him back out of his trace. But nothing worked, and the following morning, Arthur Everton was arrested for manslaughter.

After the newspapers reported on the story, hypnotists from all over the country came out of the woodwork with suggestions of their own for how to reanimate the late piano mover. One man named William Davenport, at the request of Mr. Everton, also tried his hand at bringing Mr. Simpson back.

His methods were a lot less mystical than you might imagine, though. Davenport simply leaned over Simpson's body, rested his hand upon the man's heart, and then whispered into his ear, "Bob . . . your heart! . . . your heart is beating!"

Nothing. Because Robert Simpson wasn't trapped in a catatonic state, or some sort of hypnotic trance. No, his aorta had ruptured, killing him almost instantly. But the doctors couldn't tell whether Arthur's trick had been the cause of it all, or if it had just been an unfortunate coincidence. Either way, they were certain the hypnotist was not to blame.

The grand jury soon agreed, and Arthur Everton was not charged. He returned to performing a short while later, but his business took a hit thanks to the bad publicity.

Even though every stage performer dreams of the day they might "kill it," as they say, most audiences have a very different goal.

They just want to make it out of the show alive.

GHOSTED

William Kent was a humble innkeeper in mid-1700s England. During the many months when he and his wife, Elizabeth, were expecting the birth of their first child, the woman's sister Fanny came to stay with them and help around the house. Sadly, Elizabeth died giving birth to their son, and the frail little infant passed away a short while later.

William was in turmoil, having lost both his beloved wife and his newborn son just days apart. Fanny decided to stay and help him, and eventually the two fell in love. He wanted to marry her, so he set out for London to seek counsel on how to proceed, but there was a problem. The church wouldn't let William marry Fanny, as canon law forbade it.

William was heartbroken and decided to get away—from his job, from the old house, from every bad memory he had. He and Fanny parted ways, and then he moved to London where he started a new life for himself. Fanny, however, couldn't forget William. She wrote him letters professing her love for him, and he wrote back each time. Eventually, William could no longer hide his feelings, and he invited her to stay with him.

The two lived secretly as husband and wife. They moved to a property on Cock Lane, just outside of London, which was owned by a man named Richard Parsons. Parsons was a parish clerk who owed William a debt for a loan given to him some time earlier. But there was something about the couple that didn't sit well with Parsons.

Some believe that Fanny's family had reached out and let him in on their little secret because they were upset about their daughter's behavior. However he learned the truth, he used canon law as justification to simply not repay William.

One day, William was called away to a wedding out of town, leaving a now-pregnant Fanny alone. To make sure she was watched over while he was gone, he asked Parsons's daughter, Elizabeth, to stay with her, sleeping in the same bed just in case something went wrong with the baby.

Mr. Parsons agreed to the arrangement, and then William left. That was when the scratching started. It occurred at different parts of the day and night around the home, often paired with a knocking sound. Parsons's wife said a cobbler worked nearby and that was probably what they'd heard, but when the sounds resurfaced the following Sunday—a day of rest for many tradesmen—they knew something was amiss.

Another local landlord came to inspect the house and claimed to witness a glowing, white spirit climbing the stairs. Richard Parsons confirmed he'd seen the same thing. When William returned home he moved Fanny out—not just because of the ghost, but also because of her pregnancy. She was only a few weeks away from giving birth, and he had a comfortable place ready for her to deliver in. Unfortunately, tragedy would strike once again. Fanny had contracted smallpox, and after several days of fever, she passed away.

William inherited her estate and used the money to pay her burial costs, leaving him with little left over. Nevertheless, he didn't stay down for long. He eventually remarried, and became a successful stockbroker.

With his new status and happy family, he returned to Cock Lane, taking over for the previous tenant who had left after the scratching and knocking noises became too much to bear. Richard Parsons eventually discovered the cause—his daughter, Elizabeth, claimed the ghost had returned, but now there were two, not one.

The first, which had bothered Fanny Lynes prior to her death, was thought to be her deceased sister. And the new ghost? Why, Fanny herself, of course. Parsons believed they had an important message to share, and that's why they refused to move on.

Elizabeth Lynes's presence was meant to be a warning to her sister about her death. Fanny, however, bore more shocking news. Her spirit, communicating "yes" and "no" through a series of knocks, let Parsons know the secret about her widower husband: that he had murdered her. Possibly both of them. William had allegedly poisoned Fanny with arsenic before she could have the baby, and then had her buried quickly to hide any evidence.

The church believed the ghosts were telling the truth. After all, how could you argue with a spirit? William soon became a prime suspect in the murder of Fanny. Desperate to clear his name, he asked for a séance to be held in the home so he could ask her himself. Upstairs, Richard Parsons's daughter and her sister were sleeping while William, Richard, and several others in the community gathered around a table.

They asked the spirit questions about her marriage to William, and whether he'd poisoned her. One knock meant yes, two knocks meant no. Had they been married? Two knocks. Had he poisoned her? One knock. Things weren't looking good for poor Mr. Kent, but there was something about the ghost that struck everyone as odd: she seemed to go wherever Elizabeth Parsons went. While Elizabeth was staying in another person's home, knocking sounds were reportedly heard through the night. When she returned to her home on Cock Lane just in time for another séance, so did the noise.

An investigation was conducted, as were several more séances. And present for all of them in some part of the house was Elizabeth Parsons. One night, the investigators asked her to sleep with her arms outstretched, her hands outside of the bed. No scratching or knocking was heard. Not a sound.

The experiment was repeated again the next night and the same thing happened—absolutely nothing. The truth was finally exposed when Elizabeth's maids noticed the small plank of wood she kept tucked into her clothes. They alerted investigators right away. Elizabeth, it seems, had been the ghost the entire time, knocking and scratching with the wood block. But why?

Well, because her *father* had put her up to it. He still owed William Kent money on the loan he'd taken, and he didn't want to pay it back. After Fanny had died, William had sued him for the remaining money, so Parsons exacted his revenge the only way he knew how: by pretending to be a ghost and framing him for murder.

His Scooby Doo–style plan didn't work, though. After a quick trial, Richard and his wife were ordered to pay hundreds of pounds in damages to William, and Richard was also sentenced to prison.

In the end, the lesson is obvious and simple: if you plan to skip out on your debts, you better have a really good plan, a lot of luck, and just in case things go south . . .

. . . you better knock on wood.

WARTIME
WONDERS

THE DEADLY DOUBLE

It was just a simple advertisement, and for a game, no less. There was absolutely nothing illegal or dangerous about it. And yet here they were, sitting across the table from a pair of FBI agents.

The product in question was a pretty simple dice game. And with Christmas approaching, the company had decided to run a few ads in the biggest city in America, all of them scattered throughout one single issue of *The New Yorker*. All of them were small and square, sort of like an Instagram post, and each one told interested buyers to refer to the main advertisement on page 86.

The game had been created by a company called Monarch Publishing, and the ad had been written by one of their executives, a man named Roger Paul Craig. He and his wife had spent hours trying to craft the text of the main ad, which touched on the approaching holiday season and all of the things people might have to do to be ready. The trouble wasn't in the text, though; it was in the artwork.

At the bottom of the large ad on page 86 was the big, bold title of the game, "The

Deadly Double." Beneath it was an emblem of a bird with outstretched wings, four talons, and two heads. It's what's known as an armorial device, a sort of coat of arms used for identifying individuals and groups. This particular symbol was the spitting image of the double-eagle used by the Byzantine Empire, Ivan the Terrible, and—more recently—Nazi Germany.

Add in the fact that the title of the ad included the German word "achtung," which means "danger," and it was a curious pairing, for sure. That's probably what drew the attention of the investigators, but it certainly wasn't the only thing they were worried about. The bigger problem, it seems, was inside each of the smaller ads.

Each of those were identical, and they showed a pair of dice in action. The image was hand-drawn, and had a classy tone, but the items in the ad are a bit mysterious. One of the dice showed three sides, revealing three distinct numbers: 12, 24, and the Roman numeral for 20. The other die showed the reader 5, 0, and 7.

So as Roger Paul Craig and his wife sat across the table from the FBI agents, they were starting to get nervous. The numbers, according to the investigators, were significant, and that wasn't a good thing. Twenty, they said, was awfully close to the latitude line where Pearl Harbor sat. The 12 and 7 looked a lot like December 7, the date of that infamous attack. And the 0–5 could very well have been 0500 hours, the original planned start time of the attack on Pearl Harbor.

But so what? It wasn't illegal to place historical details in an advertisement. Yes, it would be in poor taste, sure—over 2,400 lives were lost in the Battle of Pearl Harbor, so it's probably not the best subject matter for a dice game looking for gangbuster Christmas sales.

But the trouble wasn't the subject matter, it was the timing. You see, the ad that Monarch Publishing placed in *The New Yorker* was published in November, on the twenty-second, in fact. November of 1941.

Sixteen *days* before Pearl Harbor was attacked.

THE JOKER

Reggie was a bit of a practical joker. Sure, he was a physicist by training, and used his skills to help the British military defend itself from the Germans during World War II, but that trickster nature was always right there near the surface.

It's said that in the 1930s, while he was a research fellow at Oxford, he called up one of the other professors to carry out a prank. The first few times he called, Reggie immediately hung up as the man was answering. Finally, after sowing the seeds of frustration and doubt, he called and pretended to be a representative from the telephone company, and reported a faulty line.

He then went on to ask this professor to run a series of tests to see if the problem was on his end. Those tests included tapping his pencil on the phone, standing on one leg, and dipping the receiver into a bowl of cold water. Much to Reggie's enjoyment, the professor followed all of the instructions to a tee.

Let's be honest, though. The college campus is no stranger to practical jokes. In fact, Steve Wozniak, one of the founders of Apple Computer, engaged in his own fair share of fun. Wozniak actually built a sort of signal jammer for televisions, and would carry it in his pocket in the dorm and cause TV shows to cut in and out, much to every else's frustration.

But most people grow up. They move on and leave those college pranks behind them. Steve Wozniak helped create one of the most culturally significant companies of the last century, and Reggie went on to work for British Military Intelligence. His training as a physicist allowed him to help the British avoid the bombing raids that the Germans continually sent their way.

The Germans had developed a technology they called the Knickebein, which was a method for guiding airplanes to a very specific target using a pair of radio beams that intersected over the location. Reggie's first assignment was to find a way to bend one of those beams and throw off the German bombers. And it worked. Rather than dropping bombs on major cities, the German planes were guided out into the countryside where their bombs did much less damage.

One of Reggie's lesser-known projects, though, was focused on building a device known as the H2S. It was widely lauded as a savior for the British navy, who were constantly plagued by the invisible German U-boats beneath their ships. Reggie's job was to build a system that would allow British warships to locate and target these U-boats using infrared beams.

News of the H2S quickly spread, and as things have a way of working out, the Germans caught wind of it. They spent months planning countermeasures, eventually recalling every single U-boat in their fleet so they could dry-dock it and paint it with a special formula that would deceive those infrared beams.

Which is funny, because H2S never existed. Reggie and his team never built a device that could locate German submarines and help warships destroy them. They never even tried. All Reggie did was make up the rumor and then let it spread. The rest, as they always say, is history—and also *hilarious*.

Sometimes a practical joker is exactly the person you need. The work of Reginald Jones drew more than a few laughs from his friends in the military—and saved thousands of lives in the process.

Now that's a punch line I can get behind.

GOING UNDER

They say necessity is the mother of invention. When spears weren't enough to stop an enemy, bows and arrows were created. When those outlived their usefulness, along came guns and rifles to get the job done. War transformed as weapons advanced, but one thing never changed: the ingenuity of desperate men faced with impossible odds.

That ingenuity was on full display during the American Civil War, when battles weren't just fought in fields and towns, but along coastlines and rivers. These waterways were used to transport supplies, ammunition, and even soldiers from one location to another. An army controlling the water could cripple the opposing force's access to necessary items, such as food and medical equipment.

The water was also used as a venue for surprise attacks. Soldiers marching near an enemy-controlled waterway would often find themselves ambushed by waiting gunboats. Rivers and coastlines quickly became a crucial part of an army's strategy and if an enemy wanted a chance at survival, it had to either avoid the water entirely . . . or use it to its advantage.

It was at the height of the Civil War when just such an advantage presented itself. A Union blockade had been stationed in the waters off Charleston, South Carolina, led by the steam-powered sloop-of-war known as the *Housatonic*. Armed with a dozen cannons, the *Housatonic* was known for capturing Confederate ships, like the four-hundred-ton iron-hulled steamer, the SS *Georgiana*.

The Confederacy needed to break up the blockade to open up Charleston's shores, but to do so, the *Housatonic* had to go. There was only one problem: the ship was five miles off the coast. Any opposing vessel launched from the shore would be seen immediately and destroyed.

So, the Confederate Army had an outrageous idea—what if they attacked it from below? It took them two years of trial and error, but a submersible was finally developed that could carry eight men. It would travel beneath the water to the *Housatonic*, where the men would detonate a torpedo along the enemy's hull.

Something to keep in mind, though: unlike our modern torpedoes that propel themselves through the water, the *Hunley* carried what was known as a spar torpedo. It was basically a canister of explosive powder attached to the end of a long pole, which would be rammed into the opposing ship.

On the night of February 17, 1864, the *Hunley* and its crew slipped into the waters off the coast of Charleston. Powered by hand crank, it glided toward the *Housatonic*, that explosive payload leading the charge about twenty feet ahead. Later, one of the

Housatonic crew members would report that he had seen something strange in the water—something large and mysterious—but before he could alert his crewmates, it was too late.

The *Hunley* jabbed the *Housatonic*'s starboard side at 8:45 p.m., and made history. Those eight men had completed the first successful submarine attack on a warship. Five crew members aboard the *Housatonic* died as the ship sank, and if the story ended there, that alone would be enough to cement the *Hunley*'s spot in Civil War legend—but there was something else.

According to initial reports, everything had gone swimmingly. The *Housatonic* had been destroyed and the *Hunley* had begun its return to base. Except it never made it home. The sub and all eight lives inside were lost, although for almost a century and a half, no one was sure why. The mystery would remain unsolved until after the vessel was found at the bottom of Charleston's outer harbor in the mid-1990s.

In the summer of 2000, marine archeologists raised the *Hunley* from the depths, and got to work restoring the vessel. Experts spent months cleaning up the hull before opening it to see what was inside. And that's when the end of one mystery led to the start of another. You see, the eight crew members inside hadn't gotten out after the torpedo detonated. A sad end to a daring operation, for sure, but that's not the crazy part.

Upon opening up the hull, the conservation experts noticed the crew had never even made any attempt to escape. There were no external injuries or signs of drowning. The explosion, they believe, had simply been so strong that the lung and brain tissue of the men inside had been instantly obliterated.

Sometimes you win, and sometimes you lose. And sometimes . . . you do *both*.

WAR TIME

War. What is it good for? Well, if you're hoping to overthrow a government or unseat an unfavorable leader, it can help. And if you're looking out for the future of your country's imperial rule, it may be your only course of action.

That's what happened on August 27, 1896, in the island nation of Zanzibar. For years, Zanzibar had been independent of its homeland, Oman, and ruled by a long line of sultans. The United Kingdom had maintained a close relationship with the country for decades and as the years went on, that relationship grew much stronger. Some might say *too* strong.

By 1893, the British had forced Zanzibar to abolish many of their inhumane-yet-profitable industries, much to the consternation of its citizens. The sultan himself had supported the British in their endeavors and didn't see a problem with the changes, but his people had. So on August 25 of 1896, the sultan was assassinated.

The top suspect was the sultan's own cousin, who had most likely poisoned the former ruler. He took over the duties of the throne and moved into the palace—all before his cousin's funeral that very same day.

Seriously, half an hour after the old sultan had been buried, the new one was sitting on the throne. Zanzibari leaders certainly wasted no time.

Except the new ruler hit a roadblock with his grand plan. As it turned out, he'd ignored a treaty signed ten years earlier that required anyone seeking the crown to get permission from the British consul. The murderous cousin had not obtained that permission.

It didn't matter that he'd declared himself the new leader publicly, or that the palace guns had fired a salute marking the occasion that afternoon. Without approval from the *British*, he was nothing more than a pretender wearing another man's crown.

British General Lloyd Matthews urged the new sultan to step down so that a more UK-friendly ruler could take his place. The sultan, however, refused. He gathered thousands of troops in the Palace Square, armed with rifles, cannons, and a Gatling gun, and then waited to see what the British would do with their own thousand-man army.

Matthews continued to press for a surrender, but his threats of retaliation didn't sway the sultan. In fact, on the morning of August 27, he tested Matthews's resolve. British warships opened fire from the harbor, killing forces within the palace. The Zanzibari fleet returned fire on the British ships, and within moments the country officially became a war zone.

As the fighting raged on, a fire broke out that consumed the palace and killed hundreds of the sultan's soldiers. Before the war was even over, the new sultan had fled the country to seek asylum in Germany, leaving the British free to install their own choice as the new ruler. And they managed to do it without the loss of a single British life.

You might be wondering: in a war that claimed the lives of more than five hundred Zanzibari men and women, how is it possible that the British didn't lose a single person on their side? The sultan's army was well-trained and well-armed. They would have put up a fight.

But the British had a few things going for them. First, they were much more prepared for battle than the sultan's forces. Their weaponry was more advanced, and their army was much larger. Second, the palace wasn't made of concrete or stone. It was made of wood, which provided almost no protection from the incoming cannonballs or the inevitable fire that burned it all down.

In the end, the most interesting detail about this entire event is how it's recorded in the history books. Even today, it's referred to as the Anglo-Zanzibar War. And I suppose it technically was, given that two armies traded gunfire over the fate of a country's leadership. It's just that . . . well, most wars last a lot longer.

This one, you see, was the shortest war in history, clocking in at only *forty-five minutes*.

LOSING SLEEP

The Vietnam War lasted from 1955 to 1975, and in its wake almost 4 million souls were lost. A tragedy, and one they'll write books and documentaries about until the end of time. But it wasn't the only war taking place during that period. Neighboring countries waged their own campaigns alongside the turmoil going on inside Vietnam.

One such country was Laos, which—beginning in 1955—was the site of a massive civil war. On one side was the communist Pathet Lao movement, which was allied with North Vietnam. On the other, the Royal Laotian Government, allies of South Vietnam. The CIA had dubbed it the Secret War, because we had recruited and trained a Laotian hill tribe called the Hmong to fight the North Vietnamese on our behalf in order to stop the spread of communism.

The United States feared that if Laos fell to communism, nearby countries would be next. Laos had been designated a neutral territory, but by using the Hmong to fight this war, they had turned them into targets for the Pathet Lao. After the Vietnam and Secret Wars ended, the Pathet Lao didn't forget about what had happened, or who had been responsible.

They began hunting down massive numbers of Hmong people in what is now known as the Hmong genocide, which some say still goes on today. As a result, many Hmong fled to the mountains to avoid persecution, while a good number found their way to America. By 1981, that number had grown to over thirty-five thousand. But even though they managed to escape Laos, they couldn't escape the horrors of what they'd witnessed there. Death had followed them.

No one here really knew how to help them. Almost none of the Hmong spoke any English and their language was not well-known outside of their own country. It wasn't like you could go down to the local bookstore and buy a Hmong-to-English dictionary. So not only were they still suffering years after fleeing their homeland, they were doing so all on their own.

But this suffering didn't come in the form of internal bleeding or gunshots. There were no stab wounds or broken bones. Their pain was on a different level, but still just as traumatizing. And it was beyond frightening to the others around them.

One night a refugee would go to sleep and the next morning they wouldn't wake up. Eighteen Hmong refugees, mostly men, between the ages of nineteen and fifty-seven, died unexpectedly in their sleep. Doctors at the Centers for Disease Control were baffled. Autopsies revealed nothing except that the men had all been in good health.

Except there's one part of the human body that doctors can't autopsy: there's no way to cut into a person's brain and see their thoughts. The Hmong people living in the United States had been burdened with the worst memories imaginable. These memories kept many of them awake, and the ones who did manage to sleep didn't do so for long. They *couldn't,* not with the images of murdered friends and loved ones burned into their minds.

After days without sleep, their hearts, already exhausted and broken, would simply give out in the night. Doctors called it Sudden Unexplained Death Syndrome, or SUDS. In the Philippines, they gave it a name that essentially means "nightmare."

Around the time these reports of unexplained deaths hit the papers, a former professor was looking to make his mark on Hollywood. He'd already directed a small film about a family tormented by cannibals in the Nevada desert, but this was the eighties and he felt America was ready for something *truly* scary.

That's when he came across an article about the Hmong refugees who were dying in their sleep, and their story sparked a question in his mind: can our nightmares really kill us? And if so, how?

Whether or not he answered the question, this professor did go on to give birth to one of the most frightening horror films of the 1980s. Today we might view his career with enthusiasm, but Wes Craven understood that his dark stories had even darker roots.

And now you know how nightmares landed on the big screen ... all thanks to one monster: Freddy Krueger.

DOGS OF WAR

World War I, also known as the Great War, claimed the lives of 40 million civilians and military personnel from all over the world. It lasted for four years and was commonly referred to as "the war to end all wars." Obviously, that name didn't stick for too long, but it was a particularly brutal and devastating event in world history.

The United States stayed out of the fray for most of the war, until 1917, when it joined Britain, France, and Russia. Together, these allies combated the Central Powers of Germany, the Austrian-Hungarian Empire, the Ottoman Empire, and Bulgaria across Europe.

World War I saw the rise and fall of some pretty prominent individuals. Woodrow Wilson, Winston Churchill, Tsar Nicholas II, and Vladimir Lenin all made headlines throughout those tumultuous four years, but there was one name that kind of slipped under the radar (which was actually invented during World War II, but let's not get technical, okay?).

He was known as "Sergeant Stubby" and he was from Connecticut. He liked to hang around the Yale University campus, which was where members of the 102nd Infantry trained for their eventual deployment. He and another soldier, Corporal Robert Conroy, had struck up a friendship and, not wanting to wish his best friend goodbye for possibly the last time, Stubby snuck on board Conroy's ship before it set off for France.

He was soon discovered, but charmed the infantry's commanding officer and was allowed to stay—much to everyone's surprise. Stubby found himself in the trenches for eight months alongside his new family, including Conroy. He began his military career in early February of 1918 and never shied away from battle, quickly getting used to the constant barrage of gunfire exploding overhead day and night.

Three months later, Stubby was wounded in the leg by a German hand grenade and spent weeks at the rear recovering. With two new wound stripes on his uniform, he was back at the front lines helping his regiment.

He learned how to detect mustard gas to warn his unit, and he was the only soldier capable of finding wounded troops in "no-man's-land" without getting shot. No-man's-land was an uncrossable stretch of terrain between two enemy trenches. Anyone who tried to cross it was almost instantly killed. But not Stubby.

During one battle in Argonne, Stubby had come across a German spy and held him captive until reinforcements arrived to take the enemy away.

By the end of the war, Sergeant Stubby had fought in four major offensives and seventeen battles, and became a bit of a celebrity back home. The military and numerous other organizations awarded him three service stripes, a Yankee Division YD Patch, a Purple

Heart, a New Haven World War I Veterans Medal, and seven other honors. He marched in a number of victory parades, and even went on to meet President Woodrow Wilson.

Stubby had demonstrated his abilities as a new breed of soldier. I don't mean he was more ruthless or cunning than the others. He was literally a new breed of soldier. A mixture of Boston and American Bull Terrier. Sergeant Stubby was Corporal Conroy's dog.

In 1921, Conroy swapped the frontlines for Georgetown University, where he received his law degree with Stubby by his side. The mutt soon became the university's mascot and made appearances at football games, running around the field at halftime to entertain the fans.

Stubby had lived a full and rewarding life, more so than any other dog, and he'd been rewarded handsomely for his service.

After his death in 1926, *The New York Times* ran a half-page obituary for him, longer than any that most of his human contemporaries had received. And if you visit Washington, DC, stop by the National Museum at the Smithsonian Institution, where you'll find Stubby on display in his military uniform adorned with his many medals. Corporal Conroy donated Stubby's taxidermied remains to the facility in 1956.

Dogs are loyal, faithful companions. They have a keen intuition and know when we're sick or sad or even in danger. They will protect us, as Sergeant Stubby did the 102nd Infantry, and as many dogs do for today's soldiers. Stubby never asked to be a hero, but he certainly became one simply by being Conroy's friend.

You might even say he was that man's *best* friend.

TWO SHIPS PASSING

War requires sacrifice. Of course lives are lost, but war takes its toll on everyone, from the soldier's mother waiting for that fateful knock at her door, to the unemployed workers in the recessions that follow. It even forces people to adapt. Spies assume new identities so they can infiltrate enemy lines, while taxicabs and libraries turn into ambulances and infirmaries when the real things are in short supply. That's what happened with two ships during a maritime battle at the start of World War I.

In September of 1914, two ships, the British HMS *Carmania* and the German SS *Cap Trafalgar,* engaged in a contentious duel in the South Atlantic. Dozens died and by the end, it was Britain's pride and joy, the *Carmania,* that had defeated the Germans' *Cap Trafalgar* and sent it to the bottom of the ocean.

I know. I'm kind of giving away the ending right up front. But bear with me. All will become clear in a moment. I promise.

See, both vessels had begun life as passenger ships, carrying folks to various ports all over the world. Brazil, Argentina, and Uruguay had all been intended destinations, but in August of 1914, the *Cap Trafalgar* was commandeered by the German Imperial Navy and turned into a warship. A naval crew outfitted her with guns and other artillery, while the *Carmania* underwent similar treatment by the British, including having its red and black funnels painted gray to match the rest of the hull.

Not only did their respective militaries deck them out with all the latest weapons, but they'd also made their ships as stealthy as possible, allowing them to sneak by the enemy undetected. Once complete, both vessels were released back into the ocean to perform their new jobs: hunt down and sink the enemy.

The *Carmania*'s crew had gotten word of the *Cap Trafalgar*'s position off the coast of Trinidad in the Caribbean. They were closing in, but the area was swimming with German ships. It was time to for the *Carmania*'s crew to put their stealthy efforts to the test.

They spotted the *Cap Trafalgar* in the exact spot they'd been told. At least, they thought it was the *Cap Trafalgar*. It fit the description and had just left a German supply base with a fresh belly full of coal, but something felt off. That ship looked awfully familiar, like the *Carmania* crew had seen it before somewhere else.

The *Cap Trafalgar* tried to get away, but the British were right behind them. The *Carmania* fired first, straight across the bow of the enemy ship, and the *Cap Trafalgar* stopped running. It returned fire with its main gun, firing out 56-pound shells at half a mile per second.

That was it. The battle had begun. They fought for over two hours, firing bullets into each other's hulls. Wood splintered off and fell into the water as metal exploded inward, leaving gashes in the sides of each ship. The *Cap Trafalgar*'s machine guns turned the *Carmania* into Swiss cheese, but the *Carmania* managed to hit the other ship's bow and start a fire.

Both vessels did their best to take out each other's guns and water lines, but it was the *Carmania* that proved victorious. The *Cap Trafalgar* started taking on too much water and the crew was forced to either flee in lifeboats or jump into the waves below to escape the sinking ship.

All told, about sixty sailors died that day between the two ships, and another twenty-six were wounded. Those who managed to escape the *Cap Trafalgar*'s sinking were rescued by another German ship and taken to Buenos Aires for safety. Though, to those who witnessed the sinking, it might have looked a little different.

It might have looked as though the *Carmania* had been sunk in battle instead.

As it turned out, the crew of the *Cap Trafalgar* had intended to entrap British merchant ships off the Trinidadian coast. To do so, it had to look friendly, like one of Britain's own ships, so the crew took down her forward funnel and painted the remaining two funnels with red and black tops.

In other words, they had disguised the *Cap Trafalgar* to look like the *Carmania*. And the *Carmania*? Well, it must have been like looking into a mirror . . . or seeing a ghost.

CODE WORD CONFUSION

War requires a lot from a soldier: intuition, dedication, and resourcefulness. From medic to MacGyver, a soldier's role can change from one moment to the next and oftentimes, the only tools they have to work with are the objects on their person at the time. You might not think you could patch up a wound with only a rifle, a knife, and some leaves you found on the ground, but when you're under enemy fire, you find a way. The United States military had to find a way when they ran afoul of the Chinese Army during the Korean War.

The Chang Jin mountain reservoir, known by American forces as the Chosin Reservoir, became a hotbed of action during the Chinese Second Offensive in 1950. The war appeared to be over as UN forces advanced into North Korea in order to unite the two sides, but reunification wasn't going to happen if the People's Republic of China had anything to say about it.

Approximately 120,000 Chinese soldiers infiltrated North Korea in an effort to stop the UN's advancement. They reached the

Chosin Reservoir first while a special group of United States soldiers known as the X Corps approached from the coast. I know, they sound like characters out of a Marvel comic book, but trust me, they were real superheroes. Fifteen thousand men from the Marines and the US Army were ready to end the war once and for all, and bring stability to the region.

You might be wondering *why* only fifteen thousand if the Chinese had deployed *eight times* that amount to the area? That's because the United States forces had no idea the Chinese Army was waiting for them. They snuck in and fortified their position, waiting for the Americans to arrive.

The X Corps held their own for over two weeks against the Chinese military, but the harsh terrain and brutal fighting had left them all but defeated. Stuck in freezing temperatures and outgunned, the X Corps, the best of the best, were running out: out of ammo, out of food, and out of time. They were surrounded. The enemy was closing in on thousands of US soldiers, many of whom had nothing to defend themselves with except broken guns and equally broken *spirits*.

Worst of all, the mortar shells they used to beat back the Chinese forces had run dry, so they called in an air drop. "Tootsie Rolls" they called them. It sounds silly, but code names like that were necessary to prevent the other side from knowing what was coming in case someone happened to be listening in.

Unfortunately, whoever took the air drop order didn't understand the code name either. The X Corps got their supplies. Boxes and boxes of what they thought were mortar shells ready to launch. What they received, however, was far less . . . explosive. Their pleas for Tootsie Rolls had gotten them exactly what they'd asked for: Tootsie Rolls. Little chocolate candies wrapped up in wax paper.

This might have signaled the end for the US forces, now without an escape plan and their chances of survival dwindling. After all, you can't win a war with chocolate as your only supply . . . unless you're the X Corps. The men were revitalized by the sugar rush bestowed upon them from overhead, and they quickly realized the little candies, though hardened by the reservoir's freezing winds, became soft and pliable when warmed up in their mouths.

They chewed them into a putty-like substance, which they then spread over the holes in their weapons, letting the wind freeze them in place. With their bellies full and their guns back in action, the X Corps were once again a formidable threat. They managed to fight back just enough to get out of enemy territory, and make their way to the nearest coast where they could regroup.

It sounds almost too strange to be true. The idea that a simple chocolate candy saved the lives of so many American soldiers in Korea, but as it turned out, Tootsie Rolls made as good a patching material as they did a *candy*.

Now that I think about it, it's a good thing they didn't call for an air drop of Life Savers.

SHIPS AHOY!

Jon Kabat-Zinn, professor emeritus at the University of Massachusetts Medical School, once said, "When you pay attention to boredom, it gets incredibly interesting." Recent studies have shown boredom to be a terrific catalyst for creativity. When the mind is starved for stimulation, it begins to wander, which leads to fascinating discoveries and creations.

These days, boredom is a rarity. The blinking devices we carry in our pockets occupy every spare second with cat videos and a scrolling feed of celebrity rumination. However, during the early nineteenth century, boredom was a fact of life, especially during the Napoleonic Wars. I know, a war doesn't scream "boredom," but to the French prisoners of war biding their time until rescue, boredom was all they had.

As Napoleon's Empire fought throughout Europe between 1803 and 1815, numerous French soldiers fell to bullets and bayonets in the pursuit of total domination. Those who weren't killed were taken as prisoners of war, where they waited for weeks, months, and sometimes even years to be released. Their British captors were particularly kind, giving them an ounce of Scotch, a half a pound of meat or fish, and vegetables every day.

Between meals, captive soldiers were left to their own devices, filling their time with sleep, exercise, and staring at the wall. Not a very fulfilling lifestyle, but they made the best of it. Some even developed hobbies. With such a dearth of pastimes available to them, they started fashioning what was around them into trinkets and models. Tiny dioramas, watch displays, and houses were crafted from the refuse left behind after each meal.

For example, a model guillotine featured an array of guards at the base of a long ramp, leading up to the blade dangling precariously over an unfortunate victim. Ornate filigrees adorned the thin fence around the perimeter of the model, and simple hearts had even been carved in the center of each panel.

However, the most *popular* creations made among the eighty thousand prisoners of war were ships. Like the kind of wooden models that might adorn a living room mantel, these ships were finely carved to look like the French and British gunships of the time.

The men tightly wove their own hair into sail rigging, and folded scraps of tissue paper into sails. Once the British officers saw the work coming from their prisoners, they started smuggling in their own materials, such as silk and turtle shells. Tools were even brought in, an act that could have ended disastrously if any of the prisoners had decided to use them to escape.

But despite their circumstances and lack of freedom, they were treated respectfully, fed daily, and assisted in their unique style of arts and crafts. Of course, with wood in short supply in a prison cell, the tissue sails and hair rigging had to be fastened to something. Like I said, the soldiers used whatever they could find to build their models out of, and nothing was in greater supply than one specific item left behind after every meal: bone.

After they'd finished eating their daily fish or lamb, the men would boil the bones and bleach them in the sun to make them easier to carve. Larger bones were used for the ship bodies, while fish bones and tinier pieces were turned into masts and cannons.

The pigs that would roam the POW camp also aided in bone production. Not their own, mind you. The pigs belonged to the soldiers, but any truffle hunter knows the value of a pig's snout. Except instead of truffles, the hogs would sniff out shallow graves that still held human remains. The idea of slicing up human bones into model ships sounds morbid, I know, but French soldiers thought dying of boredom was a much worse fate.

When completed, the ships became ob-jects of desire among British naval officers. The money earned from their sale went back to the soldiers to buy more supplies, thus allowing them to produce more ships. What no one's been able to explain in more than two hundred years, however, is just how the prisoners were able to craft such accurate representations of ships . . . that they couldn't see from their cells.

While they were not built to scale, the level of artistry and precision in each model makes one imagine that perhaps the men were sneaking out each night to study the real thing before getting back to work. A ludicrous thought, but no more ludicrous than what has become of the ships today.

They're still around, and just as in demand as they were two centuries ago. French prisoner of war "bone ships" can sell at auction for thousands of dollars. In fact, a model of the British Royal Navy's HMS *Victory* sold for more than fifty-five thousand dollars back in 2007.

Not too shabby for something made from spare parts in a prison cell.

BY A HARE

Napoleon Bonaparte's military career was defined by success. More than sixty battles fought, and only eight losses. That's a record very few can live up to.

Maybe it's because he planned obsessively, analyzing every detail and preparing for every potential outcome. Perhaps it was because he was annoyingly practical, having expanded on tactics put forth by his predecessors in order to carry out his grand plans for conquest. Or heck, maybe it was both of those things.

Despite Napoleon's strategic genius, though, there were some battles he simply couldn't prepare for, no matter how long he researched. In one instance, the opposing army was too unpredictable, too ferocious, too difficult to comprehend. And it resulted in one of the most devastating losses of his military career.

In July of 1807, Napoleon's French army had just won a major battle against the Russian Empire. With that victory, he brought an end to the hostilities between the two factions, which resulted in a peace treaty. Once signed, Napoleon decided the best course of action would be to celebrate. He instructed his chief of staff, Louis-Alexandre Berthier, to organize a luncheon for the highest ranking men in the French military.

But it wasn't just a luncheon. No, these men were soldiers. They didn't just want to eat, they wanted to *kill* the food they would enjoy together, and nothing would have been more sporting than a good, old fashioned rabbit hunt. Berthier, not someone to carry out a task for his boss lightly, arranged cages teeming with thousands of rabbits along the perimeter of a vast, grassy meadow. After a period of mingling and talking shop, the men picked up their rifles, boarded a carriage, and set out for the hunt.

Once the men arrived, the cages were opened, and the rabbits hopped into the field. Except they didn't scatter. They weren't afraid at all. They took one look at Napoleon and his hunting party, and their agenda became clear.

The hunters had become the hunted. An ocean of bunnies charged toward them, waves of fur and ears coming for the seasoned French officers. And rather than aiming their guns, they simply watched and laughed. After all, what kind of harm could a bunch of rabbits do?

As an aside, I'm sure most of you have heard the phrase, "a murder of crows," right? A "murder" is a quasi-technical term for a group of crows, like a "pride of lions." For rabbits, the options are a bit less entertaining. A "warren," a "herd," or even a "husk." But my personal favorite is a "trip." And that's what Napoleon's officers were facing down: a trip of bunnies.

As the incursion grew closer, Napoleon's

good nature quickly turned to one of fear. The rabbits surrounded the hunters, climbing up their legs and torsos as the men tried hopelessly to brush them off. They used their riding crops, nearby sticks, and anything else they could get their hands on to beat back the onslaught of furry friends. But nothing worked.

The rabbits kept attacking, and Napoleon—not one to run from a battle—knew defeat when he saw it. He had no choice but to retreat, so he and the men jumped back into their carriage hoping to escape. But the bunnies seemed to have learned some military strategy of their own, like divide and conquer. They split into two groups and flanked the carriage on all sides. Some even managed to make it *inside* as it was rolling away.

It wasn't until the carriage was out of sight that the animals finally calmed down. The most brilliant military man in genera-tions had been outdone by an invading army of rabbits. But at least Napoleon had someone else to blame for the fiasco: his chief of staff, Berthier.

You see, on such short notice, it had been impossible for Berthier to find enough wild hares to satisfy a party full of hunters, so he'd put the word out to local farmers that he wanted to buy their rabbits.

Only too happy to oblige a man so prominent within Napoleon's army, the farmers had agreed, and sold him all the rabbits they had. If only Berthier had done his research, he would have learned that farm-raised rabbits were conditioned. They had come to identify the presence of a human being as a sign that food was on its way.

They weren't attacking so much as they were looking for their next meal. And Napoleon? Well, he suffered the most humiliating defeat of his career.

One might even say . . . it tripped him up.

LADY BE BAD

Not long after Italy declared war against France and Britain during World War II, the country became a major target for allied bombers. Out of all their targets, Naples held the title as the most bombed Italian city of the war.

Hospitals and churches were leveled. Residential neighborhoods became battlegrounds. And roughly sixty thousand Italian civilians had been killed in bombing raids by the end of the war. While the country bounced back relatively quickly, so much had already been lost and would never be recovered.

The bombers had carried out the attacks as a form of liberation—from tyranny, from fascism, from the clutches of an autocratic dictator—swooping in, dropping their payloads, and flying back to their respective bases.

Bombing raids became standard fare during the war, but pilots always had unpredictable factors to deal with. Sure, there were enemy planes to watch out for, as well as return fire from soldiers on the ground, but a pilot's deadliest enemy—inside or outside of war—has always been the weather.

Blue skies could turn gray in seconds, and suddenly a routine flight home meant negotiating high winds and lightning while also struggling to remain in the air. And for one particular B-24 bomber, nicknamed "Lady Be Good," the weather would prove to be a more dangerous foe than any Nazi.

Lady Be Good's crew had just wrapped up a bombing run over Naples on the afternoon of April 4, 1943, when it ran into trouble. The mission had been simple: a squadron of twelve bombers would fly over the city first, followed by another group of thirteen bombers right after.

Lady Be Good had taken off from Benghazi, Libya just after 3:00 p.m., when a sandstorm kicked up, making visibility almost impossible. The B-24 fell behind from the rest of the planes, but eventually made it to Naples several hours later, along with three others. When their mission was over, they turned around, and headed back to base.

But Lady Be Good's navigation system started acting up. The pilot, Lieutenant William Hatton, radioed for a landing location, but it never came. Hatton flew directly over the base, taking his crew and his plane deep into the Sahara Desert.

Hours passed and fuel was running low. With no way to land safely, Hatton instructed his men to put on their parachutes and abandon the plane. At 2:00 a.m., nine men jumped from the Lady Be Good, allowing the plane to fly solo to its final resting place in the dark of night.

Rescue efforts were launched the next day, with teams scouring the desert and the Mediterranean Sea for any signs of wreckage. When they found nothing, the men and their Lady were presumed lost.

It wasn't until fifteen years later when British Petroleum workers spotted something from the air over the Calanshio Sand Sea. They'd been scouting locations for potential drilling and radioed authorities at a local air base about their discovery. No one had any idea what was out there. There were no records of any wrecks that far into the desert.

A few months later, more reports of a downed plane started pouring into the base, so on May 26, 1959, a recovery team started investigating the claims. And there it was: the Lady Be Good, broken into two pieces, but otherwise intact.

The plane had been remarkably well preserved, no doubt due to the dry desert environment. The machine guns still worked. There were food and water rations onboard, too. Even a thermos of tea had been found with the liquid inside still drinkable. By all appearances, it seemed the crew that had abandoned the plane midflight never found her again.

In the winter of the following year, the US Army began sweeping the desert for signs of the plane's crew. They found the bodies of five of the men, including Lieutenant Hatton, while most of the others were eventually discovered later having been buried in the sand. Only the gunner, Staff Sergeant Vernon Moore, remained unaccounted for.

After Lady Be Good's discovery, some of her parts were sent back to the United States to be evaluated by teams of engineers. The military, hoping to save a little money, saw an opportunity to repurpose those parts on other aircraft, a decision they would soon come to regret.

Transmitters from the Lady Be Good were installed in a C-54 Skymaster, a transport plane, that was forced to abandon its cargo in an emergency landing after suffering from propeller problems. Another transport plane was fitted with the bomber's radio receiver . . . before it disappeared into the Mediterranean.

Even inconsequential pieces from the Lady Be Good seemed cursed after being installed in other craft. A single-engine prop plane crashed off the coast of Libya, almost all of it lost beneath the waves except for an armrest that had washed ashore—an armrest that had come from the Lady Be Good.

Despite its amazing resilience, it seems that the Lady Be Good just couldn't live up to its name.

It was, after all, more than a little bad.

SOLDIER OF MISFORTUNE

Communication is key. It's the corner-stone of all successful relationships. Effective communication can bring people closer together, help them understand each other better, and even stop certain problems before they start. In the case of Hiroo Onoda, communication could have saved him and the Japanese military a whole lot of headaches.

Onoda had been stationed in the Philippines during World War II. An intelligence officer by trade, he had been given strict orders to do everything within his power to hinder all enemy attacks on the island. The airstrip and the pier at the harbor became his primary targets, and should he be caught, he was to fight until death. Capture and suicide were not allowed.

Once Onoda arrived on the island, he fell in with a group of Japanese soldiers who had already been stationed there. He was of a lower rank than them, and so had to follow their orders instead. His mission had stopped before it ever started, and it wasn't long before the United States took over the island with the Philippine Commonwealth in February of 1945, seven months before the official end of the war.

The other soldiers had been given orders, too: fight, which they did. But they were no match for the Allied forces. It would have been much easier had they allowed Onoda to carry out his original mission, but it was too late. All but a handful fell, leaving Onoda the acting commander. He ordered the remaining men to retreat into the nearby hills where they would be safe.

He and three other Japanese soldiers lived in the Philippine wilderness for months, building huts out of bamboo and stealing food from local villages. When they got desperate, they slaughtered cows and ate their meat. Their time in the mountains changed them, too, and the men eventually grew paranoid of anyone who dared venture near their camp. Stray islanders were often mistaken for enemy guerrillas, and killed without question.

The soldiers managed to avoid all American and Filipino search parties for a time, until their position was compromised and a shootout killed two of them. A third surrendered to the authorities while Onoda ventured deeper into the mountains.

And no one heard from him after that. Lieutenant Onoda was declared dead by the Japanese government in 1959. All search party efforts had failed to locate him, and after the killings stopped, they stopped looking.

Then, in 1974, a Japanese student named Norio Suzuki set out to find the missing soldier. Well, he set out to find three things, really: "Lieutenant Onoda, a panda, and the Abominable Snowman."

And four days after his journey began, he found him. Alive. Suzuki tried to coax the soldier off the island, to return to the modern world back home, but Onoda wouldn't listen. He was still awaiting orders from his commanding officer.

Unable to convince the soldier to leave with him, Suzuki took some pictures as proof and let the Japanese government handle the recovery of their missing asset. Government officials asked Onoda's superior officer, Major Yoshimi Taniguchi, to fly out to the Philippines to deliver the orders as he had promised years earlier.

Once the orders had been given, Onoda surrendered and handed over all the weapons he had amassed during his time on the island. For over thirty years, Hiroo Onoda believed World War II was still being fought all over the world. He had no idea that atom bombs had been dropped on Hiroshima and Nagasaki, or that the Allies had won. The Japan he came home to was like an alien planet, with tall glass buildings all around him, and cars clogging up the streets.

He became a celebrity of sorts back home, and eventually released a book about his experiences on the island, how he'd fought his own war on behalf of a country that had left him behind. But he found fitting into the new world difficult. So much had changed while he was gone. Unable to handle living in a modern Japan, he traveled to Brazil, got married, and established schools to help troubled kids both at home and abroad.

Hiroo Onoda had been lost in time for most of his life. He'd missed so much and had come back to a world he did not recognize. Yet, despite his hesitation and wariness, he never forgot his primary mission: survive at all costs.

And thankfully . . . he *succeeded*.

GUARDIAN ANGELS

In war, a soldier's primary goals are to kill the enemy and stay alive. During the Civil War, however, that second part wasn't so easy. Musket balls did immense damage as they tore through flesh, often taking winding routes and remaining lodged in the body.

This led to infections, which turned into high fevers and, eventually, death. Treatment was rudimentary and scarce. Many who survived often lost limbs to gangrene. Penicillin hadn't been discovered yet.

The Civil War saw the birth of an organized ambulance system as a way to safely and quickly rush injured soldiers to local hospitals. Trains were also used as mobile medical units, but care itself had not advanced in any meaningful way. It wasn't like there was time, either, with a war raging across the country.

However, some soldiers suffering from gunshot wounds found themselves being healed by something outside the realm of modern medicine. It was a phenomenon that had to be seen to be believed. You might say they had a guardian angel watching over them.

In early April of 1862, more than forty thousand Union soldiers had been camped out along the Tennessee River near the little town of Shiloh. A second division of roughly twenty thousand additional troops were on their way, but the Union soldiers, led by General Ulysses S. Grant, still had no idea of what was coming.

Meanwhile, forty thousand Confederate troops were moving in from the south, hoping to catch the Union forces off guard. On the morning of April 6, Confederate soldiers emerged from the nearby woods and surprised Grant's army, beginning what would become the bloodiest battle of the war.

The Battle of Shiloh lasted two days. Between both sides, more than twenty-three thousand lives were lost—more casualties than in any other battle in American history up to that moment. The surprise attack didn't matter anyway. The Confederates, with their antiquated weapons, were forced to retreat while both sides tended to their dead and wounded.

The night after the fight, rains started moving into the area. The soil turned to mud. Injured soldiers waited for medical support. Then they noticed something odd about their wounds—they were glowing.

No one had expected such a sight. Being in the middle of nowhere, with no access to proper medicine—as limited as it was at the time—didn't leave them feeling hopeful. But a miraculous thing happened. The soldiers whose wounds had emitted a soft, blue glow survived more often than the ones whose wounds had not. They healed faster. There were fewer cases of infection and amputations. Those who witnessed it started referring to it as Angel's Glow.

If only it had been that . . . divine. Sadly, angels had not descended upon Shiloh to save the Union troops. In fact, the truth about their glowing wounds had nothing to with guardian angels at all. As it turned out, the whole area was crawling with nematodes—tiny worms that ate insect larvae they found in the mud.

Well, they didn't exactly eat the larvae. They burrowed inside it and vomited up a special kind of bacteria called *Photorhabdus luminescens*. And the bacteria was special for two reasons: first, it killed the larvae from the inside for the nematodes to eat. Secondly, it gave off a soft blue glow.

That's what the soldiers were seeing: glowing blue bacteria thrown up by hungry worms. Kind of gross, I know, but that's not all. The bacteria didn't just eat insect larvae. It ate pretty much anything in its path, including other bacteria that might have caused infections. Those soldiers had survived at a much higher rate than the rest of the army did so because of nematode vomit.

The medical profession might not have learned much about proper care during the worst of the Civil War, but the soldiers sure learned something else: a cure could always be found in nature, even in the most unlikely of places.

NEVER FORGET

War changes everything. The landscape. The economy. The people in it and around it. War is a stampede of wild elephants leaving nothing but rubble in their wake. The costs are unfathomable. Some countries never recover, while others take years to get back even a piece of what they lost. And the soldiers who fight often lose a piece of themselves as well.

But then there are wars that don't change much. It's true. It does happen. In 1859, a British-owned black boar was shot by an American farmer on an island off the coast of Washington. The dispute that ensued resulted in a war lasting a matter of weeks between the United States and Great Britain. Eventually a deal was worked out and the conflict, known today as the Pig War, ended without a single life lost—well, except for the boar's.

The Napoleonic Wars, however, changed a whole lot. Millions were killed over a span of twelve years as Napoleon worked his way across Europe. The United Kingdom, Austria, Sweden, and other countries worked to fight off the invading French Empire, eventually defeating Napoleon in 1815 at Waterloo.

Spain was also heavily involved in the

conflict. Its leaders had lost control of the country around 1808, and for six years they fought alongside the British, and were able to push the French forces out by 1814. But one town had been ready to get its hands dirty from day one. The small town of Huescar, in the province of Granada, didn't have much. They didn't even have an army. Only about eight guards to protect the town.

But they wanted to help Spain put Ferdinand VII back on the throne, so in 1809 they declared war on Napoleon and his allies—specifically Denmark. Napoleon eventually lost (no thanks to Huescar) and his brother, the acting king, was banished from the throne.

Spain and Denmark signed the Treaty of Paris in 1814, which established France's borders and gave other countries their land back, thus ending Spain's fraught battle with the Emperor. Huescar, however, never backed down. Even though Spain had found peace with France, the people of the small Spanish town remained at war with the Danes for years. One hundred and seventy-two, in fact. And yet no shots were fired and neither side suffered a single casualty.

So how could an entire country and a small Spanish town be at war for that long without anyone dying or even hearing about it? For that, we can thank Vicente Gonzalez. Vicente was an official from Huescar who found the original declaration . . . in 1981.

As it turned out, after the treaty had been signed, the town simply forgot about the war. For 172 years, the two sides were engaged in a conflict neither was aware of.

Once the declaration was made public, a Danish ambassador traveled to the small town on Armistice Day of 1981 and signed a treaty, officially bringing an end to the war. Gifts were exchanged, with the mayor of Huescar receiving a photo of the Danish Queen as well as books by famous Danish children's author Hans Christian Andersen.

In return, Huescar renamed one of its streets Calle Dinamarca—or, Denmark Street. Townspeople got the day off from work to celebrate and drink free wine while thousands of tourists flooded into town. Word has it a bus full of Scandinavian women even showed up dressed as Vikings.

Two years later, the village of Lijar, about seventy miles from Huescar, *also* declared peace with France—and it only took a hundred years. The king of Lijar had been offended during a visit to Paris in 1883 and retaliated with a formal declaration of war. But neither side made a move and so the declaration, just like Huescar's, was lost to time.

We're often reminded after major conflicts to "never forget" so we don't repeat the mistakes of the past. Unfortunately for Huescar and Lijar, somebody *did* forget—and the conflict almost never stopped.

EDDIE'S MONSTER

When you're fighting a certain kind of enemy, it's not always about who has more guns or more soldiers. The ability to understand the opposing side and develop a solid strategy can lead to shorter wars and less bloodshed. During and after World War II, when the United States needed help handling a foreign power as quickly as possible, they called on one man.

His name was Edward Lansdale and he was a United States Air Force officer. His specialty was psychological warfare—getting into the heads of his enemies and using their beliefs against them. For example, in Vietnam in the 1950s, he helped lead half a million Catholic refugees out of communist-led North Vietnam by spreading religious propaganda. The pamphlets and flyers claimed "Christ has gone to the South" and insinuated a nuclear bomb would be dropped on Hanoi at any moment.

The plan worked, and the mass migration allowed South Vietnam to take over as the majority half of the country. However, Lansdale's efforts there were fairly tame compared with some of his other attempts at military manipulation. Upon discovering the Vietnamese people's belief in prophecy, he paid local fortune tellers and astrologers to write predictions for an astrological almanac he was publishing.

Once completed, he snuck it across enemy lines and let it do its work. The book forecasted problems for the people in the North, encouraging them to move to the south where it was safer.

But perhaps his wildest idea came in the mid-1950s while he was working to quash a communist uprising in the Philippines. Soldiers who didn't want to be associated with the rich Manilan Filipinos embraced communism and formed their own rebel militia called the Huks. And their numbers were growing.

Lansdale was sent in to stop them. Unfortunately, the Huks had taken a prime position at the top of a hill in Luzon and US forces were unable to get to them without sustaining significant casualties. But Lansdale had an idea. He knew what the rebels were afraid of and it wasn't guns or bombs. It was called an *aswang*—a creature with a long tongue and sharp teeth that drained its victims' blood, kind of like a vampire.

Lansdale went to work spreading rumors about an aswang feeding nearby, hoping to spook the Huks, but rumors wouldn't be enough to convince them to leave their position. He had his troops wait along a known route for enemy patrols. As the Huks passed, Lansdale's men snatched the last rebel in line, a poor guy who had fallen behind enough so as not to not be heard as he was carried off into the woods.

He was strung upside down and his neck was punctured, leaving two small holes. He was then drained of his blood and tossed back on the road where he'd been taken from. After that, it was just a matter of waiting for him to be discovered.

The rebel soldiers returned looking for their fallen friend. And there he was: pale, lifeless, and brandishing the telltale signs of an aswang attack. The next day, the Huks left the hill for a safer position. Lansdale's ruse had worked flawlessly, although he wasn't done just yet.

One aswang attack would not end the whole rebellion. So he went on to paint all-seeing eyes on the doors of homes where it was thought that rebels might be hiding. He also had low-flying planes transmit messages to make the Huks think there were spies everywhere.

Not long after, the Huks surrendered, ending their rebellion and earning Edward Lansdale a place in history as someone who didn't suck at winning wars—even if he had to pretend to be a vampire to do it.

ACKNOWLEDGMENTS

The stories we tell are a product of the people around us. Thankfully, I'm surrounded by a lot of kind and talented human beings.

First and foremost, thanks to Harry Marks for going on this journey with me, and for sharing the joy that comes from finding raw story deep inside the mines of history and then cutting it free to give it a shine. You've put words in my mouth, and that's turned out to be a very good thing.

Thanks to my agent, Todd Shuster, and my editor, Michael Homler. I couldn't have asked for a better team to help me get this book over the finish line.

I'm also grateful to the amazing creators I get to call friends, who provide me with a community full of love and support: Chad Lawson, Nora McInerny, Amy Bruni, Misha Collins, Carlos Foglia, Josh Gates, Genevieve and Jared Padalecki, Lauren Shippen, Chuck Wendig, Delilah Dawson, Glen Morgan, Dana Schwartz, and Mike Wolfe.

Special thanks to the talented humans who work alongside me and Harry every day at Grim & Mild, crafting weird historical podcasts: Robin Miniter, GennaRose Nettercott, Cassandra de Alba, Sam Alberty, Jamie Vargas, Alexandra Steed, and Alex Robinson.

And finally, thank you to my wife and daughters, who fill my days with laughter, joy, and a whole lot of conversation. You've put up with a lot of my bizarre stories at the dinner table, and given me a healthy outlet for all my dad jokes and puns. You might not be grateful for that, but I certainly am.

SOURCES

SECOND LIFE

"The True Story of the Short-Lived State of Franklin," smithsonianmag.com, https://www.smithsonianmag.com/smart-news/true-story-short-lived-state-franklin-180964541

SHOTS FIRED

"The Speech That Saved Teddy Roosevelt's Life," smithsonianmag.com, https://www.smithsonianmag.com/history/the-speech-that-saved-teddy-roosevelts-life-83479091/

"Theodore Roosevelt," wikipedia.org, https://en.wikipedia.org/wiki/Theodore_Roosevelt.

"Mount Rushmore," wikipedia.org, https://en.wikipedia.org/wiki/Mount_Rushmore

"John Flammang Schrank," wikipedia.org, https://en.wikipedia.org/wiki/John_Flammang_Schrank

"Teddy Roosevelt, The Birth of the Progressive Party, and the Speech That Slowed a Bullet," by Natalie Childs. stmuhistorymedia.org, https://www.stmuhistorymedia.org/i-will-deliver-this-speech-or-die-the-bull-moose-and-the-speech-that-stopped-a-bullet/

PONY UP

"Pony Express," wikipedia.org, https://en.wikipedia.org/wiki/Pony_Express

"10 Things You May Not Know About the Pony Express" by Evan Andrews. history.com, https://www.history.com/news/10-things-you-may-not-know-about-the-pony-express

"First Inaugural Address," abrahamlincolnonline.org, http://www.abrahamlincolnonline.org/lincoln/speeches/1inaug.htm

"Pony Bob," by Russell Alan Spreeman. americancowboy.com, https://www.americancowboy.com/ranch-life-archive/pony-bob

"Pony Express Historical Timeline," ponyexpress.org, http://ponyexpress.org/pony-express-historical-timeline/

BY A HAIR

"Locket Containing George and Martha Washington's Intertwined Hair," ripleys.com, https://www.ripleys.com/weird-news/locket-washingtons-hair/

"Memento mori," wikipedia.org, https://en.wikipedia.org/wiki/Memento_mori

"George Washington," wikipedia.org, https://en.wikipedia.org/wiki/George_Washington

"Mount Vernon," history.com, https://www.history.com/topics/landmarks/mount-vernon

"Martha Washington: The Custis Years," marthawashington.us, http://marthawashington.us/exhibits/show/martha-washington—a-life/the-custis-years/page-3

"Martha Washington: The War for Independence," marthawashington.us, http://marthawashington.us/exhibits/show/martha-washington—a-life/the-war-for-independence

"Martha Washington: The 1790s," marthawashington.us, http://marthawashington.us/exhibits/show/martha-washington—a-life/the-1790s

"18 Haunting Pieces of Memento Mori," by Leonora Epstein, buzzfeed.com, https://www.buzzfeed.com/leonoraepstein/haunting-pieces-of-memento-mori

ACTING OUT

"Edwin Booth," wikipedia.org, https://en.wikipedia.org/wiki/Edwin_Booth

"Edwin Booth," biography.com, https://www.biography.com/people/edwin-booth-39624

TIME TRAVELER

"Sylvester Magee," Wikipedia.org, https://en.m.wikipedia.org/wiki/Sylvester_Magee

"Sylvester Magee Claimed To Be 130 Years Old—And That's Not Even the Craziest Part," by Katie Serena, allthatsinteresting.com, https://allthatsinteresting.com/sylvester-magee

"Top 10 Longest Living Animals," onekindplanet.org, https://onekind planet.org/top-10/top-10-worlds -longest-living-animals/

"How Many People Live to 100?" geneaologyintime.com, http://www .genealogyintime.com/Genealogy Resources/Articles/how_many _people_live_to_100_page1.html

"Civil Rights Act of 1964," wikipedia .org, https://en.wikipedia.org/wiki /Civil_Rights_Act_of_1964

AMERICAN ICON

"Robert G. Heft," ohiohistorycentral .org, http://www.ohiohistorycentral .org/w/Robert_G._Heft

"Robert G. Heft," wikipedia.org, https://simple.wikipedia.org/wiki /Robert_G._Heft

"Flag of the United States," wikipe dia.org, https://en.wikipedia.org /wiki/Flag_of_the_United_States

BONE TO PICK

"Why Was Benjamin Franklin's Basement Filled with Skeletons?," by Colin Schultz, smithsonianmag .com, https://www.smithsonianmag .com/smart-news/why-was-benja min-franklins-basement-filled-with -skeletons-524521/

"That Time They Found Those Bodies in Ben Franklin's Basement," by Matt Soniak, mentalfloss.com, http://mentalfloss.com/article /30448/time-they-found-those -bodies-ben-franklins-basement

"Benjamin Franklin . Worldly Ways . England | PBS," pbs.org, https:// www.pbs.org/benfranklin/exp _worldly_england.html

"Dr. William Hewson," findagrave.com, https://www.findagrave.com/memorial /143691934/william-hewson

"William Hewson (surgeon)," wikipedia .org, https://en.m.wikipedia.org /wiki/William_Hewson_(surgeon)

CLOWNING AROUND

"Dan Rice," wikipedia.org, https:// en.m.wikipedia.org/wiki/Dan_Rice

"Dan Rice, the Clown Who Ran for President," by Marc Hartzman, blogs.mycentraljersey.com. http:// www.weirdhistorian.com/dan -rice-the-clown-who-ran-for-pre sident/

"Dan Rice: American Clown," britannical.com, https://www .britannica.com/biography /Dan-Rice

"Ringling Bros. and Barnum & Bailey Circus," wikipedia.org, https:// en.m.wikipedia.org/wiki/Ring ling_Bros._and_Barnum_%26_Bai ley_Circus

BATTLE PLANS

"Reagan and Gorbachev Agreed to Fight Aliens Together," by Colton Kruse, ripleys.com, https://www .ripleys.com/weird-news/alien -invasion-agreement/

"Declassified Lunar Space Weapons," by Colton Kruse, ripleys.com, https://www.ripleys.com/weird -news/lunar-space-weapons/

"Reykjavík Summit," wikipedia.org, https://en.wikipedia.org/wiki/Reykjav %C3%ADk_Summit

"The Reykjavik Summit," the reaganvision.org, https://www .thereaganvision.org/the-reykjavik -summit-the-story/

"How Two Sci-Fi Writers Fueled a U.S. President's Wild Quest to Weaponize Space," by John Wenz, thrillist.com, https://www .thrillist.com/entertainment/nation /strategic-defense-initiative-reagan -star-wars-jerry-pournelle-larry -niven

"The End of the Cold War," ushis tory.org, http://www.ushistory.org /us/59e.asp

"Mikhail Gorbachev," wikipedia. org, https://en.wikipedia.org/wiki /Mikhail_Gorbachev

UPSIDE DOWN

Strange Stories, Amazing Facts of America's Past (The Reader's Digest Association, Inc., 1989), pp. 23, 305.

THE RUNDOWN

Mysteries of the Unexplained (The Reader's Digest Association, Inc., 1989), p. 72.

THE GIFT

Mysteries of the Unexplained (The Reader's Digest Association, Inc., 1989), p. 70.

SOMETHING BORROWED

Mysteries of the Unexplained (The Reader's Digest Association, Inc., 1989), p. 75.

LUCK OF THE IRISH

"The Woman Who Survived All Three Disasters Aboard the Sister Ships: The Titanic, Britannic, and Olympic," todayifoundout.com, http://www.todayifoundout.com /index.php/2014/01/woman -survived-sinking-titanic-britannic -collision-olympic

"Violet Jessop," wikipedia.org, https:// en.wikipedia.org/wiki/Violet_Jessop

PUT A RING ON IT

The Life, Death, Afterlife, and Curse of Rudolph Valentino," the13th floor.tv, http://www.the13thfloor .tv/2016/07/11/the-life-death-after life-and-curse-of-rudolph-valen tino/

"Rudolph Valentino's Cursed Ring Remains Locked in a Hollywood Vault," ripleys.com, https://www .ripleys.com/weird-news/cursed -ring/

"Rudolph Valentino," wikipedia.org, https://en.m.wikipedia.org/wiki /Rudolph_Valentino

DAM IT ALL

"Hoover Dam," wikipedia.org, https://en.wikipedia.org/wiki /Hoover_Dam

"Purpose of the Hoover Dam," by Rita Kennedy. usatoday.com,

https://traveltips.usatoday.com/purpose-hoover-dam-62077.html

"Hoover Dam," usbr.gov, https://www.usbr.gov/lc/hooverdam/faqs/damfaqs.html

"Dark Synchronicity and Strange Deaths," by Brett Swancer. mysteriousuniverse.org, https://mysteriousuniverse.org/2017/07/dark-synchronicity-and-strange-deaths/

"Father and Son Died on the Same Day, 14 Years Apart While Working on Hoover Dam," by Henry Brean. theguardian.com, https://www.reviewjournal.com/local/local-las-vegas/father-and-son-died-on-the-same-day-14-years-apart-while-working-on-hoover-dam/

WIZARD'S COAT

"'Wizard of Oz' Coat Belonged to L. Frank Baum?," snopes.com, https://www.snopes.com/fact-check/coat-of-baums/

"1939 in Film," wikipedia.org, https://en.wikipedia.org/wiki/1939_in_film#cite_note-5

"L. Frank Baum," wikipedia.org, https://en.wikipedia.org/wiki/L._Frank_Baum

"The Wizard of Oz (1939 Film)," wikipedia.org, https://en.wikipedia.org/wiki/The_Wizard_of_Oz_(1939_film)

BROTHERS GRIM

"Coincidental Twin Tragedy in Bermuda: Facts," by Siddhartha Vookoti, hoaxorfact.com, http://anomalyinfo.com/Stories/1913-patient-bullet

"586 Deaths on Bermuda's Roads Since 1962," bernews.com, http://bernews.com/2015/01/586-road-deaths-since-1962/

"Bermuda really is another world: the stats," by Sarah Lagan, royalgazette.com, http://www.royalgazette.com/drive-for-change/article/20180129/bermuda-really-is-another-world-stats

"Bermuda Triangle," wikipedia.org, https://en.wikipedia.org/wiki/Bermuda_Triangle

"10 Facts About Bermuda That Are Weirder Than the Triangle," by Helen Raine, listverse.com, http://listverse.com/2018/04/21/10-facts-about-bermuda-that-are-weirder-than-the-triangle/

"Hamilton, Bermuda," wikipedia.org, https://en.wikipedia.org/wiki/Hamilton,_Bermuda

THE HAND-ME-DOWN

"The Curse of James Dean's "Little Bastard," jalopnik.com, https://jalopnik.com/5113390/the-curse-of-james-deans-little-bastard

"James Dean's Death," by Jennifer Rosenberg, thoughtco.com, https://www.thoughtco.com/james-dean-dies-in-car-accident-1779341

RS550 specs, type550.com, http://type550.com/blueprint/rs5501500-specs/

"Porsche 550," wikipedia.org, https://en.wikipedia.org/wiki/Porsche_550

BOTTOM OF THE NINTH

"Curse of the Ninth," futilitycloset.com, https://www.futilitycloset.com/2006/11/14/curse-of-the-ninth/

"Curse of the Ninth," wikipedia.org, https://en.m.wikipedia.org/wiki/Curse_of_the_ninth

"Ludwig van Beethoven," wikipedia.org, https://en.m.wikipedia.org/wiki/Ludwig_van_Beethoven

"Enneaphobia," wikipedia.org, http://phobia.wikia.com/wiki/Enneaphobia

"Fear of Friday The 13th Phobia—Paraskevidekatriaphobia or Friggatriskaidekaphobia," fearof.net, https://www.fearof.net/fear-of-friday-the-13th-phobia-paraskevidekatriaphobia-or-friggatriskaidekaphobia/

"What is the Meaning of the Number 13?," by Medium Maria, linkedin.com, https://www.linkedin.com/pulse/what-meaning-number-13-medium-maria

"Gustav Mahler," wikipedia.org, https://en.m.wikipedia.org/wiki/Gustav_Mahler

"Anton Dvořák," wikipedia.org, https://en.m.wikipedia.org/wiki/Anton%C3%ADn_Dvořák

"Symphony No. 9 (Mahler)," wikipedia.org, https://en.m.wikipedia.org/wiki/Symphony_No._9_(Mahler)

"Das Lied von der Erde," wikipedia.org, https://en.m.wikipedia.org/wiki/Das_Lied_von_der_Erde

BAD OMEN

"Halley's Comet," wikipedia.org, https://en.wikipedia.org/wiki/Halley%27s_Comet

"Battle of the Catalaunian Plains," wikipedia.org, https://en.wikipedia.org/wiki/Battle_of_the_Catalaunian_Plains#Battle

"Battle of the Catalaunian Plains," britannica.com, https://www.britannica.com/event/Battle-of-the-Catalaunian-Plains

"First Jewish-Roman War," wikipedia.org, https://en.wikipedia.org/wiki/First_Jewish–Roman_War#Fall_of_Jerusalem

"A Brief History of Halley's Comet," by Evan Andrews, history.com, https://www.history.com/news/a-brief-history-of-halleys-comet-sightings

"6 Famous Coincidences," by Sarah Pruitt, history.com, https://www.history.com/news/6-famous-coincidences

"Norman Conquest of England," wikipedia.org, https://en.wikipedia.org/wiki/Norman_conquest_of_England

"Mark Twain," wikipedia.org, https://en.wikipedia.org/wiki/Mark_Twain

VERY SUPERSTITIOUS

"Arnold Schoenberg" wikipedia.org, https://en.wikipedia.org/wiki/Arnold_Schoenberg#Superstition_and_his_death

"25 Otherworldly Curses in the Music Industry," by Jacob Shelton . ranker.com, https://www.ranker .com/list/curses-in-the-music -industry/jacob-shelton

"10 Most Interesting, Superstitious Rituals of Professional Athletes," by Chris Giblin. mensjournal.com, https://www.mensjournal.com /sports/10-most-interesting -superstitious-rituals-of -professional-athletes/wade -boggsae-pre-game-chicken -tradition/

"Friday the 13th, Arnold Schoenberg and Triskaideka phobia," interlude.hk, http:// www.interlude.hk/front/friday -the-13tharnold-schoenberg -and-triskaidekaphobia/

"Fear of 13 and Other Superstitions Embedded in Compositions," wqxr.org, https://www.wqxr.org /story/fear-13-other-super stitions-embedded-compositions/

COLD-BLOODED

Edward Payson Evans, *The Criminal Prosecution and Capital Punishment of Animals* (W. Heinemann, 1906), pp. 155–56.

GETTING AHEAD

"Mike The Headless Chicken," MikeTheHeadlessChicken.org, http://www.miketheheadless chicken.org/mike/page/history.

"1904, November 12: Biddy, the Headless Chicken," AnomalyInfo .com, http://anomalyinfo.com /Stories/1904-november-12-biddy

"Chicken," wikipedia.com, https:// en.wikipedia.org/wiki/Chicken

"Mike the Headless Chicken more popular than Clinton," by Amy Reiter, salon.com, https://www .salon.com/1999/05/12/snl/

"Here's Why a Chicken Can Live Without Its Head," by Rebecca Katzman, modernfarmer .com, https://modernfarmer .com/2014/08/heres-chicken-can -live-without-head/

HORSING AROUND

"Clever Hans," wikipedia.org, https:// en.wikipedia.org/wiki/Clever_Hans

"Clever Hans," futilitycloset.com, https://www.futilitycloset.com /2006/10/06/clever-hans/

"Cold Reads & More: How Fraudulent Mediums Obtained Information," prairieghosts.com, http://www .prairieghosts.com/coldreads.html

SMALL WONDERS

"Wonders of Minute Workmanship," futilitycloset.com, https://www .futilitycloset.com/2006/11/16 /wonders-of-minute-workmanship/

"Flea circus," wikipedia.org, https:// en.wikipedia.org/wiki/Flea_circus

"Performing Animals: History, Agency, Theater," books.google .com, https://books.google.com /books?id=_l4yDwAAQBA J&pg=PT98&lpg=PT98&d q=mark+scaliot+miniatures &source=bl&ots=oxTL5B _5oh&sig=vytaSHGGhjPSe GgJK3XaxQVmrmM&hl= en&sa=X&ved=2ahUKEwi5h _uu0eDeAhWLdd8KHTSAC tAQ6AEwCXoECAIQAQ#v=o nepage&q=mark%20scaliot%20 miniatures&f=false

"Black Death," wikipedia.org, https:// en.wikipedia.org/wiki/Black_Death

"Revive the Charm of an 1800s Show with These Modern-Day Flea Circuses," acmefleacircus.blogspot .com, http://acmefleacircus.blogspot .com/2017/11/smithsonian-maga zine-website-november.html

BEAR NECESSITIES

"MacFarlane's Bear," wikipedia.org, https://en.wikipedia.org/wiki/ MacFarlane's_bear

"Roderick Ross MacFarlane," by Edward A. Preble. jstor.org, https:// www.jstor.org/stable/pdf/4073952 .pdf

"Hudson's Bay Company," wikipedia .org, https://en.wikipedia.org/wiki /Hudson%27s_Bay_Company

"Inopinatus—The Unexpected," by George G. Goodwin, strangeark .com, http://www.strangeark.com /macfarlane-bear

"Roderick MacFarlane," inuvialuitlivinghistory.ca, http://www.inuvialuitliving history.ca/wiki_pages/Roderick %20MacFarlane

"Fort Rae," fortwiki.com, http://www .fortwiki.com/Fort_Rae

"Caspar Whitney," wikipedia.org, https://en.wikipedia.org/wiki /Caspar_Whitney

PRINCE OF WHALES

"A Whale in Vermont? The Story Behind the State's Most Famous Fossil," by Mitch Wertlieb and Melody Bodette, vpr.org, https:// www.vpr.org/post/whale-vermont -story-behind-states-most-famous -fossil

"Dead Humber Estuary whale was 'rare' species," wikipedia.org, https://www.bbc.com/news/uk -england-humber-15104896

"Thompson's Biography," wikipedia .org, https://www.uvm.edu/vtnatu ralhistory/thompsons-biography

"The Charlotte Whale," uvm.com, https://www.uvm.edu/perkins/char lotte-whale

PIG HEADED

"A Learned Pig?," thelearnedpig .org, http://www.thelearnedpig.org /a-learned-pig

"The tragedy of Samuel Bisset," perthshirediary.com, http:// www.perthshirediary.com/html /day0426.html

"Learned pig," wikipedia.org, https:// en.wikipedia.org/wiki/Learned_pig

"Attaboy," futilitycloset.com, https:// www.futilitycloset.com/2008/01/10 /attaboy-2/

GREAT ESCAPE

"Can Animals Think?," by Eugene Linden, time.com, http://content

.time.com/time/magazine/article
/0,9171,30198,00.html

"This epic zoo escape story shows
how fantastically smart orangutans
can be," by James Gaines, upworthy
.com, https://www.upworthy.com
/this-epic-zoo-escape-story-shows
-how-fantastically-smart-orangutans
-can-be

"Koko (gorilla)," wikipedia.org,
https://en.m.wikipedia.org/wiki
/Koko_(gorilla)

MONSTER MASS

"The Crawfordsville Monster," by
Chandler Lighty, blog.newspapers
.library.in.gov, https://blog.news
papers.library.in.gov/crawfordsville
-monster/

"Killdeer," wikipedia.org, https://
en.m.wikipedia.org/wiki/Killdeer

"Crawfordsville monster," wikipedia
.org, https://en.m.wikipedia.org
/wiki/Crawfordsville_monster

"Ice cutting," wikipedia.org, https://
en.m.wikipedia.org/wiki/Ice_cutting

"The Crawfordsville Monster,"
futilitycloset.com, https://www
.futilitycloset.com/2008/02/20
/the-crawfordsville-monster/

"1891, September 5: The Crawfordsville Monster," by Charles Fort,
anomalyinfo.com, http://anomaly
info.com/Stories/1891-september
-5-crawfordsville-monster

THE STOWAWAY

"How Simon the Cat Earned a
Military Medal," by Colton Kruse,
ripleys.com, https://www.ripleys
.com/weird-news/simon-the-cat/

"Simon (cat)," wikipedia.org, https://
en.m.wikipedia.org/wiki/Simon_(cat)

"Dickin Medal," wikipedia.org,
https://en.m.wikipedia.org/wiki
/Dickin_Medal

GOOD BOY

"Owney (dog)," wikipedia.org,
https://en.m.wikipedia.org/wiki
/Owney_(dog)

"For a Productive Workplace Let Your
Office Go to the Dogs," by Pratik
Dholakiya, entrepreneur.com,
https://www.entrepreneur.com
/article/237982

"Owney," futilitycloset.com, https://
www.futilitycloset.com/2008/03/19
/owney/

RAT RACE

"1508: The Trial of the Autun Rats,"
duhaime.org, http://www.duhaime
.org/LawMuseum/LawArticle
-1529/1508-The-Trial-of-the
-Autun-Rats.aspx

"Representing Rats," futilitycloset
.com, https://www.futilitycloset
.com/2008/06/02/representing
-rats/

"Bubonic plague," wikipedia.org,
https://en.m.wikipedia.org/wiki
/Bubonic_plague

"Barthélemy de Chasseneuz," wiki
pedia.org, https://en.m.wikipedia
.org/wiki/Barth%C3%A9lemy_de
_Chasseneuz

ON STRIKE

David J. Hand, *The Improbability
Principle: Why Coincidences,
Miracles, and Rare Events Happen
Every Day* (Macmillan, 2014),
p. 161.

OUTLASTED

"Will Purvis," murderpedia.org,
http://murderpedia.org/male.P/p
/purvis-will.htm

ROUGH LANDING

"Vesna Vulović," wikipedia.org,
https://en.wikipedia.org/wiki
/Vesna_Vulović.

"How Do People Survive Plane
Crashes?" curiosity.com, https://
curiosity.com/topics/how-do
-people-survive-plane-crashes
-oJJtN3Xy/

"JAT Flight 367," wikipedia.org,
https://en.wikipedia.org/wiki
/JAT_Flight_367

WEST SIDE STORY

"Church Explosion Spares Choir,"
snopes.com, https://www.snopes
.com/fact-check/choir-non-quorum/

"Why The Choir Was Late ~ an
Amazing Synchronicity Story,"
sillysutras.com, https://sillysutras
.com/why-the-choir-was-late
-an-amazing-synchronicity-story/

CRADLE WILL FALL

"There Once Was a Man Hit on the
Head by a Falling Baby, Twice!,"
todayifoundout.com, http://
www.todayifoundout.com/index
.php/2011/09/there-once-was-a
-man-hit-on-the-head-by-a-falling
-baby-twice/

"Falls," who.int, http://www.who.int
/news-room/fact-sheets/detail/falls

OVER A BARREL

"Queen of the Mist," futilitycloset
.com, https://www.futilitycloset
.com/2007/06/20/queen-of-the
-mist/

"Annie Edson Taylor," wikipedia
.org, https://en.wikipedia.org/wiki
/Annie_Edson_Taylor

"Goat Island," wikipedia.org, https://
en.wikipedia.org/wiki/Goat
Island(New_York)

ONE-TRICK PENNY

"Pocket penny that saved soldier's
life sold at auction," bbc.com,
https://www.bbc.com/news/uk
-england-derbyshire-47667031

"For Sale: A Penny That Stopped
a Bullet and Saved a Life," by
Matthew Taub, atlasobscura.com,
https://www.atlasobscura.com
/articles/for-sale-a-penny-that
-stopped-a-bullet-and-saved-a-life

"Lucky Penny That Saved WWII
Soldier's Life When It Deflected
a Bullet Aimed at His Chest
Is Discovered More Than 100
Years Later," thenewstalkers
.com, https://thenewstalkers.com
/community/discussion/45076
/lucky-penny-that-saved-wwii

-soldiers-life-when-it-deflected-a
-bullet-aimed-at-his-chest-is-discov
ered-more-than-100-years-later

"Britannia," wikipedia.org, https://
en.wikipedia.org/wiki/Britannia

"Coin-Penny, Queen Victoria,
Great Britain, 1889," collections
.museumvictoria.com.au, https://
collections.museumvictoria.com
.au/items/82241

COLD TRUTH

"A Girl Was Frozen in Sub-Zero
Temperatures and Survived," ripleys
.com, https://www.ripleys.com
/weird-news/frozen-subzero/

"Hypothermia," mayoclinic.org,
https://www.mayoclinic.org/diseases
-conditions/hypothermia/symptoms
-causes/syc-20352682

"Jean Hilliard," wikipedia.org, https://
en.m.wikipedia.org/wiki/Jean_Hilliard

UNBALANCED

"Charles Blondin," wikipedia.org,
https://en.m.wikipedia.org/wiki
/Charles_Blondin

"Tempting Fate," futilitycloset
.com, https://www.futilitycloset
.com/2008/03/01/tempting-fate/

"The Ravel Family," travsd
.wordpress.com, https://travsd
.wordpress.com/2012/11/08
/the-ravel-family-2/

"The Daredevil of Niagara Falls," by
Karen Abbott, smithsonianmag
.com, https://www.smithsonianmag
.com/history/the-daredevil-of
-niagara-falls-110492884/

THE OLD MAN AND THE PLANES

"When Ernest Hemingway Walked
Away from Two Plane Crashes
Just Hours Apart," mentalfloss
.com, September 20, 2023, https://
www.mentalfloss.com/posts/ernest
-hemingway-two-plane-crashes
-hours-apart

"Ernest Hemingway and His Wife
Survived Two Plane Crashes Just

One Day Apart," smithsonian
mag.com, September 12, 2023,
https://www.smithsonianmag.com
/smart-news/hemingway-and-his
-wife-survived-two-plane-crashes
-just-one-day-apart-180982884/

"Murchison Falls," ugandawildlife
.org, date unknown, https://
ugandawildlife.org/national-parks
/murchison-falls-national-park/

DARKNESS FALLS

"Remembering New England's 'Dark
Day,'" history.com, https://www
.history.com/news/remembering
-new-englands-dark-day

"New England's Dark Day," wikipedia
.org, https://en.m.wikipedia.org
/wiki/New_England%27s_Dark
_Day

WHAT ALES YOU

"London Beer Flood," wikipedia.org,
https://en.wikipedia.org/wiki/London
_Beer_Flood.

"1814, October 17: Beer Flood of
London," anomalyinfo.com, http://
anomalyinfo.com/Stories/1814
-october-17-beer-flood-london

Horse Shoe Brewery," wikipedia.
org, https://en.wikipedia.org/wiki
/Horse_Shoe_Brewery

MAKE IT RAIN

"When San Diego Hired a Rainmaker
a Century Ago, It Poured," JSTOR
Daily, December 2015, https://
daily.jstor.org/charles-hatfield
-rainmaker

"In 1915, San Diego Hired a
Rainmaker and Floods Ensued,"
WBUR, June 2015, http://www
.wbur.org/hereandnow/2015/06/02
/rainmaker-1915-san-diego

ASCENSION

"Found Empty Coffin in 'Tomb' of
Monarch," Highland Recorder,
Number 11, March 19, 1926:
https://virginiachronicle.com
/cgi-bin/virginia?a=d&d
=HR19260319.2.29

BOMB'S AWAY

"1958 Mars Bluff B-47 nuclear
weapon loss incident," wikipedia
.org, https://en.wikipedia.org
/wiki/1958_Mars_Bluff_B-47
_nuclear_weapon_loss_incident

"Operation Snow Flurry," wikipedia
.org, https://en.wikipedia.org/wiki
/Operation_Snow_Flurry

"Atomic Bombings of Hiroshima and
Nagasaki," wikipedia.org, https://
en.wikipedia.org/wiki/Atomic
_bombings_of_Hiroshima_and
_Nagasaki

STEAMY DREAMS

Stephen E. Braude, *Immortal Remains:
The Evidence for Life After Death*
(Rowman & Littlefield Publishers,
2003), pp. 262–63.

Isaac Kaufman Funk, *The Widow's
Mite and Other Psychic Phenomena*
(Funk & Wagnalls, 1911),
pp. 383–85.

LOOKING UP

"The Mystery Airship of 1896," The
Museum of Unnatural Mystery,
unmuseum.org, http://www
.unmuseum.org/airship.htm

J. Allan Danelek, *The Great Airship
of 1897: A Provocative Look at the
Most Mysterious Aviation Event in
History* (SCB Distributors, 2013).

ALL SHOOK UP

"1970 Ancash earthquake," wikipedia
.org, https://en.m.wikipedia.org
/wiki/1970_Ancash_earthquake

"Huascaron," wikipedia.org, https://
en.m.wikipedia.org/wiki/Huascarán

"American Scientists Predicted a
Devastaing Avalanche in Peru, but
No One Listened. Unfortunately,
They Were Right!," amazing
factblog.wordpress.com,
https://amazingfactblog
.wordpress.com/2014/04/17
/american-scientists-predicted
-a-devastaing-avalanche-in
-peru-but-no-one-listened-unfortu
nately-they-were-right/

"Yungay, Peru," wikipedia.org, https://en.m.wikipedia.org/wiki/Yungay,_Peru

"In 1962 Peru Banned the Scientists Who Predicted Their Mountains Would Collapse," by Samuel Reason, blitzlift.com, http://blitzlift.com/in-1962-peru-banned-the-scientists-who-predicted-their-mountains-would-collapse/

A COOL DREAM

"The Ice Palace," futilitycloset.com, https://www.futilitycloset.com/2008/01/28/the-ice-palace/

"Ice Palace," wikipedia.org, https://en.wikipedia.org/wiki/Ice_palace

"Pyotr Yeropkin," wikipedia.org, https://en.wikipedia.org/wiki/Pyotr_Yeropkin

"Russo-Turkish War (1735–1739)," wikipedia.org, https://en.wikipedia.org/wiki/Russo-Turkish_War_(1735–1739)

"Anna of Russia," wikipedia.org, https://en.wikipedia.org/wiki/Anna_of_Russia

DEAD WEIGHT

"Frank Hayes (jockey)," wikipedia.org, https://en.wikipedia.org/wiki/Frank_Hayes_(jockey)

"Usain Bolt," wikipedia.org, https://en.wikipedia.org/wiki/Usain_Bolt

"Jim Thorpe," wikipedia.org, https://en.wikipedia.org/wiki/Jim_Thorpe

"Frank Hayes: The Dead Man Who Won a Horse Race," ripleys.com, https://www.ripleys.com/weird-news/frank-hayes/?ref=suggested post

"Frank Hayes: The jockey who won a race despite being dead," by Bianca Britton, cnn.com, https://www.cnn.com/2018/12/10/sport/frank-hayes-sweet-kiss-belmont-park-intl-spt/index.html

HOLD ON

"In 1990, British Airways Flight 5390 Pilot Survived Being Sucked Out Window!," ripleys.com, https://www.ripleys.com/weird-news/flight-5390/

"British Airways Flight 5390," wikipedia.org, https://en.wikipedia.org/wiki/British_Airways_Flight_5390

"What Are the Odds of Being Struck by Lightning?," discovertheodds.com, https://discovertheodds.com/what-are-the-odds-of-being-struck-by-lightning/

"'Am I Going Down?' App Tries to Help Anxious Flyers by Telling Them Odds of Plane Crash," by Gillian Edevane, newsweek.com, https://www.newsweek.com/what-are-odds-dying-plane-crash-app-892008

DREAMS OF PARADISE

"Perish, then Publish: Jacopo Alighieri and the 13 Missing Cantos," EsoterX, November 2016, https://esoterx.com/2016/11/22/perish-then-publish-jacopo-alighieri-and-the-13-missing-cantos

OPEN MIND

Nicola Bown, Carolyn Burdett, and Pamela Thurschwell, *The Victorian Supernatural* (Cambridge University Press, 2004), pp. 44–61.

TRIFLES

Ely Liebow, *Dr. Joe Bell: Model for Sherlock Holmes* (Popular Press, 1982).

Michael Sims, *Arthur and Sherlock: Conan Doyle and the Creation of Holmes* (Bloomsbury Publishing USA, 2017).

RED LIKE BLOOD

Mark Twain, *Life on the Mississippi* (J. R. Osgood and Company, 1883), pp. 237–45.

Albert Bigelow Paine, *Mark Twain, a Biography: The Personal and Literary Life of Samuel Langhorne Clemens, Volume 1* (Harper & Bros., 1912), pp. 132–44.

EXPELLED

Strange Stories, Amazing Facts of America's Past (The Reader's Digest Association, Inc., 1989), p. 16.

APRIL FOOL

"Isaac Bickerstaff," wikipedia.org, https://en.wikipedia.org/wiki/Isaac_Bickerstaff

"John Partridge (astrologer)," wikipedia.org, https://en.wikipedia.org/wiki/John_Partridge_(astrologer)

"The Tatler (1709 journal)," wikipedia.org, https://en.wikipedia.org/wiki/Tatler_(1709_journal)

"Jonathan Swift," wikipedia.org, https://en.wikipedia.org/wiki/Jonathan_Swift

OH MY

"O. Henry," wikipedia.org, https://en.wikipedia.org/wiki/O._Henry

Inflation Calculator, https://www.usinflationcalculator.com

"O. Henry," brittanica.com, https://www.britannica.com/biography/O-Henry

BURNING MAD

"Strange Case of Dr Jekyll and Mr Hyde," wikipedia.org, https://en.wikipedia.org/wiki/Strange_Case_of_Dr_Jekyll_and_Mr_Hyde#Reception

"The Strange Case of Fanny Stevenson and Literary Partnership," incitingsparks.org, https://incitingsparks.org/2016/03/21/the-strange-case-of-fanny-stevenson-and-literary-partnership/

"Treasure Island," wikipedia.org, https://en.wikipedia.org/wiki/Treasure_Island

"William Ernest Henley," wikipedia.org, https://en.wikipedia.org/wiki/William_Ernest_Henley

"The Story of Dr Jekyll, Mr Hyde and Fanny, the Angry Wife Who Burned the First Draft," by John Ezard. theguardian.com, https://

www.theguardian.com/uk/2000
/oct/25/books.booksnews

IT'S ALIVE

"George Forster (murderer),"
wikipedia.org, https://en.wikipedia
.org/wiki/George_Forster
_(murderer)

"Giovanni Aldini," wikipedia.org,
https://en.wikipedia.org/wiki
/Giovanni_Aldini

"Luigi Galvani," wikipedia.org,
https://en.wikipedia.org/wiki
/Luigi_Galvani

"Galvanism," wikipedia.org, https://
en.wikipedia.org/wiki/Galvanism

"Mary Shelley," biography.com,
https://www.biography.com/people
/mary-shelley-9481497

"Giovanni Aldini," corrosion-doctors
.org, https://corrosion-doctors.org
/Biographies/AldiniBio.htm

"George Foster," exclassics.com,
https://www.exclassics.com/new
gate/ng464.htm

"The real-life gruesome experiments
that inspired Frankenstein," thenext
web.com, https://thenextweb
.com/syndication/2018/12/18/real
-life-gruesome-science-experiments
-that-inspired-frankenstein/

HEAD SPACE

"Shakespeare's Stolen Skull," ripleys
.com, https://www.ripleys.com
/weird-news/shakespeares
-stolen-skull/

"What Happened to Shakespeare's
Skull?," by Lee Jamieson,
Thoughtco.com, https://www
.thoughtco.com/what-happened
-to-shakespeares-skull-4019536

"The Argosy vol. 28," books.google
.com, https://books.google.com
/books?id=RtIYAQAAIAAJ&p
g=PA270&dq=Frank+Chambers
+Ragley+Hall&hl=en&sa
=X&ved=0ahUKEwjis8_l6tnLAh
WLqx4KHTonBuQQ6AEIH
DAA#v=onepage&q=Frank%20
Chambers%20Ragley%20Hall&f
=false

"Shakespeare's Skull May Have Been
Stolen by Grave Robbers," by
Laura Geggel, scientificameri
can.com, https://www.scientific
american.com/article/shakespeare
-s-skull-may-have-been-stolen-by
-grave-robbers/?redirect=1

LIVING A DREAM

"The Ansel Bourne Identity: A 19th
Century Mystery," hsp.org, https://
hsp.org/blogs/hidden-histories
/the-ansel-bourne-identity-a-19th
-century-mystery

"Ansel Bourne," wikipedia.org,
https://en.m.wikipedia.org/wiki
/Ansel_Bourne

"The Bourne Identity (Novel),"
wikipedia.org, https://en.m
.wikipedia.org/wiki/The_Bourne
Identity(novel)

"William James," wikipedia.org,
https://en.m.wikipedia.org/wiki
/William_James

INTEL INSIDE

Gerald M. Levitt, *The Turk, Chess
Automaton* (Jefferson, N.C.:
McFarland, 2000).

DRESSED DOWN

"World War I," wikipedia.org, https://
en.m.wikipedia.org/wiki/World_War_I

"World War One: How the German
Zeppelin wrought terror," bbc
.com, https://www.bbc.com/news
/uk-england-27517166

"Eleven other things France
has given the US," thelocal.fr,
https://www.thelocal.fr/20150617
/what-else-has-france-given-the
-united-states

"The Modern Origins of 5 Totally
Ordinary Things," themodern
rogue.com, https://www.themodern
rogue.com/articles/2018/3/7/the
-bizarre-origins-of-5-totally
-ordinary-things

HAPPY ACCIDENT

"Silly Putty,'" wikipedia.org, https://
en.wikipedia.org/wiki/Silly_Putty

"Make It Do—Scrap Drives in World
War II," sarahsundin.com, http://
www.sarahsundin.com/make-it-do
-scrap-drives-in-world-war-ii-2/

"Make It Do—Tire Rationing in World
War II" sarahsundin.com, http://
www.sarahsundin.com/make-it
-do-tire-rationing-in-world-war-ii/

"Weird Science: The Accidental Invention of Silly Putty"
kidsdiscover.com, https://www
.kidsdiscover.com/quick-reads
/weird-science-the-accidental
-invention-of-silly-putty/

EVENING READING

"Night Writing,'" wikipedia.org,
https://en.m.wikipedia.org/wiki
/Night_writing

"Louis Braille and the Night Writer,"
historytoday.com, https://www
.historytoday.com/stephen-bert
man/louis-braille-and-night-writer

"Napoleon's Influence on Braille"
hankeringforhistory.com, http://
hankeringforhistory.com/napoleons
-influence-on-braille/

"Charles Barbier," wikipedia.org,
https://en.m.wikipedia.org/wiki
/Charles_Barbier

"Timeline of the Napoleonic Era,"
wikipedia.org, https://en.m
.wikipedia.org/wiki/Timeline_of
_the_Napoleonic_era#Early_years

KID ICARUS

"The Alchemist Who Thought He
Could Fly," scotsman.com, https://
www.scotsman.com/lifestyle/the
-alchemist-who-thought-he-could
-fly-1-466848

"One Thousand and One Nights,"
wikipedia.org, https://en.wikipedia
.org/wiki/One_Thousand_and
_One_Nights

"Elixir of Life," wikipedia.org, https://
en.wikipedia.org/wiki/Elixir_of_life

"Leonardo da Vinci," wikipedia.org,
https://en.wikipedia.org/wiki
/Leonardo_da_Vinci

"The Bird Man of Stirling," bbc.co
.uk, https://www.bbc.co.uk

/history/scottishhistory/renaissance
/oddities_renaissance.shtml

NO-MAN BAND

"The Phonoliszt Violina is a 1907
Robotic Orchestra," ripleys.com,
https://www.ripleys.com/weird
-news/phonoliszt-violina/

"Best Invention; Invention Is the
Mother Of Necessity," by Jared
Diamond, nytimes.com, https://
www.nytimes.com/1999/04/18/mag
azine/best-invention-invention-is-the
-mother-of-necessity.html

"Hupfeld Phonoliszt Violina the 8th
Wonder of the world," antique-hq
.com, https://www.antique-hq.com
/hupfeld-phonoliszt-violina-the
-8th-wonder-of-the-world-114/

"The Self-Playing Violins That
Mastered Chopin," by Michael
Waters, atlasobscura.com, https://
www.atlasobscura.com/articles
/phonoliszt-violin-self-playing
-instruments-player-piano-ludwig
-hupfeld

SHOCKING

*Mysteries of the Mind, Space, and Time:
The Unexplained, Volume 2*
(H. S. Stuttman, Inc, 1992), p. 154.

"The Mysteryus Baghdad Battery,"
Historic Mysteries, December
2010, https://www.historicmysteries
.com/baghdad-battery.

TOGETHER FOREVER

"The Man Buried in a Pringles Can,"
time.com, June 4, 2008, https://
content.time.com/time/business
/article/0,8599,1811730,00.html

"Grave of Fredric J. Baur," atlasobscura
.com, January 31, 2017, https://
www.atlasobscura.com/places
/grave-of-frederic-j-baur

"Fred Baur," wikipedia.org, date
unknown, https://en.wikipedia.org
/wiki/Fred_Baur

FLIGHT OF FANCY

*Mysteries of the Mind, Space, and
Time: The Unexplained, Volume 2*

(H. S. Stuttman, Inc, 1992),
pp. 153–54.

"The Saqqara Bird," Time.com,
June 2010, http://techland.time
.com/2010/06/09/cryptids-the
-saqqara-bird.

THE SHAWL

Strange Stories, Amazing Facts
(Reader's Digest Association,
1976) p. 399.

THIN AIR

"Mysterious Vanishings with Bizarre
Phone Calls," Journal Online, June
2017, http://www.journal.com.ph
/editorial/mysteries/mysterious-vani
shings-with-bizarre-phone-calls

MAKING WAVES

"Spy Radio 'Number Stations' Are
Still Broadcasting," ripleys.com,
https://www.ripleys.com/weird
-news/number-stations/

"How to Listen to Real Spy Broadcasts Right Now," by Alan Henry,
lifehacker.com, https://lifehacker
.com/how-to-listen-to-real-spy
-broadcasts-right-now-5961035

"5 Creepiest Number Station
Sounds Ever Recorded," youtube
.com, https://www.youtube.com
/watch?v=u0F984w4vLQ

"NATO Phonetic Alphabet,"
wikipedia.org, https://en.wikipedia
.org/wiki/NATO_phonetic_alphabet

"Shortwave radio," wikipedia.org,
https://en.wikipedia.org/wiki
/Shortwave_radio#Propagation
_characteristics

"Numbers in the Air," users.telenet
.be, http://users.telenet.be/d
.rijmenants/en/numbers.htm

ROYAL TREATMENT

"The Sumerian King List Still Puz-
zles Historians After More than a
Century of Research," ancient
-origins.net, https://www.ancient
-origins.net/myths-legends-asia
/sumerian-king-list-still-puzzles

-historians-after-more-century
-research-001287

"Sumerian King List," wikipedia.org,
https://en.wikipedia.org/wiki
/Sumerian_King_List

"Sumer," wikipedia.org, https://
en.wikipedia.org/wiki/Sumer

"Sumer," history.com, https://www
.history.com/topics/ancient-middle
-east/sumer

"Cuneiform," wikipedia.org, https://
en.wikipedia.org/wiki/Cuneiform

"Mesopotamia," wikipedia.org,
https://en.wikipedia.org/wiki
/Mesopotamia

"Is The Sumerian King's List
Indication of a Lost Civilization?,"
gaia.com, https://www.gaia.com
/article/sumerian-kings-list

WORDSMITH

"Decipherment of Rongorongo,"
wikipedia.org, https://en.wikipedia
.org/wiki/Decipherment_of
_rongorongo

"The mysterious Rongorongo writing
of Easter Island," ancient-origins
.net, https://www.ancient-origins
.net/unexplained-phenomena
/mysterious-rongorongo-writing
-easter-island-002242

"Tangata manu," wikipedia.org,
https://en.m.wikipedia.org/wiki
/Tangata_manu

"Hanau epe," wikipedia.org, https://
en.m.wikipedia.org/wiki/Hanau
_epe

"Eugène Eyraud," wikipedia.org,
https://en.m.wikipedia.org/wiki
/Eugène_Eyraud

"Petroglyph," wikipedia.org, https://
en.m.wikipedia.org/wiki/Petroglyph

"Easter Island," wikipedia.org, https://
en.m.wikipedia.org/wiki/Easter
_Island

"Rongorongo," wikipedia.org, https://
en.m.wikipedia.org/wiki/Rongorongo

URAL HISTORY

"The Dashka Stone Map: 120 Million
Years Old," knittingittogether.

com, https://knittingittogether
.com/2016/11/07/the-dashka
-stone-map-120-million-years-old/

"The Controversial Dashka Stone:
120 Million-Year-Old Map?"
ancient-origins.net, https://www
.ancient-origins.net/artifacts
-ancient-writings/controversial
-dashka-stone-120-million-year
-old-map-006589

"Human evolution," wikipedia.org,
https://en.m.wikipedia.org/wiki
/Human_evolution#Evidence
_from_the_fossil_record

"Dashka Stone," creationwiki.org,
https://www.creationwiki.org
/Dashka_stone

DISC MEN

"Minoan Civilization," wikipedia.org,
https://en.m.wikipedia.org/wiki
/Minoan_civilization

"Arthur Evans," wikipedia.org,
https://en.m.wikipedia.org/wiki
/Arthur_Evans

"Scientists Finally Crack the Code
of the Ancient 'Phaistos Disk,'" by
Jacqueline Howard, huffpost.com,
https://www.huffpost.com/entry
/ancient-cd-rom-phaistos-disk
-code_n_6055178

MESMERIZING

"The Man Who Gave Us the Law of
Attraction," by Mitch Horowitz,
harvbishop.com, https://www
.harvbishop.com/the-man-who
-gave-us-the-law-of-attraction/

"Chapter 8: Visions and Predictions
of the Poughkeepsie Seer | Story
of Andrew Jackson Davis," by
Nandor Fodor, survivalafterdeath
.info, https://www.survivalafter
death.info/library/fodor/chapter8
.htm

"Galen," wikipedia.org, https://
en.m.wikipedia.org/wiki/Galen

"The List of Child Prodigies," wikipedia
.org, https://en.m.wikipedia.org
/wiki/List_of_child_prodigies

"Animal Magnetism," wikipedia.org,
https://en.m.wikipedia.org/wiki
/Animal_magnetism

"Wolfgang Amadeus Mozart,"
wikipedia.org, https://en.m.wikipedia
.org/wiki/Wolfgang_Amadeus
_Mozart

"Andrew Jackson Davis, the Seer of
Poughkeepsie," madammayo
.blogspot.com, https://madammayo
.blogspot.com/2014/02/andrew
-jackson-davis-seer-of.html

"Andrew Jackson Davis," wikipedia
.org, https://en.m.wikipedia.org
/wiki/Andrew_Jackson_Davis

SHARK ATTACKED

"A Locked-Room Murder,"
futilitycloset.com, https://www
.futilitycloset.com/2008/03/14/a
-locked-room-murder/

"Joseph Bowne Elwell," wikipedia.org,
https://en.m.wikipedia.org/wiki
/Joseph_Bowne_Elwell

"The Murder of Joseph Bowne Elwell,"
bridgebum.com, http://www.bridge
bum.com/joseph_bowne_elwell
.php

"The Impossible Murder of Joseph
Bowne Elwell," by Skunk Uzeki,
criminal.media, https://criminal
.media/the-impossible-murder
-of-joseph-bowne-elwell

"The Ziegfeld Midnight Frolic,"
blog.mcny.org, https://blog.mcny
.org/2014/07/01/the-ziegfeld
-midnight-frolic/

MAN vs. WILD

"Eric Shipton," wikipedia.org, https://
en.m.wikipedia.org/wiki/Eric
_Shipton

"This Man Searched for the Yeti
for 60 Years—and Found It," by
Simon Worrall, nationalgeographic
.com, https://news.nationalgeo
graphic.com/2017/08/yeti-abomi
nable-snowman-bear-daniel-taylor/

"The Loch Ness Monster Turns
83: The Story of the Surgeon's
Photograph," by Kat Kiernan,
donttakepictures.com, https:
//www.donttakepictures.com
/dtp-blog/2017/4/19/the-loch-ness
-monster-turns-83-the-story-of-the
-surgeons-photograph

"1951, November 8: The Shipton
Photograph," anomalyinfo.com,
http://anomalyinfo.com/Stories
/1951-november-8-shipton
-photograph

"Timeline of Mount Everest
expeditions," wikipedia.org,
https://en.m.wikipedia.org/wiki
/Timeline_of_Mount_Everest
_expeditions

"Tenzing Norgay," wikipedia.org,
https://en.m.wikipedia.org/wiki
/Tenzing_Norgay

THE RUMOR MILL

"Bielefeld Conspiracy," wikipedia
.org, https://en.wikipedia.org/wiki
/Bielefeld_Conspiracy

"The City that Doesn't Exist, and
When Angela Merkel Made a
Joke—the Story of Bielefeld,"
citymetric.com

"Bielefeld," wikipedia.com,
https://en.wikipedia.org/wiki
/Bielefeld

CRASH LANDING

"Pan Am Flight 121," wikipedia
.org, https://en.wikipedia.org/wiki
/Pan_Am_Flight_121

"Gene Roddenberry," wikipedia.
org, https://en.wikipedia.org/wiki
/Gene_Roddenberry

UNBALANCED BREAKFAST

"John Harvey Kellogg," wikipedia
.org, https://en.wikipedia.org/wiki
/John_Harvey_Kellogg

"Seventh-day Adventist Church,"
wikipedia.org, https://en.wikipedia
.org/wiki/Seventh-day_Adven
tist_Church

"Battle Creek Sanitarium," wikipedia
.com, https://en.wikipedia.org/wiki
/Battle_Creek_Sanitarium

"A historical story about the Invention of Corn Flakes," youtube
.com, https://www.youtube.com
/watch?v=QQypgxfSkSg

"C.W. Post," wikipedia.org, https://
en.wikipedia.org/wiki/C._W._Post

GETTING AHEAD

"Up, Up, and Away!" snopes.com, https://www.snopes.com/fact -check/up-up-and-away/

"Larry Walters," wikipedia.org, https://en.wikipedia.org/wiki /Larry_Walters

ART IMITATES LIFE

"Petrus Gonsalvus," wikipedia.org, https://en.wikipedia.org/wiki /Petrus_Gonsalvus

"Beauty and the Beast (2017)," history vshollywood.com, http://www .historyvshollywood.com/reelfaces /beauty-and-the-beast/

"Beauty and the Beast," wikipedia .org, https://en.wikipedia.org/wiki /Beauty_and_the_Beast

SPACE CASE

"The Jet-Propelled Couch: Part I," by Robert Mitchell Lindner .harpers.org, https://harpers.org /archive/1954/12/the-jet-propelled -couch/

"The Jet-Propelled Couch: Part II," by Robert Mitchell Lindner. harpers.org, https://harpers.org /archive/1955/01/the-jet-propelled -couch-2/

"Kirk Allen," wikipedia.org, https://en.wikipedia.org/wiki /Kirk_Allen

LOVE NOTES

"The Creepy Origins of Valentine's Day," ripleys.com, https://www .ripleys.com/weird-news/the -creepy-origins-of-valentines-day/

"St. Valentine Beheaded," history .com, https://www.history.com /this-day-in-history/st-valentine -beheaded

"Claudius Gothicus," wikipedia.org, https://en.wikipedia.org/wiki/Clau dius_Gothicus#Saint_Valentine

"Prohibition in the United States," wikipedia.org, https://en.wikipedia .org/wiki/Prohibition_in_the _United_States

AND THE WINNER IS . . .

"Louis B. Mayer," wikipedia.org, https://en.wikipedia.org/wiki/Louis _B._Mayer

"Metro-Goldwyn-Mayer," wikipedia .org, https://en.wikipedia.org/wiki /Metro-Goldwyn-Mayer

"Inside the Union-Busting Birth of the Academy Awards," vanityfair .com, https://www.vanityfair.com/ hollywood/2014/02/secret-oscar -history

"1st Academy Awards," wikipedia .org, https://en.wikipedia .org/wiki/1st_Academy _Awards

"How an Oscar Statuette Is Made," www.cnn.com, March 10, 2023, https://www.cnn.com/interactive /2023/03/entertainment/oscar -statuette-design-cnnphotos/index .html#:~:text=The%20first%20 Oscar%20was%20designed, standing%20on%20a%20film%20 reel.

"Margaret Herrick," en.wikipedia .org, https://en.wikipedia.org/wiki /Margaret_Herrick

COPIED

Juanita Rose Violini, *Almanac of the Infamous, the Incredible, and the Ignored* (Weiser Books, 2009), pp. 161–62.

THE KNOCKOUT

"Strangest Knockout in History," Mystery in the History, February 2015, https://mysteryinthe history.com/strangest-knockout -in-history

MOURNING

Helen Rappaport, *Queen Victoria: A Biographical Companion* (ABC-CLIO, 2003), p. 409.

PRECIOUS CARGO

"Henry 'Box' Brown," wikipedia.org, https://

wikipedia.org/wiki/Henry _Box_Brown

"Henry 'Box' Brown," by Dr. Bryan Wells, pbs.org, http://www.pbs .org/black-culture/shows/list/under ground-railroad/stories-freedom /henry-box-brown/.

BIRD BRAIN

"How Kurt Vonnegut's Brother Settled History's Most Dubious Chicken- Tornado Debate," mentalfloss.com, http:// mentalfloss.com/article/59586 /how-kurt-vonneguts-brother-set tled-istorys-most-dubious-chick en-tornado-debate.

"Bernard Vonnegut," wikipedia.org, https://en.wikipedia.org/wiki /Bernard_Vonnegut

"Kurt Vonnegut," wikipedia.org, https://en.wikipedia.org/wiki /Kurt_Vonnegut

"Cat's Cradle," wikipedia.org, https:// en.wikipedia.org/wiki/Cat%27s _Cradle

THAT GIRL IS POISON

"Locusta the Poisoner," badassoftheweek.com, http:// www.badassoftheweek.com /index.cgi?id=15657322 4535

"Locusta," wikipedia.org, https://en.wikipedia.org/wiki /Locusta

"Gaul," wikipedia.org, https://en.wikipedia.org /wiki/Gaul

"Gnaeus Domitius Ahenobarbus (consul 32)," wikipedia.org, https:// en.wikipedia.org/wiki/Gnaeus _Domitius_Ahenobarbus _(consul_32)

"Agrippina the Younger," wikipedia.org, https://en.wiki pedia.org/wiki/Agrippina_the _Younger

"Britannicus," wikipedia.org, https://en.wikipedia.org/wiki /Britannicus

RAVENOUS

"The Horrific Story of the Man Who Couldn't Stop Eating,'" cracked.com, http://www.cracked.com/blog/the-horrific-story-man-who-couldnt-stop-eating/

"Günter Schabowski," Wikipedia.org, https://en.m.wikipedia.org/wiki/Günter_Schabowski

MUMMY DEAREST

"The enduring mystery of The Lady of Dai mummy," ancient-origins.net, https://www.ancient-origins.net/ancient-places-asia/enduring-mystery-lady-dai-mummy-001357

"China's Sleeping Beauty," by Eti Bonn-Muller. archaeology.org, https://archive.archaeology.org/online/features/mawangdui/

"Entombed in Style," by Eti Bonn-Muller, atlasobscura.com, https://archive.archaeology.org/0905/abstracts/lady_dai.html

"Guqin," wikipedia.org, https://en.wikipedia.org/wiki/Guqin

"Xin Zhui," wikipedia.org, https://en.wikipedia.org/wiki/Xin_Zhui

ROCK MUSIC

"The Musical Stones of Skiddaw," futilitycloset.com, https://www.futilitycloset.com/2007/12/06/the-musical-stones-of-skiddaw/

"Musical Stones of Skiddaw," wikipedia.org, https://en.wikipedia.org/wiki/Musical_Stones_of_Skiddaw

"Skiddaw Stones," ableton.com, https://www.ableton.com/en/packs/skiddaw-stones/

"Lithophone," wikipedia.org, https://en.wikipedia.org/wiki/Lithophone

"Hornfels," wikipedia.org, https://en.wikipedia.org/wiki/Hornfels

"The Skiddaw Stones," bestservice.com, https://www.bestservice.com/the_skiddaw_stones.html

FOOD FOR THOUGHT

"Red Lady of Paviland," wikipedia.org, https://en.m.wikipedia.org/wiki/Red_Lady_of_Paviland

"William Buckland," wikipedia.org, https://en.wikipedia.org/wiki/William_Buckland

"Animal Lover," futilitycloset.com, https://www.futilitycloset.com/2008/02/26/animal-lover/

"The Father and Son Who Ate Every Animal Possible," by Craig Donofrio, atlasobscura.com, https://www.atlasobscura.com/articles/the-father-and-son-who-ate-every-animal-possible

"The Story of the Zoologist Who Ate Everything—Including A King's Heart," by William DeLong, allthatsinteresting.com, https://allthatsinteresting.com/william-buckland

"Lewis Harcourt, 1st Viscount Harcourt," wikipedia.org, https://en.m.wikipedia.org/wiki/Lewis_Harcourt,_1st_Viscount_Harcourt

BOOKSMART

"Antonio Magliabechi," wikipedia.org, https://en.m.wikipedia.org/wiki/Antonio_Magliabechi

"Book Lover," futilitycloset.com, https://www.futilitycloset.com/2008/06/14/book-lover/

O BROTHER

"How the Marx Brothers Got Their Nicknames," todayifoundout.com, October 1, 2012, https://www.todayifoundout.com/index.php/2012/10/how-the-marx-brothers-got-their-nicknames/

"The Origin of Zeppo's name (The Marx Brothers Marxology)," marx-brothers.org, https://www.marx-brothers.org/marxology/zeppo.htm

"Marx Brothers," wikipedia.org, https://en.wikipedia.org/wiki/Marx_Brothers

"Minnie Marx," wikipedia.org, https://en.wikipedia.org/wiki/Minnie_Marx

"Vaudeville: The World that Gave Rise to the Marx Brothers," cincyplay.com, November 17, 2017, https://www.cincyplay.com/blog-single-post/cinncinati-blog/2017/11/17/vaudeville-the-world-that-gave-rise-to-the-marx-brothers

"Gummo Marx," wikipedia.org, https://en.wikipedia.org/wiki/Gummo_Marx

"Art Fisher and Groucho the Monk (The Marx Brothers Marxology)," marx-brothers.org, https://www.marx-brothers.org/marxology/fisher.htm

THE WAITING GAME

"The Crypt of Civilization," damninteresting.com, https://www.damninteresting.com/the-crypt-of-civilization

"A Peek Inside the Crypt of Civilization," scientificamerican.com, https://blogs.scientificamerican.com/anecdotes-from-the-archive/a-peek-inside-the-crypt-of-civilization

POTPOURRI

Alice Gerard, *Glozel: Bones of Contention* (iUniverse, 2005).

RESTLESS

"The Mystery of Moving Coffins in Barbados' Chase Vault," brilio.net, https://en.brilio.net/scary/the-mystery-of-moving-coffins-in-barbados-chase-vault—170412k.html#

MEDIUM-SIZED TOWN

"Cassadaga, Florida," wikipedia.org, https://en.wikipedia.org/wiki/Cassadaga,_Florida

"Welcome to the Strange, Tiny Town of Cassadaga: Psychic Capital of the World," by Anna Hider, chronicles.roadtrippers.com, https://chronicles

.roadtrippers.com/tiny-strange
-settlement-florida-psychic-capital
-world/

"The Curious & Clairvoyant Town of
Cassadaga," ripleys.com, https://
www.ripleys.com/weird-news
/curious-clairvoyant-town-cassa
daga/

"Inside Cassadaga, the Psychic Capital of the World," by Christopher
Balogh, vice.com, https://www
.vice.com/en_us/article/nn4g87
/inside-cassadaga

"Mediumship," wikipedia.org, https://
en.wikipedia.org/wiki/Medium
ship#Trance_mediumship

IMPULSE BUY

"Stonehenge," wikipedia.org, https://
en.wikipedia.org/wiki/Stonehenge

"Cecil Chubb," wikipedia.org,
https://en.wikipedia.org/wiki
/Cecil_Chubb

"Stonehenge," history.com, https://
www.history.com/topics/british
-history/stonehenge

"History of Stonehenge," english
-heritage.org.uk, https://www
.english-heritage.org.uk/visit
/places/stonehenge/history-and
-stories/history/

"The Man Who Bought Stonehenge
at Auction," by Colton Kruse,
ripleys.com, https://www.ripleys
.com/weird-news/man-bought
-stonehenge/

AMUSE IT OR LOSE IT

"Salina Turda," atlasobscura.com,
https://www.atlasobscura.com
/places/salina-turda

"Transylvania," wikipedia.org, https://
en.wikipedia.org/wiki/Transylvania

"There Is an Underground Amusement Park in Transylvania," by
Sophia Softky, awol.junkee.com,
https://awol.junkee.com/there-is
-an-underground-amusement
-park-in-transylvania/4784

"Amazing Transylvania Amusement
Park Is Underground," by Samuel
Reason, blitzlift.com, http://blitzlift

.com/amazing-transylvania
-amusement-park-is-underground/

"The World's Largest Trampoline Is
in an Underground Cave," awol
.junkee.com, https://awol.junkee
.com/the-worlds-largest-tram
poline-is-in-an-underground
-cave/12553

WINDY CITY

"The Windmills of Iran That Are
Over 1,000 Years Old," by Emily
Hirsch, blitzlift.com, http://blitzlift
.com/the-windmills-of-iran-that
-are-over-1000-years-old/

"Nashtifan Windmills," wikipedia.
org, https://www.atlasobscura.com
/places/nashtifan-windmills

"Iran's Centuries-Old Windmills May
Soon Stop Turning," by Brian
Clark Howard, nationalgeographic
.com, https://news.nationalgeo
graphic.com/2017/01/nashtifan
-iran-windmills/

"Massive sandstorm turns daylight
into darkness as it sweeps through
city in Iran," by Alexander
Maveal, globalnews.ca, https://
globalnews.ca/news/4152742
/massive-sandstorm-turns-day
light-into-darkness-as-it-sweeps
-through-city-in-iran/

"Iran sandstorm kills at least four in
Tehran," bbc.com, https://www
.bbc.com/news/world-middle-east
-27669395

FIRESTARTER

"Peshtigo," futilitycloset.com, https://
www.futilitycloset.com/2009/04/16
/peshtigo/

"Fire in Everglades Ecosystems-
Everglades National Park (U.S.
National Park Service)," nps.gov,
https://www.nps.gov/ever/learn
/management/inevergladeseco
systems.htm

FANCY FOOTWORK

"Object of the Month: First World
War Amputees," by William Birnie
wellcomecollection.wordpress

.com, https://wellcomecollection
.wordpress.com/tag/carl-her
mann-unthan/.

"Carl Unthan, the Armless Fiddler,"
neatorama.com, https://www
.neatorama.com/2007/09/24/carl
-unthan-the-armless-fiddler/

"Carl Herman Unthan," wikipedia
.org, https://en.wikipedia.org/wiki
/Carl_Herman_Unthan

NICK OF TIME

"Curiosities of Clocks and Watches:
From the Earliest Times," by
Edward J. Wood, 1866, https://books
.google.com/books?id=__M3A
QAAMAAJ&q=chevalley#v=snippet
&q=chevalley&f=false.

"A Brief History of Clocks and
Calendars," localhistories.org, http://
www.localhistories.org/clocks.html

"Clock," wikipedia.org, https://
en.wikipedia.org/wiki/Clock

CLIMB EVERY MOUNTAIN

"Goran Kropp," wikipedia.org,
https://en.wikipedia.org/wiki
/Göran_Kropp.

"Historical Badass: Goran Kropp, the
Man Who Rode to Everest,"
adventure-journal.com, https://www
.adventure-journal.com/2016/06/hist
orical-badass-goran-kropp-the-man
-who-rode-to-everest.

THE LITTLE GIANT

"World's Littlest Giant: The Curious
Case of Adam Rainer," thechirur
geonsapprentice.com, https://web
.archive.org/web/20150206050935
/http://thechirurgeonsapprentice
.com/2015/01/20/worlds-littlest
-giant-the-curious-case-of-adam
-rainer/

"List of Humans with Gigantism,"
wikipedia.org, https://en.wiki
pedia.org/wiki/List_of_humans
_with_gigantism

"Acromegaly," niddk.nih.gov, https://
www.niddk.nih.gov/health-in
formation/endocrine-diseases
/acromegaly

TALL ORDER

"Jeffrey Hudson," wikipedia.org, https://en.wikipedia.org/wiki/Jeffrey_Hudson

"The Court Dwarf Served in a Pie to a King," by Marea Harris, thevintagenews.com, https://www.thevintagenews.com/2018/08/22/sir-jeffrey-hudson/

"English Civil Wars," history.com, https://www.history.com/topics/british-history/english-civil-wars

"Anti-Catholicism in the United Kingdom," wikipedia.org, https://en.wikipedia.org/wiki/Anti-Catholicism_in_the_United_Kingdom

YOU MUST REMEMBER THIS

"Daniel McCartney," wikipedia.org, https://en.wikipedia.org/wiki/Daniel_McCartney

"What Is Hyperthymesia and Who Has It?," hyperthymesia.org, http://www.hyperthymesia.org

BIG MISTAKE

"The Irish Giant and a Hunter Named Hunter," by Colton Kruse, ripleys.com, https://www.ripleys.com/weird-news/irish-giant/

"Charles Byrne (giant)," wikipedia.org, https://en.wikipedia.org/wiki/Charles_Byrne_(giant)

"John Hunter (surgeon)," wikipedia.org, https://en.wikipedia.org/wiki/John_Hunter_(surgeon)#Contributions_to_medicine

"Royal College of Surgeons of England," wikipedia.org, https://en.wikipedia.org/wiki/Royal_College_of_Surgeons_of_England#Hunterian_Museum

MATCHING SET

Strange Stories, Amazing Facts of America's Past (The Reader's Digest Association, Inc., 1989), pp. 187.

NUTSHELL

"Frances Glessner Lee," Harvard Magazine, 2005, https://harvardmagazine.com/2005/09/frances-glessner-lee-html

"How a Gilded-Age Heiress Became the 'Mother of Forensic Science,'" theatlantic.com, https://www.theatlantic.com/science/archive/2017/10/nutshells-frances-glessner-lee/542757/

"Murder Is Her Hobby: Frances Glessner Lee and the Nutshell Studies of Unexplained Death," americanart.si.edu, https://americanart.si.edu/exhibitions/nutshells

"Frances Glessner Lee," wikipedia.org, https://en.wikipedia.org/wiki/Frances_Glessner_Lee

"Nutshell Studies of Unexplained Death," wikipedia.org, https://en.wikipedia.org/wiki/Nutshell_Studies_of_Unexplained_Death

LAST DANCE

"The Erdington Murders: Two Eerily Similar Slayings—157 Years Apart," the-line-up.com, https://the-line-up.com/erdington-murders-coincidences

"The Eerie Coincidences of the Erdington Murders," huffingtonpost.com, https://www.huffingtonpost.com/the-lineup/the-eerie-coincidences-of_b_8682392.html

UNLUCKY HAND

Juanita Rose Violini, Almanac of the Infamous, the Incredible, and the Ignored, https://books.google.com/books?id=s8d0F4pCFLYC&pg=PA76&lpg=PA76&dq=Robert+Fallon+1858+poker&source=bl&ots=JO69Y07wUh&sig=jrId7ayV6MqUUqygPBIwEsqEVE4&hl=en&sa=X&ei=_xOEUs6-M-qY2AXPpYCwDA&ved=0CFgQ6AEwBA#v=onepage&q=Robert%20Fallon%201858%20poker&f=false

"Top 15 Amazing Coincidences," bytesdaily.blogspot.com, http://bytesdaily.blogspot.com/2013/08/top-15-amazing-coincidences.html

"San Francisco at Statehood," sfmuseum.org, http://www.sfmuseum.org/hist5/oldsf.html

PROS AND CONS

"Victor Lustig," wikipedia.org, https://en.wikipedia.org/wiki/Victor_Lustig

"The Weird Story of Victor Lustig, the Con Artist Who Sold the Eiffel Tower and Scammed Al Capone," theuijunkie.com, https://theuijunkie.com/victor-lustig-eiffel-tower-al-capone/

"Victor Lustig's Ten Commandments for Con Men," smileandgun.wordpress.com, https://smileandgun.wordpress.com/2015/09/02/464/

BANK ROLLED

"Charles Deville Wells: The Man Who Broke the Bank at Monte Carlo," roulette17.com, https://www.roulette17.com/stories/charles-deville-wells/

"Charles Wells (gambler)," wikipedia.org, https://en.m.wikipedia.org/wiki/Charles_Wells_(gambler)

"Charles Wells: The Man Who Broke the Bank at Monte Carlo," gamblingsites.org, https://www.gamblingsites.org/biographies/charles-wells/

KILLER ACT

"A Case of Hypnotism Gone Wrong and a Desperate Attempt to Make it Right," by Marc Hartzman, weirdhistorian.com, http://www.weirdhistorian.com/a-case-of-hypnotism-gone-wrong-and-a-desperate-attempt-to-make-it-right/

"Hypnotized to Death," by Greg Gillette, blogs.mycentraljersey.com, http://blogs.mycentraljersey.com/hillsborough/2011/02/23/hypnotized-to-death/

"Is Hypnosis Real? And 16 other Questions, Answered" by Kimberly

Holland, healthline.com, https://www.healthline.com/health/is-hypnosis-real

GHOSTED

"Cock Lane ghost," by wikipedia.org, https://en.m.wikipedia.org/wiki/Cock_Lane_ghost

"The Cock Lane Ghost," futilitycloset.com, https://www.futilitycloset.com/2008/06/16/the-cock-lane-ghost/

THE DEADLY DOUBLE

Mysteries of the Unexplained (The Reader's Digest Association, Inc., 1989), p. 73.

GOING UNDER

"H. L. Hunley (submarine)," wikipedia.org, https://en.wikipedia.org/wiki/H._L._Hunley_(submarine)

"Conservation-Restoration of the *H.L. Hunley*," wikipedia.org, https://en.wikipedia.org/wiki/Conservation-restoration_of_the_H.L._Hunley

"The River War," battlefields.org, https://www.battlefields.org/learn/articles/river-war

"USS Housatonic (1861)," by Amy Reiter, wikipedia.org, https://en.wikipedia.org/wiki/USS_Housatonic_(1861)

"The Mystery of a Spooky Confederate Submarine Might Finally Be Solved," by Rachel Feltman, popsci.com, https://www.popsci.com/hunley-confederate-submarine-mystery

WAR TIME

"Anglo-Zanzibar War," wikipedia.org, https://en.wikipedia.org/wiki/Anglo-Zanzibar_War

LOSING SLEEP

"Nightmares Suspected in Bed Deaths of 18 Laotians," by Wayne King, 1981, nytimes.com, https://www.nytimes.com/1981/05/10/us/nightmares-suspected-in-bed-deaths-of-18-laotians.html

"Pathet Lao," wikipedia.org, https://en.wikipedia.org/wiki/Pathet_Lao

"Laotian Civil War," wikipedia.org, https://en.wikipedia.org/wiki/Laotian_Civil_War

"The Secret War and Hmong Genocide," umn.edu, https://sites.google.com/a/umn.edu/historpedia/home/politics-and-government/the-secret-war-and-hmong-genocide-fall-2012

DOGS OF WAR

"Sergeant Stubby," wikipedia.org, https://en.wikipedia.org/wiki/Sergeant_Stubby.

"Sergeant Stubby," futilitycloset.com, https://www.futilitycloset.com/2006/06/04/sergeant-stubby/

"Stubby: Dog, Hoya Mascot, and War Hero," americanhistory.si.edu, http://americanhistory.si.edu/blog/2011/05/stubby-dog-hoya-mascot-and-war-hero.html

"Famous People of the First World War," biographyonline.net, https://www.biographyonline.net/military/wwi/people-first-world-war.html

"World War I: Beginnings and the Aftermath," mtholyoke.edu, https://www.mtholyoke.edu/~raina20s/ww1/play.html

TWO SHIPS PASSING

"The Battle of Trindade," historychannel.com.au, https://www.historychannel.com.au/h100/the-battle-of-trindade/

"A Desperate Fight to the Death: RMS Carmania vs. SMS Cap Trafalgar 1914," warhistoryonline.com, https://www.warhistoryonline.com/instant-articles/desperate-fight-death-rms-carmania-vs-sms-cap-trafalgar-1914.html

"'Carmania' sinking the 'Cap Trafalgar' off Trinidade Island in the South Atlantic, 14 September 1914," collections.rmg.co.uk, http://collections.rmg.co.uk/collections/objects/204091.html

CODE WORD CONFUSION

"Battle of the Chosin Reservoir," brittanica.com, https://www.britannica.com/event/Battle-of-the-Chosin-Reservoir

"Tootsie Rolls Saved Troops at the Battle of the Chosin Reservoir," ripleys.com, https://www.ripleys.com/weird-news/battle-chosin-reservoir/

"Battle of Chosin Reservoir," wikipedia.org, https://en.wikipedia.org/wiki/Battle_of_Chosin_Reservoir

SHIPS AHOY!

"Mystery Objects," by Sara Putterman. sothebys.com, https://www.sothebys.com/en/articles/mystery-objects

"Ships Made with Human Bones," ripleys.com, https://www.ripleys.com/weird-news/ships-made-with-human-bones/

"How Being Bored Out of Your Mind Makes You More Creative," by Clive Thompson. wired.com, https://www.wired.com/2017/01/clive-thompson-7/

"Macabre Ship Models Made from Human Bones by POWs," by Keith Veronese, gizmodo.com, https://io9.gizmodo.com/macabre-ship-models-made-from-human-bones-by-pows-5923127

"Napoleonic Wars," wikipedia.org, https://en.wikipedia.org/wiki/Napoleonic_Wars#Overview

BY A HARE

"The Time Napoleon Was Attacked by Rabbits," by Lucas Reilly, mentalfloss.com, https://mentalfloss.com/article/51364/time-napoleon-was-attacked-rabbits

"Tamam Shud case," wikipedia.org, https://en.wikipedia.org/wiki/Tamam_Shud_case

"Napoleon's Strategy and Tactics," napolun.com, http://www.napolun .com/mirror/napoleonistyka .atspace.com/Napoleon_tactics.htm

"Treaty of Tilsit," wikipedia.org, https://en.wikipedia.org/wiki /Treaties_of_Tilsit

"Battle of Friedland," wikipedia.org, https://en.wikipedia.org/wiki /Battle_of_Friedland

"Napoleon and the Battle of the Rabbits: Faced with the implacable animal horde, the Emperor beat a hasty retreat," Barbara Stepko, thevintagenews.com, https://www .thevintagenews.com/2018/05/18 /napoleon-and-the-battle-of-the -rabbits/

LADY BE BAD

"Lady Be Good (aircraft)," wikipedia .org, https://en.wikipedia.org/wiki /Lady_Be_Good_(aircraft)

"One Mean Plane," futilitycloset .com, https://www.futilitycloset .com/2007/09/01/one-mean -plane/

"C-54 Skymaster," wikipedia.org, https://en.wikipedia.org/wiki /Douglas_C-54_Skymaster

"Bombing, States and Peoples in Western Europe 1940–1945," humanities.exeter.ac.uk, https:// humanities.exeter.ac.uk/history /research/centres/warstateandsociety /projects/bombing/italy/

SOLDIER OF MISFORTUNE

"Hiroo Onoda, Soldier Who Hid in Jungle for Decades, Dies at 91," by Robert D. McFadden, nytimes.com, https://www.nytimes .com/2014/01/18/world/asia/hiroo

-onoda-imperial-japanese -army-officer-dies-at-91.html

"Hiroo Onoda," wikipedia.org, https://en.wikipedia.org/wiki /Hiroo_Onoda

"2nd Lt. Hiroo Onoda," wanpela .com, http://www.wanpela.com /holdouts/profiles/onoda.html

GUARDIAN ANGELS

"Battle of Shiloh," wikipedia.org, https://en.wikipedia.org/wiki /Battle_of_Shiloh

"Medicine in the American Civil War," by Dr. Mary Williams, R.N., D.C., cprcertified.com, https:// www.cprcertified.com/medicine -in-the-american-civil-war

"Angel's Glow: The Bacterium That Saved Civil War Soldiers," kidsdiscover.com, https://www .kidsdiscover.com/quick-reads /angels-glow-the-bacterium-that -saved-civil-war-soldiers/

"Shiloh: Pittsburgh Landing," battle fields.org, https://www.battlefields .org/learn/civil-war/battles/shiloh

"Glowing Civil War Flesh Wounds," ripleys.com, https://www.ripleys .com/weird-news/glowing-civil-war -flesh-wounds/

NEVER FORGET

"The Town of Huescar Declared War on Denmark and Forgot for 172 Years," by Samuel Reason, blitzlift .com, http://blitzlift.com/the-town -of-huescar-declared-war-on -denmark-and-forgot-for-172-years/

"Economic Consequences of War on U.S. Economy: Debt, Taxes and Inflation Increase; Consumption and Investment Decrease," by Mi-

chael Shank, huffpost.com, https:// www.huffpost.com/entry/economic -consequences-of_b_1294430

"6 Wars Fought for Ridiculous Rea- sons," by Evan Andrews, history .com, https://www.history.com /news/6-wars-fought-for-ridiculous -reasons

"Extra! Extra! Huescar makes peace with Denmark!," by Bjorn Edlund, upi.com, https://www.upi.com /Archives/1981/11/11/Extra-Extra -Huescar-makes-peace-with -Denmark/8195374302800/

"Treaty of Paris (1814)," wikipedia .org, https://en.wikipedia.org/wiki /Treaty_of_Paris_(1814)

"Lijar against France. Hundred Years' War in a Town of Almería," the diplotmatinspain.com, https://the diplomatinspain.com/en/2017/08 /lijar-against-france-hundred-years -war-in-a-town-of-almeria/

EDDIE'S MONSTER

"Vampire Attack Sucks Life Out of the Cold War," ripleys.com, https:// www.ripleys.com/weird-news /faked-vampire-attacks/

"Ed Lansdale's Black Warfare in 1950s Vietnam," by Marc D. Bernstein, historynet.com, https://www.historynet.com /ed-lansdales-black-warfare-in -1950s-vietnam.htm

"The 5 Most Outrageous Bluffs in the History of War," by Alex Hanton, cracked.com, https://www .cracked.com/article_20518_the-6 -most-outrageous-bluffs-in-history -war.html

"Edward Lansdale," wikipedia.org, https://en.m.wikipedia.org/wiki /Edward_Lansdale

INDEX

ABOUT THE AUTHOR

PHOTO: AARON MAHNKE

One of the most successful podcast producers in the world, **Aaron Mahnke** began his career in 2015 with the launch of *Lore*, which has racked up nearly half a million downloads, been adapted for two seasons of television on Amazon Prime, and published as a three-book set from Penguin Random House. *Beyond Lore*, Aaron has produced a number of shows, including the chart-topping *Cabinet of Curiosities* and the 2021 award-winning *Bridgewater*. He lives in the North Shore area of Massachusetts with his family.